FREUDIAN REPRESSION, THE UNCONSCIOUS, AND THE DYNAMICS OF INHIBITION

FREUDIAN REPRESSION, THE UNCONSCIOUS, AND THE DYNAMICS OF INHIBITION

Simon Boag

Routledge
Taylor & Francis Group

LONDON AND NEW YORK

First published 2012 by Karnac Books Ltd.

Published 2018 by Routledge
2 Park Square, Milton Park, Abingdon, Oxon OX14 4RN
711 Third Avenue, New York, NY 10017, USA

Routledge is an imprint of the Taylor & Francis Group, an informa business

British Library Cataloguing in Publication Data

A C.I.P. for this book is available from the British Library

ISBN 9781855757387 (pbk)

Edited, designed and produced by The Studio Publishing Services Ltd
www.publishingservicesuk.co.uk
e-mail: studio@publishingservicesuk.co.uk

CONTENTS

PART II: MAKING SENSE OF REPRESSION

PART III: EXPLAINING REPRESSION

ACKNOWLEDGEMENTS

This book represents the culmination of a body of work beginning with my doctoral research whilst at the School of Psychology at the University of Sydney, which continued through to my present position in the Department of Psychology at Macquarie University. This book was then finally completed whilst on sabbatical back in the Department of Psychology at the University of Sydney. My sincere thanks go to Mike Jones who, as Head of Department of Psychology at Macquarie University, supported this time which allowed me to finish writing, and also to Sally Andrews who warmly welcomed me back to the Department of Psychology at Sydney.

Finishing this book at the University of Sydney was apposite since it was there that I was first introduced to the realist school of psychology that now dominates my thinking and has shaped my approach to psychoanalytic theory. From there I have been particularly influenced by the work of John Maze, Terry McMullen, Joel Michell, as well as Agnes Petocz presently at the University of Western Sydney. I am particularly indebted to Joel and Agnes; their rigorous thinking and breadth of knowledge provided me with much stimulating food for thought and Joel's earlier work on conceptualizing inhibitory processes provides a foundation for my present position. I am also particularly indebted to Joel since it was not until his lectures on the concept of motivation, and his discussion of determinism and teleology based on John Maze's work, that it became clearer and clearer to me that Freud provided a view of the human organism that had the potential of satisfying both the biological and psychological requirements of a good deterministic theory. I would also like to thank Nigel Mackay for his contributions to psychoanalysis and realism which have influenced this work, as well as a special thanks to Matthew Erdelyi for both his encouragement towards my work (even if reminding me of Freud's distaste for philosophy) and for his ongoing and extensive contributions to demystifying psychoanalysis for the general psychology community. Vesa Talvitie also deserves special mention for his thoughtful correspondence whilst writing this book and I am also grateful for his research emphasizing the importance of resolving conceptual issues for progress in psychoanalytic thinking. A special thanks also goes to Julie Fitness who, as Head of Department of Psychology at Macquarie University when I arrived in 2006, has consistently encouraged my research and also to Colin Wastell, also at Macquarie University, for appreciating the value of teaching the history and philosophy of psychology. I am also grateful to the people at Karnac who made this book possible and special thanks here go to Lucy Shirley and Kate Pearce, as well as to the production team at The Studio Publishing Services Ltd. Lastly, an enormous thanks to my long-suffering partner Michelle who has learnt much more about Freud than she ever wished for.

Simon Boag is a senior lecturer in the Department of Psychology at Macquarie University, Sydney, Australia, where he teaches personality and psychoanalysis, psychological theory, and philosophy of science. Since being awarded his PhD on the topic of Freudian repression, he has published extensively on the topic, addressing misconceptions of repression and theoretical developments in psychoanalytic theory and neuroscience. His paper on repression and pathological science prompted an exchange with Harvard Professor Richard McNally and featured in York University's *Advances in the History of Psychology*. Additionally, his paper "Freudian dream theory, dream bizarreness and the disguise-censor controversy" was a target article in the journal *Neuropsychoanalysis*, where he discussed the role of repression in dreaming and its relationship to neuroscientific findings.

For Annika

Introduction

The problematic concept of repression

Of all the concepts and theoretical innovations to emerge from Freudian psychoanalysis, the concepts of "repression" and the dynamic unconscious has remained the most controversial and problematic. At its simplest, *"the essence of repression lies simply in turning something away, and keeping it at a distance, from the conscious"* (Freud, 1915d, p. 147, his italics) and, for Freud, repression provided insight into the mind's dynamics contributing to dreams and psychopathology. Freud's claim that repression "was a novelty, and that nothing like it had ever before been recognised in mental life" (Freud, 1925d, p. 30, cf. 1914d, p. 15) might be an overstatement, given that similar ideas are found prior to Freud (e.g., Johann Herbart's inhibition of "ideas"—see Jones, 1953, pp. 407ff; cf. Erdelyi, 1993, p. 127; Laplanche & Pontalis, 1973, p. 392). Nevertheless, it is the *dynamic* unconscious whereby mental content is actively prevented from becoming conscious due to mental conflict which is specifically psychoanalytic (Blum, 2003a, p. 501). As Brenner (1957) notes, repression "introduced into psychopathology the fundamental theoretical concept that *intrapsychic conflict* and its consequences were of essential significance in the formation of neurotic symptoms" (p. 20, his italics; cf. Beres, 1962; Eagle, 2000a; Gill, 1963; Jones, 1993; May, 1999; Wollheim, 1991).

The theoretical significance of repression allows Freud to write that the "theory of repression is the corner-stone on which the whole structure of psycho-analysis rests" (Freud, 1914d, p. 16) and that it "is possible to take repression as a centre and bring all the elements of psycho-analytic theory into relation with it" (Freud, 1925d, p. 30). In fact, Eagle notes that "it is with his introduction of the concept of repression that Freud's theorising becomes distinctively psycho-analytic. The concept of repression constitutes a dividing line between Freud's prepsychoanalytic and psychoanalytic writing" (Eagle, 2000a, p. 1, cf. Eagle, 1998, p. 87). As such, providing a coherent theoretical account of repression takes on added significance with respect to justifying the foundational characteristic of psychoanalysis. However, both advocates and critics alike have identified problems with the theory. Repression's scientific status, for example, has been repeatedly questioned and Nesse (1990) writes that, although clinically important, "[repression] remains an anomalous and awkward concept that has kept psychoanalysis apart from the rest of science" (p. 262). The place of repression in contemporary psychoanalysis is similarly unclear, and while one still finds reference to repression as the "cornerstone of psychoanalysis" (McIlwain, 2007, p. 542), it would be difficult to claim this centrality in contemporary psychoanalytic discussions. Eagle (2000a), in fact, observes that it is his "strong impression that one finds far more frequent references to 'dissociation' than to repression in contemporary psychoanalytic literature" (p. 22). Furthermore, in terms of psychoanalytic therapy, the concept of repression also receives mixed support. On the one hand, Eagle (2000b) writes that "the therapeutic value of the lifting of repressions remains as one of the core theoretical assumptions underlying psycho-analytic, as well as other, related treatments" (p. 168; cf. Blum, 2003a, p. 501), whereas, in contradistinction, Fonagy (1999) writes that "[t]he removal of repression is no longer to be considered a key to therapeutic action" (p. 218).

An additional reason for why repression remains problematic—but also intriguing—is with respect to providing a coherent explanation for how it occurs. Freud's (1915d) apparently straightforward claim that *the essence of repression lies simply in turning something away, and keeping it at a distance, from the conscious* (p. 147) conceals a major theoretical stumbling block, and careful examination of Freud's theory reveals that maintaining repression appears to require the impossible: *knowing in order not to know* (Maze & Henry, 1996). Freud writes,

> The process of repression is not to be regarded as an event which takes place *once*, the results of which are permanent, as when some living thing has been killed and from that time onward is dead; repression demands a persistent expenditure of force, and if this were to cease the success of the repression would be jeopardized, so that a fresh act of repression would be necessary. We may suppose that the repressed exercises a continuous pressure in the direction of the conscious, so that this pressure must be balanced by an unceasing counter-pressure. Thus the maintenance of a repression involves an uninterrupted expenditure of force, while its removal results in a saving from an economic point of view. [Freud, 1915d, p. 151, his italics]

As Maze and Henry (1996) note, if the ego as "repressing agency" is to continuously guard against the repressed becoming known, then repression entails a paradox whereby the ego must know what it is not meant to know. Various responses to this problem have been proposed and some authors (following Freud's lead) propose a censor (or censors) guarding the ego from knowledge of the repressed. More recently, some explanatory strategies attempt to explain repression solely in terms of neural processes, denying any need for psychological processes in repression. Whether such approaches are sustainable is questionable (see Boag, 2006b), and it remains to be seen whether a coherent account of repression can be provided. A particular difficulty for any satisfactory explanation is coming to grips with Freud's claim that repression involves what he refers to as being "afflicted by that blindness of the seeing eye" (Freud in Breuer & Freud, 1895d, p. 117n), which entails somehow *both* knowing and not knowing the repressed. Subsequent discussions of repression invite the same apparent paradoxical descriptions. Consider, for instance, Fayek's (2005) claim that with repression "the unconscious element remains in consciousness unattended to" (p. 537), which implies an unconscious consciousness, or the common assertion that after repression is lifted that the analysand somehow knew the repressed all along (e.g., Talvitie, 2009). Repression appears to necessarily entail "unconscious knowing" and becomes essentially the psychoanalytic phenomenon and challenge to explain *par excellence*.

Freud's theory of repression and pathological science

The controversial nature of repression also stems from its enmeshment within the possibility of recovered memories, a debate "that has been at the heart of one of the most bitter controversies ever to affect our field" (McNally, 2007, p. 360). Smith (2006) here comments that "[r]epression has long been the battleground in psychology's family feud. No other issue has seen such contentious and emotional brawling among psychologists as the question of repression" (p. 534), and the myriad claims and counter-claims of the validity of these assertions have come to make up the "memory wars" (Crews, 1995). However, while Freud is commonly invoked in discussions of "repressed memories", after 1900—and for the majority of Freud's research— Freud discusses repression with respect to the targets being representatives of "instinctual impulses" (Freud, 1915d), a not unproblematic translation, but quite specific, nevertheless, for anyone reading Freud's often cited paper titled "Repression" (Freud, 1915d). The opening line of that paper reads: "One of the vicissitudes an instinctual impulse may undergo is to meet with resistances which seek to make it inoperative. Under certain conditions . . . the impulse then passes into a state of 'repression'" (Freud, 1915d, p. 146). However, this same paper has been cited to attack Freud's theory of repressed *memories* (e.g., Henderson, 1999; Loftus & Ketcham, 1994), and, thus, something is evidently amiss.

It is, though, true that until 1897 Freud gave credence to reports of child sexual abuse as universally causally relevant to later psychopathology (what has come to be known as the "seduction hypothesis"), but, as noted by many (Brenner, 1957; Davies, 1996; Jones, 1993; Maze & Henry, 1996; Oliner, 2000), after the seduction hypothesis was abandoned as early as 1897 (mentioned in a letter to his friend Wilhelm Fliess, dated 21 September 1897, see Masson, 1985), Freud recognized that repression mainly operates on *phantasies* and *wishes* rather than actual memories of prior (sexual) experiences. The childhood seductions that he first held to be true were, in fact, fantasy, and "childhood" memories sometimes arise as "screens" to avoid remembering the actual state of affairs (infantile desires) (Freud, 1899a, 1901b). While not denying that child sexual abuse occurs, Freud concludes that "the neurotic symptoms were not directly related to actual events but to wishful phantasies, and that as far as the neurosis was concerned psychical reality was of more importance than material reality" (Freud, 1925d, p. 34, cf. 1906a, p. 274). What had been missing from the picture for Freud was the theory of infantile sexuality, and the characterization of repression that follows from this revision emphasizes conflict and instinctual demands. Repression needs to considered as a form of defence which is initiated by conflict and provides "protection . . . against instinctual demands" (Freud, 1926d, p. 164), whereby wishes and desires that require satisfaction also constitute a threat. The contrast of the Freudian account with the "common view" is noticeable in the following:

> As a result of the experience, an instinctual demand arises which calls for satisfaction. The ego refuses that satisfaction, either because it is paralysed by the magnitude of the demand or because it recognises it as a danger . . . The ego fends off the danger by the process of repression. The instinctual impulse is in some way inhibited, its precipitating cause, with its attendant perceptions and ideas, is forgotten. [Freud, 1939a, p. 128]

The significance of conflict is further seen in the distinction between *psychoneuroses* and the conflict-free *traumatic neuroses* which arise after "frightening experiences or severe accidents, without any reference to a conflict in the ego" (Freud, 1919d, p. 209) and, thus, the association of Freud's theory of repression with the recovered memory debate appears then to be a gross oversimplification of Freudian theory, and one which has become entrenched and resistant to correction. Hence, Sandler and Sandler (1997) note the need for clarification of the theory:

> The psychoanalytic concept of repression is frequently invoked in discussions of the validity of recovered memories of abuse, and "forgotten" memories are nearly always thought of as having been relegated by repression to the 'the unconscious'. Such a broad formulation is inevitably imprecise, and it is important that the psychoanalytic meaning and usage of the repression concept, as well as that of 'the unconscious', be clarified. [p. 163]

Given the extent of the problem, there might be reason to suspect something more occurring than simply error. A "pathology of science" occurs when there is a breakdown in the scientific process whereby researchers are prevented from the recognition of error (Michell, 2000) and in an earlier paper (Boag, 2006a) I had argued that there was such a breakdown with respect to the scientific assessment of Freud's theory of repression whereby, after first oversimplifying his theory to propose that repression simply targets unpleasant and traumatic memories (e.g., Holmes, 1990), critics of Freud are then quick to cite the common occurrence of false memories as evidence against Freudian theory (e.g., Rofé, 2008). Ironically, Freud, for his part, was well aware of the fallibility and reconstructive nature of memory. Given that one generally sees oneself as an object in childhood memories (rather than from the perspective of the subject during the initial event), Freud writes that

> it is evident that such a picture cannot be an exact repetition of the impression that was originally received ... [since] ... the subject sees himself in the recollection as a child. Whenever in a memory the subject himself appears in this way as an object among other objects this ... may be taken as evidence that the original impression has been worked over. [Freud, 1899a, p. 321]

Pugh (2002), in fact, here claims that

> Freud is revealed as one of the first to write about the distinction between the recall of a memory from the perspective of one who is part of the scene and from the perspective of the onlooker—the field/observer distinction. [p. 1379]

In a response to my 2006 paper, McNally (2007) raises some reasonable counter-arguments to my claim that the discussion of Freudian repression and traumatic memories constitutes pathological science. Whereas I had suggested that one causal factor for this state of affairs (among many) might be that of resistance (Boag, 2006a, p. 82), as Freud had predicted (Freud, 1925e), McNally notes that there are other less "pathological" reasons to consider primarily. In particular, the current debate on repression remains primarily interested in the issue of repressed *memories*: "The continued focus on Freud's trauma theory occurs precisely because it is this version of repression, not the later version, that has been the crux of the recovered memory debate" (McNally, 2007, p. 360) and "mature psychoanalysis was a step backward, not an advance" (p. 359).

Nevertheless, the situation is not so clear-cut. Shortly after my 2006 paper, Rofé published a paper citing Boag (2006a) and purporting to explicitly "evaluate Freudian repression" (Rofé, 2008). Like McNally (2007), Rofé discusses the repression of memories and his conclusion is sweeping: "the fact remains that the Freudian notion of repression cannot be used as a scientific psychological concept, as its empirical status precludes this possibility" (Rofé, 2008, p. 76). However, what is striking about Rofé's (2008) paper, which explicitly purports to evaluate *Freudian* repression, is that there is very little evidence that Freud's work actually has been read. Rofé's "reading" of Freud appears mostly derived from secondary critical sources (e.g., Bonanno & Keuler, 1998), and ones that would not typically be considered as authorities of Freudian theory (e.g., the *DSM-IV-TR*, American Psychiatric Association, 2000). From that latter source, Rofé attributes to Freud the claim that "the unconscious is supposedly capable of controlling and manipulating over 100 personalities" (Rofé, 2008, p. 71), a viewpoint which is nowhere to be seen in any of Freud's writings. Rofé does, however, cite Freud's paper "The unconscious" (Freud, 1915e) to propose that Freud's assumes "an autonomous *unconscious entity*, which activates the repressive process, preserves the anxiety-provoking contents, and controls the manifestation of repression in the form of psychiatric disorders" (p. 63, his italics). However, inspection of that paper (and other relevant publications where Freud discusses unconscious processes, e.g., Freud, 1912g) reveals that Freud discusses unconscious processes in *descriptive*, *dynamic*, and *systemic* terms, none of which are explicitly addressed by Rofé. Rofé's "reading" of Freud is precisely the issue with respect to pathological science: Rofé's work is typical of accounts dismissing Freudian theory yet demonstrating a sustained failure to actually assess what Freud has to say or to sufficiently grasp psychoanalytic concepts.

Repression and the problem of "the unconscious"

None of this is to say, however, that there are not problems with Freud's theory, and it is precisely the notion of "the unconscious" which, while essential for understanding repression, remains theoretically obscure. This is not a small issue, since any theoretical problem with understanding unconscious processes can only cast doubt on psycho-analysis. Freud, in fact, describes psychoanalysis as *"the science of the unconscious mind"* (Freud, 1923a, p. 252, his italics), and Fonagy and Target's (2000) claim that "[t]he hallmark of psychoanalytic theory is the attention to unconscious mental processes and unconscious motivation in the explanation of complex and often paradoxical human behaviour" (p. 414) demonstrates that this position endures. Nevertheless, conceptualizing the unconscious remains a perennial problem. Erdelyi (1985) writes that "[t]he unconscious has led a difficult existence within psychology" (p. 57) and Cramer (1998) writes that the postulation of unconscious mentality has led to psychoanalysis to being "banished to the land of mysticism, parapsychology, and other "non-scientific" areas of discourse" (Cramer, 1998, p. 882). However, more than this, there is something about the psychoanalytic account that is particularly difficult given the general acceptance of the so-called "new unconscious" (Kihlstrom, 1987). Summarizing the problems, Uleman (2005) writes,

> the psychoanalytic unconscious is widely acknowledged to be a failure of scientific theory because evidence of its major components cannot be observed, measured precisely, or manipulated easily. The theory's complexity renders it largely unfalsifiable . . . [and] it does not provide an influential framework for unconscious processes in academic or scientific circles. [p. 5]

Furthermore, even those sympathetic to psychoanalysis still struggle with reconciling "unconscious mentality", preferring to equate the unconscious with neural processes rather than psychological ones (e.g., Searle, 1992; Talvitie, 2009; Talvitie & Tiitinen, 2006).

Evaluating Freud's theory of repression

Since *ad hominem* attacks against Freud are not uncommon (Lothane, 1999; Weinberger & Westen, 2001), an important starting point for evaluating Freud's theory involves distinguishing "Freud the person" from Freudian theory. In fact, several authors have noted that simple association with Freud's name is grounds for dismissing psychoanalytic concepts (Cramer, 1998; Talvitie, 2009; Westen, 1999). Naturally, the acceptance or rejection of any theory is independent of the person saying it, which, of course, extends to using Freud's "author-ity" as a basis for argument. This aside, making sense of the complex-ity of Freud's thinking on repression is not necessarily always easy, for a variety of reasons. Aside from the difficulty with understanding "the blindness of the seeing eye", Freud's account of repression developed and turned in various directions according to his theoretical and clin-ical insights. Subsequently, Madison (1956, p. 75; cf. Compton, 1972a, p. 3) notes that Freud's writings

> represent an historical account of an adventurous explorer developing a system of concepts that changed and grew continuously and unevenly over a half-century of creative effort . . . [subsequently he] left behind a trail of complex ideas unevenly developed and never integrated into a logical, systematic whole.

Shill (2004) further notes that most post-Freudian discussion of conflict and defence "generally reflects the unresolved contradictions in Freud's writings" (p. 125). Subsequently, the "difficulties in deci-phering Freud's work" and "problems in the theoretical presentation of the concept of repression led to misinterpretations in its translation into a laboratory setting" (Geisler, 1985, p. 254; Madison, 1961, p. 6). However, while all of this might be true, this is not to say that every aspect of the theory is incomprehensible or that all apparent contradic-tions are irreconcilable: instead, to assess the merits of Freud's theory of repression so that it can stand up to tests of empirical evaluation requires first of all theoretical and conceptual clarification.

Theoretical and conceptual clarification

Unfortunately, psychoanalysis, too, has long suffered from termino-logical confusion and vague and ambiguous constructs (Erdelyi, 1985; Fonagy & Target, 2000; Sandler, Dreher, & Drews, 1991) and while "[p]art of the problem of current analytic discourse resides in analysts using the same term with different meanings" (Blum, 2003b, p. 510), Talvitie and Tiitinen (2006) recently write that "with the use of psycho-analytic terminology, there seem to be specific *psychoanalytic* prob-lems" (p. 178, their italics; cf. Talvitie & Ihanus, 2005, p. 666). However, general psychology is certainly not immune to conceptual ambiguity and vagueness, and while there are serious conceptual difficulties associated with psychoanalytic theory, such difficulties can be clarified via conceptual research.

Conceptual research has a long history in science generally (Machado & Silva, 2007) and specifically within psychoanalysis (e.g., Dreher, 2005; Laplanche & Pontalis, 1973; Richfield, 1954; Sandler, Dreher, & Drews, 1991) and is logically prior to empirical tests of theory since the theory must be clarified *prior* to empirical assessment (Boag, 2007c; Michell, 2000). In fact, as Mackay (2006) notes, it would be futile to even attempt to assess empirically any theory that fails logically as it could never refer to the actual state of affairs, and so, "in the evaluation of any substantive theory and its evidence priority must go to the logical test of the theory's propositions" (p. 40). Accordingly, we cannot compare psychoanalytic theory with empirical evidence until we have clarified what we are talking about first. With respect to the empirical evaluation of repression, this first step, for the most part, has been neglected (see Boag, 2006c, 2007c) and, consequently, any claim that Freud's theory of repression lacks empirical support is premature (see Boag, 2006a). Instead, any evaluation of Freud's theory of repression requires a careful exposition of the theory, acknowledgement of any problems and contradictions, and rejection of unworkable elements.

The problem of metaphor

A particular difficulty with clarifying the Freudian account is, however, Freud's use of metaphor and analogy when describing the mind's workings. This is particularly so with respect to Freud's theory of repression, where many note a tension between Freud's explanation via mechanisms and his use of anthropomorphic metaphors, whereby he describes the mind's workings in terms of agents (Gouws, 2000; Grossman & Simon, 1969; Sartre, 1956; Thalberg, 1982). Nagel (1959), for instance, writes:

> Although psychoanalysis explicitly proclaims the view that human behaviour has its roots in the biophysical and biochemical organization of the body, it actually postulates a veritable "ghost in the machine" that does work which a biologically orientated psychology might be expected to assign to the body. [Nagel, 1959, p. 47]

Explaining behaviour and cognition with respect to an internal agent invokes the problematic homunculus (or internal little person), and Freud's model of personality has been criticized for postulating multiple homunculi (e.g., id, ego, and superego) (Grossman & Simon, 1969; Laplanche & Pontalis, 1973, Wiedeman, 1972). As Grossman and Simon (1969) note, the "person-within-the-person" model simply defers explanation, since explaining the "person's" behaviour with reference to another "person" simply means that the homunculus's behaviour must itself be explained without reference to another homunculus (to avoid an infinite regress of homunculi—Gardner, 1993; Grossman & Simon, 1969; Maze, 1983, 1987; Wegner, 2005). That is, any explanation in terms of agents or persons requires further explanation (ultimately in terms of causal antecedents and mechanisms) if a vicious regress of explanations to (sub) persons is to be avoided. Alternatively, if the homunculus has "free will", then "the homunculus causes things merely by deciding, without any prior causes leading to these decisions" (Wegner, 2005, p. 20), which, as Wegner correctly notes, makes behaviour literally inexplicable. However, Gillett (1990) also observes that anthropomorphic language "can be useful and acceptable as long as it is clear how it can be translated into causal terms" (p. 560), and anthropomorphic descriptions of the psyche might be appropriate if one takes into account the influence of object-relations in the development of the psyche (see Beres, 1965; Gardner, 1993; Hopkins, 1995b).

The problem of metaphor is also not limited to Freudian theory and the issue extends to general psychology, particularly with respect to the computer metaphor and the widespread appeal to "models" (see Oliphant, 1994). All fields of science make use of metaphors and analogy for illustrative purposes (Cheshire & Thomä, 1991; Petocz, 2006) and making sense of these requires knowing the necessary points of contrast ("marking off the area of negative analogy"), which entails spelling out the relevant characteristics of both the phenomenon and metaphor:

> The claim that some entity or system (say A) is a metaphor, or a model, for some other entity or system (say B) is a claim that in some respects A is the same as B, but in other respects A is different from B; it's a claim about A, and about B, and about the relationship between the two. Now, in order to be able to evaluate that claim we obviously need to know what the relevant characteristics of A are, what the

relevant characteristics of B are, and exactly what the mapping is between the first set of characteristics and the second set of characteristics. [Oliphant, 1994, p. 36]

Thus, for Freud's theory of repression to be scientifically workable requires a careful assessment of any metaphor, simile, or analogy, and we must know what aspects are to be retained and which are to be rejected.

The challenge facing neuropsychoanalysis

Conceptual and theoretical research is also important with respect to evaluating the increasing integration of psychoanalysis and neuroscientific research (e.g., Epstein, 1998; Kandel, 1999; Kaplan-Solms & Solms, 2000; Peled, 2008; Ramachandran, 1994, 1996; Schore, 2002, 2009; Solms, 1995, 1997a,b, 2005; Solms & Turnbull, 2002; Turnbull & Solms, 2004). Such a venture presents conceptual and theoretical challenges with respect to physical and psychological interactions. Talvitie and Ihanus (2006) here note that "a need exists for a 'philosophy of neuropsychoanalysis'" (p. 96) and Bennett and Hacker (2003) have recently drawn attention to the myriad conceptual issues and confusions involved in neuroscientific theorizing. Freud, of course, began his research as a neurologist and saw no essential problem with postulating a neurobiological foundation for psychodynamic processes (Freud, 1950[1895]) but, as Petocz (2006) notes, Freud's own position on the matter was inconsistent: "[i]t is possible to find in Freud's writings almost every major position on the mind–body relationship" (p. 50). Furthermore, Hutterer and Liss (2006) note that there might be certain tensions between neuroscientific and dynamic *explanations* with, for instance, whether psychological explanations should be reduced to biological ones. Accordingly, a theoretical framework is required for understanding the relationship between mind and body.

Freudian psychology and realism

The theoretical framework adopted here is one which fits with Freud's broad commitment to the natural scientific approach (Freud, 1940b, p. 282), which entails realism, empiricism,[1] and determinism (see

Freud, 1933a, p. 182, 1940a, pp. 158–159). A central tenet of psycho-analytic thinking is (even if not always consistently espoused) that "there is, of course, no such thing as arbitrary determination in the mind" (Freud, 1901a, p. 680; cf. 1898b, p. 294, 1906c, pp. 104–105) and, since making sense of the world involves understanding its causal relations, "[t]hose who are interested in mind's workings will naturally take up a determinist position" (Anderson, 1936, p. 125). Determinism is simply the thesis that all events arise out of antecedent conditions and go on to cause other things, and it should not be equated with biological fatalism. Admittedly, determinism appears unpalatable to some (e.g., Erdelyi, 1985; Weinberger & Westen, 2001) and while it is not my purpose here to mount a detailed defence of determinism, it is the position accepted here that without a determin-istic outlook, the scientific study of behaviour, or any other phenome-non, would not be possible, since random, non-causal fluctuations could pervade any field of research (see Maze, 1983, 1987). Any account of repression must, therefore, be explicable in deterministic terms (causal antecedents and mechanisms) and, for all its faults, Freud's theory is the only major framework for understanding human persons that comes close to being satisfying in this respect (cf. Kandel, 1999). As summarized by Maze (1983): "Freud's metapsychology, though unfinished, was the one great systematic attempt in modern psychology to outline a deterministic, physiologically based theory of motivation and extend it to embrace all of human behaviour, bodily and mental" (Maze, 1983, pp. 142–143).

The aim of the present work

The aim of this book is to demonstrate that Freud's account of repres-sion is both coherent and defensible (albeit, after refinement). To achieve this will necessitate making sense of the "blindness of the see-ing eye", which will necessarily involve a discussion of conscious and unconscious processes, before proposing an account of repression in terms of selective inattention (which places repression within a com-prehensible framework of normal psychology) and neural inhibition, which makes the more intriguing aspects of repression intelligible.

This book is divided into three parts. Part I involves an extraction and analysis of various directions within the development of Freud's thinking on repression, with the aim to identify core workable ideas and components, and major gaps and weaknesses. This exegesis of the developments in Freud's thinking is designed to allow extraction of elements for a preferred account of repression, via criticisms of elements and themes that are to be rejected. Part II involves closer consideration of the components involved in Freudian repression (e.g., unconscious and conscious processes, etc.), with an effort to build up the overall context required for providing a workable model of repression. Specifically, this part will address and clarify the terms and relations involved in repression to provide a basis for both evaluating various accounts of repression and providing a foundation for the model to be proposed here. The approach here appreciates Freud's theory as situated within, and extending, the ordinary folk-psychological "desire plus belief model" (Cavell, 1991, 1993; Gardner, 1993; Hopkins, 1988, 1995b; Mackay, 1996, 1999; Pataki, 2000; Petocz, 1999; Wollheim, 1991, 1993). Although Freud's account is problematic in several critical aspects, the contention here is that after rejecting certain unworkable elements of the theory and clarifying others, Freud provides a solid basis for an account of repression. Part III will examine various approaches to explaining repression, and highlight the ways in which these attempts fail—notable because they fail to appreciate the requirements identified in Part II—before proposing an account of repression that involves both psychological and neurological processes.

Note

1.   Throughout this work, empiricism simply refers to knowledge through experience and should not be confused with experimentalism. While well-conducted experiments provide systematic observations, objective knowledge is not contingent upon them.

PART I

REPRESSION WITHIN
FREUDIAN THEORY

CHAPTER ONE

The beginning of the theory of repression

Background influences

Two main sources of influence appear to have shaped Freud's thinking and the beginnings of psychoanalysis. One of these was the mechanistic and physicalist approach of figures such as Brücke, Meynert, and Helmholtz. The other, a psychological interest in neurotic phenomena and hypnosis, derived from figures such as Möbius, Charcot, Liébeault, Bernheim, Janet, and Breuer (Jones, 1953; Wollheim, 1991). In the latter camp, Josef Breuer's case of Anna O is historically significant, since it provided the first insight into psychoanalytic explanation. Anna O suffered from, among other complaints, a rigid paralysis to the right side of her body and various thought disturbances. Breuer discovered that her symptoms related to specific psychological *traumas*, where memories of unpleasant experiences had been split off from her consciousness and subsequently become pathogenic. Recalling the traumatic experience (and attendant emotions) with the aid of hypnosis appeared to remove the symptoms. This method was applied to other cases published by Breuer and Freud in *Studies on Hysteria* (Breuer & Freud, 1895d), which, according to Freud (on at least one occasion), marked the birth of psychoanalysis

(Freud, 1913m, p. 207). This was a period of intensive thought for Freud, evidenced not only by his publications, but also by letters to his friend Wilhelm Fliess, and the posthumously published *Project for a Scientific Psychology* (1950[1895]). Although Freud's thinking was to develop in various ways, many of the core assumptions underlying the theory of repression, as well as psychoanalytic theory as a whole, remained consistent with views developed during this time.

The dynamic viewpoint

The first reference to the "repressed" (*verdrängt*) occurs in Breuer and Freud's *Preliminary Communication* (1893, in Breuer & Freud, 1895d) where "traumatic" memories are inaccessible due to *motivated forgetting*. Unlike Janet's conclusion that hysteria was due to a congenital degeneracy (cf. Freud, 1894a, p. 46, 1913m, p. 207), Breuer and Freud write that, with hysteria, "it was a question of things which the patient wished to forget, and therefore intentionally repressed from his conscious thought and inhibited and suppressed" (Breuer & Freud, 1895d, p. 10). The postulation of repression is significant, since it proposes to explain psychopathology formation in terms of mental *dynamics*. That is, some forms of psychopathology, first referred to as "defence neuroses" and then later as "psychoneuroses", resulted from *psychical conflict*, "a struggle between *motive* forces of different degrees of strength or intensity" (Freud, in Breuer & Freud, 1895d, p. 270, my italics). Thus, from the beginning, the central role of motivational conflict is evident and, according to Freud,

> had the merit of entering into the interplay of the psychical forces and of thus bringing the mental processes in hysteria nearer to normal ones, instead of characterising the neurosis as nothing more than a mysterious disorder insusceptible to further analysis. [Freud, 1906a, p. 276]

From very early on, Freud recognizes the importance of unpleasure and pain as a motivating factor in all of human behaviour, writing in the *Project*: "The nervous system has the most decided inclination to a *flight from pain*" (Freud, 1950[1895], p. 307, his italics). Pain as a motivating stimulus implies that defence and repression are part of ordinary functioning, as seen in a comment in a draft sent to

Fliess (Draft K, enclosed in a letter to Fliess dated 1 January 1896), where he writes that "there is a normal trend towards defence—that is, an aversion to directing psychic energy in such a way that unpleasure results" (Masson, 1985, p. 163). Repression is described as a "fending off" of "incompatible ideas" that arouse unpleasure (such as shame, self-reproach, or psychical pain) with the consequence of preventing the repressed ideas from association with conscious thinking (Breuer & Freud, 1895d, p. 157). Thus, repression is comparable to a withdrawal from painful stimuli and acts to minimize the immediate distress following "psychical traumas": "The basis of repression can only be a feeling of unpleasure, the incompatibility between the single idea that is to be repressed and the dominant mass of ideas constituting the ego" (Freud, in Breuer & Freud, 1895d, p. 116).

"Trauma" was initially used in a very general sense where "[a]ny experience which calls up distressing affects—such as those of fright, anxiety, shame or physical pain—may operate as a trauma of this kind" (Breuer & Freud, 1895d, p. 6). Thus, the *type* of experience, the *nature* of distress, and *intensity* of the affective response appear not to be important for defining whether an experience was traumatic or not. However, Krystal (1978) discerns two identifiable models of trauma that emerge in Freud's account: the *unbearable situation* model, emphasizing overwhelming affective states (e.g., fright) and the *dynamics of pathogenesis* model, hereafter referred to as the *conflict* model, where trauma results from psychical conflict and the "incompatibility" of desires. An example of this latter incompatibility is where one's desires conflict with one's moral beliefs. Awareness of this "contradiction" leads to distress and "mental torment" (Freud, in Breuer & Freud, 1895d, p. 165), and the "traumatic moment" is defined as an idea coming "into distressing opposition to the patient's ego" (Freud, 1896b, p. 162):

> The actual traumatic moment, then, is the one at which the incompatibility forces itself upon the ego and at which the latter decides on the repudiation of the incompatible idea. [Freud, in Breuer & Freud, 1895d, p. 123]

Hence, the motivation for repression is unpleasure and distress resulting from the recognition of incompatibility. Repression, therefore, is a motivated psychological activity, comprehensible in terms of defensive pain-avoiding responses (see Boag, 2007a,b).

The ego and repression

The view that repression is motivated by the recognition of incompatibility between desires and morality and the subsequent experience of unpleasure brings us to the role of the "ego" (*Ich*). According to Freud, it is the ego that suffers the trauma and which instigates repression:

> The patient's ego had been approached by an idea which proved to be incompatible, which provoked on the part of the ego a repelling force of which the purpose was defence against this incompatible idea. [Freud, in Breuer & Freud, 1895d, p. 269]

> Thus a psychical force, aversion on the part of the ego, had originally driven the pathogenic idea out of association . . . [Freud, in Breuer & Freud, 1895d, p. 269; cf. Freud, 1896b, p. 170]

The term *Ich* or "I" (translated as the Latin "ego") appears in Freud's earlier writings to simply refer non-technically to a notion of "self" (Bettelheim, 1983; Brenner, 1957). However, while this is generally true, there are also early indications that Freud was developing a view of the ego that was comparable to the ego as the structured functional system found in his later formulations (e.g., Freud, 1923b). In Freud's *Project* (1950[1895]), written during this period, the ego is an organization of constantly cathected neurones operating to maximize "discharge" of Q (*quantity*, the hypothesized psychophysical energy) from the psychophysical apparatus (Freud, 1950[1895], p. 323), a position also hinted at in the *Studies* (e.g., Breuer & Freud, 1895d, p. 269). It is generally correct to say that Freud entertained both positions throughout his work (McIntosh, 1986), and what is consistent between the two views is that the ego is intimately bound up with *consciousness*. On a number of occasions, Freud refers to "ego-consciousness" (e.g., Breuer & Freud, 1895d, pp. 291, 299), comparing this to a "defile" (Breuer & Freud, 1895d, p. 291). Repression, accordingly, is the blocking of the defile:

> If there are difficulties in the way of mastering this single pathogenic memory—as, for instance, if the patient does not relax his resistance against it, if he tries to repress or mutilate it—then the defile is, so to speak, blocked . . . the single memory which is in a process of breaking through remains in front of the patient until he has taken it up into

the breadth of his ego. The whole spatially-extended mass of psychogenic material is in this way drawn through a narrow cleft and thus arrives in consciousness cut up, as it were, into pieces or strips. [Breuer & Freud, 1895d, p. 291]

This use of a spatial metaphor for understanding the ego's role in repression is fairly common in Freud's writings. For instance, at other times, repression is described as a "barrier erected by the will" (Freud, 1894a, p. 50), and one question that requires resolving is exactly how such metaphors are to be understood.

Repression as an intentional activity

Since repression is a motivated activity, instigated by the ego in response to "trauma", the question is then whether repression is a simple act of avoiding painful stimuli that can be described as voluntary or "intentional". Breuer and Freud's early reference to repression explicitly refers to repression in intentional terms with respect to it being "a question of things which the patient wished to forget, and therefore *intentionally* repressed from his conscious thought and inhibited and suppressed" (Breuer & Freud, 1895d, p. 10, my italics). Freud's editor, Strachey, however, believes that Freud did not mean by this reference to intentionality that repression involves any implication of ordinary voluntary intention of which the subject might be conscious. Instead, Strachey writes,

> On some of its earlier appearances the term 'repressed' is accompanied . . . by the adverb 'intentionally' (*'absichtlich'*) or by 'deliberately' (*'willkürlich'*). This is expanded by Freud in one place [Freud, 1894], where he states that the act of repression is 'introduced by an effort of will, for which the motive can be assigned'. Thus the word 'intentionally' merely indicates the existence of a motive and carries no implication of *conscious* intention. [Strachey, in Breuer & Freud, 1895d, p. 10*n*, his italics]

That is, repression is simply a motivated response to pain that could occur without knowledge of its occurrence (Strachey, in Breuer & Freud, 1895d, p. 10*n*), a position that has been taken to justify the prevailing viewpoint that repression necessarily occurs unconsciously (see Boag, 2010a). That repression necessarily must be unconscious has been vigorously challenged by Erdelyi (1990, 1993, 2001, 2006), who notes that if repression can occur consciously then there is no dispute that repression exists in terms of ordinary selective attention (2006, p. 500). However, whether repression necessarily must be unconscious hinges partly upon what is precisely meant by the terms "unconscious" and "conscious" and it is interesting to note that Freud's description of events in the *Studies* can, at times, easily be interpreted along the lines that repression could occur with awareness. For example, both Erdelyi (1990, p. 13) and Macmillan (1991, pp. 102–103) note that Freud's description of the case of Miss Lucy R in the *Studies* explicitly demonstrates that the act of repression occurred with the subject's knowledge. Her initial "act of will", bringing repression into operation against the love for her employer, was easily recalled. Miss Lucy R had desires for her employer that "she had thought intentionally to leave in obscurity and had made efforts to forget" (Freud, in Breuer & Freud, 1895d, p. 117). For a time, she had been aware of these desires, but after realizing that these were unfulfillable, "she decided to banish the whole business from her mind" (Freud, in Breuer & Freud, 1895d, p. 118). In an exchange where Miss Lucy R agrees with Freud's interpretation of her repressed desire creating her hysteric conversion, Freud asks her, "But if you knew you loved your employer why didn't you tell me?", and she responds: "I didn't know—or rather, I didn't want to know. I wanted to drive it out of my head and not think of it again; and I believe latterly I have succeeded" (in Breuer & Freud, 1895d, p. 117). Thus, both Erdelyi and Macmillan's position appear justified, since Miss Lucy R appears aware of the act of repression.

On the other hand, some commentators claim that although Freud initially postulated repression as a conscious process, he quickly came to abandon this point of view in favour of repression as an unconscious process (Brenner, 1957; Eagle, 2000a). Presumably, this must occur somewhere between the time of the *Studies'* publication (1895) and subsequent writing, since, by 1896, we find Freud referring to repression as "the psychical mechanism of (unconscious) *defence*" (Freud, 1896b, p. 162, his italics) and "that it is impossible for the ego to direct to the repressed material the part of the psychical energy to which conscious thought is linked" (Draft K, in Masson, 1985, p. 167). However, no clear point of transition occurs, since Freud (1895c) also notes early on that "the expulsion of the incompatible idea is brought about in an unconscious manner which has left no trace in the patient's memory" (pp. 79–80) and that rather than changing views, there is another interpretation to be considered. This interpretation involves an apparent paradox with respect to whether it is possible to both know and yet not know something at the same time. In the case of Miss Lucy R, cited above, Freud writes in a footnote that this paradoxical state of affairs explicitly is the case, writing,

> I have never managed to give a better description than this of the strange state of mind in which one knows and does not know a thing at the same time. It is clearly impossible to understand it unless one has been in such a state oneself. [Breuer & Freud, 1895d, p. 117n]

After then providing a similar example from his own experience, Freud describes this as being "afflicted by that blindness of the seeing eye" (p. 117n), all of which suggests that the debate as to whether repression is *either* conscious *or* unconscious is too simplistic and something much more complex is occurring. This, it will be argued, is the central difficulty with understanding unconscious processes, subliminal perception, and so forth, and reconciling this apparent paradox provides the key to understanding repression and, to some extent, unlocking the dynamics of the mind.

Repression and awareness of the target

One issue that is much clearer in Freud's writings is that in so far as repression is motivated by conflict and ensuing unpleasure, it must involve awareness and evaluation of the "offending target". As Freud recognized, for repression to occur there must be awareness of the distressing idea (a "traumatic moment") on *at least one* occasion:

> Consciousness, plainly, does not know in advance when an incompatible idea is going to crop up. The incompatible idea that, together with its concomitants, is later excluded and forms a separate psychical group must originally have been in communication with the main stream of thought. Otherwise, the conflict that led to their exclusion could not have taken place. It is these moments, then, that are to be described as "traumatic" . . . .. [Breuer & Freud, 1895d, p. 167; cf. Draft K, in Masson, 1985, pp. 164–165]

Additionally, Freud notes that after the initial repression there could be several other instances when the distressing idea becomes known again (Breuer & Freud, 1895d; Freud, 1894a). These "auxiliary" moments occur "whenever the arrival of fresh impressions of the same [as the repressed] succeed in breaking through the barrier erected by the will", supplying the "weakened idea with fresh affect and . . . re-establishing for a time the associative link between the two psychical groups" (Freud, 1894a, p. 50). Auxiliary moments, in turn, require further defensive acts, and Freud's position then is that both "traumatic" and "auxiliary" moments include knowing the target of repression.

The "return of the repressed": the seduction hypothesis and diphasic repression

The ideas arousing unpleasure and leading to repression were generally considered to be "immoral", and though Freud's theory of sexuality (including infantile sexuality) had not yet explicitly emerged, the desires arousing conflict were often "sexual" in a broad sense, ranging from "tender inclinations and wishes, daydreaming and infatuations to the consummated sexual act" (May, 1999, p. 777). An example here can be seen in the *Studies* case of Elisabeth von R, where her sexual desires (and related "ideas") towards her brother-in-law were "incompatible" with her moral standards: "This girl felt towards her brother-in-law a tenderness whose acceptance into consciousness was resisted by her whole moral being" (Freud, in Breuer & Freud, 1895d, p. 157). This conflict between her sexual desires and moral tendencies created distress, and, subsequently, the offending ideas related to the desires were repressed. The antagonism between sexuality and morality was, of course, set to emerge as a major source of conflict in Freud's theory, and although morality and sexuality were not singled out as the only possible source of conflict, Freud states that given prevailing social mores "it is easy to see that it is precisely sexual life which brings with it the most copious occasions for the emergence of incompatible ideas" (Freud, 1894a, p. 52). The prevailing moral and social climate cultivated a shameful outlook towards sexuality, motivating repression. Accordingly: "Where there is no shame . . . or where no morality comes about . . . or where disgust is blunted by the conditions of life . . . there too no repression . . ." (Draft K, in Masson, 1985, p. 163).

In the *Studies*, Freud discusses the repression of traumatic memories during adult life (cf. the case of Miss Lucy R, above). However, between 1895 and 1897, Freud developed a line of thinking referred to as the *seduction hypothesis*, where he believed that adult neuroses could be traced to still earlier childhood sexual experiences. A necessary condition for later repressions of sexuality in adulthood was a sexual seduction during childhood (Freud, 1896a,b): "'Repression' of the memory of a distressing sexual experience which occurs in maturer years is only possible for those in whom that experience can activate the memory-trace of a trauma in childhood" (Freud, 1896b, p. 166; cf. pp. 197, 199). From this viewpoint, repression can be described as diphasic, in so far as there are two distinct stages separated by puberty. The first stage was a necessary condition for the second stage and involved a sexually immature child becoming the victim of an *actual* sexual seduction, either by an adult or another child. Freud believed that the sexually immature child could not assimilate the sexual experiences, but that these experiences persisted, nevertheless, as "unconscious memories" (Freud, 1896c, p. 211). Such unconscious memories themselves were not sufficient for producing pathogenic effects, however. It was only after these memories of seduction were revived after puberty that problems would occur: "it is not the [seduction] experiences themselves which act traumatically but their later revival as a *memory* after the subject has entered sexual maturity" (Freud, 1896b, p. 164, his italics). The diphasic nature of sexuality results in the earlier infantile sexual experiences becoming more powerful than when they had first occurred, since, although memories are typically less vivid than an actual experience, the memory of the sexual seduction has a greater excitatory effect than the original experience if aroused during or after puberty, since puberty increases the capacity for sexual reaction:

> The trend toward defence becomes detrimental, however, if it is directed against ideas which are also able, in the form of memories, to release fresh unpleasure—as in the case with sexual ideas. Here, indeed, is the one possibility realised of a memory's having a greater releasing power than was produced by the experience corresponding to it. Only one thing is necessary for this: that puberty should be interpolated between the experience and its repetition in memory—an event which thus strongly increases the effect of the revival. [Draft K, in Masson, 1985, p. 163]

The memories from infantile sexual experiences behave, then, as current events after their re-arousal (Freud, 1896b; Freud's letter to Fliess dated 6 December 1896, in Masson 1985, p. 209), and the feelings and associated memories subsequently become compulsive and incapable of normal inhibition:

> If *A*, when it was current, released a particular unpleasure and if, when it is re-awakened, it releases fresh unpleasure, then this cannot be inhibited. If so, the memory is behaving as though it were some current event. This can only occur with sexual events, because the magnitudes of the excitations which these release increase of themselves with time (with sexual development). [Freud's letter to Fliess dated 6 December 1896, in Masson, 1985, p. 209]

A summary of this scheme is provided by Freud (1896b): (i) an early sexual seduction during sexual immaturity leads to unassimilated "unconscious memories", (ii) at sexual maturation self-reproaches (i.e., conflict) become attached to the *memory* of the seduction, (iii) both memory and self-reproach are repressed and replaced by primary symptoms of defence, typically conscientiousness, shame, and self-distrust, (iv) there is a period of apparent health (successful defence), until finally, (v) *illness proper* "characterised by *the return of the repressed memories*—that is, therefore, by the failure of defence" (p. 169, his italics).[1]

While in the above scheme Freud writes that it is the *memory* of the seduction which is targeted by defence, elsewhere Freud writes that the unassimilated memories of childhood operate *unconsciously* (Freud, 1896b, pp. 166–167; cf. p. 167*n*). Repression in adulthood requires an "incompatible idea" having some (logical or associative) connection with the "unconscious memories" of the seduction experience:

> *The defence achieves its purpose of thrusting the incompatible idea out of consciousness if there are infantile scenes present in the (hitherto normal) subject in the form of unconscious memories, and if the idea that is to be repressed can be brought into logical or associative connection with an infantile experience of that kind.* [Freud, 1896c, p. 211, his italics]

On this account, rather than actual memories of the event being targeted by repression, what is repressed in adulthood is material bearing some associative connection with those same memories. For instance, adult sexual feelings might arouse shame due to feelings associated with the infantile unconscious memories.

The significance of the seduction hypothesis is that the repression of sexual mental content in infancy creates conditions for symptoms of the psychoneuroses (or the "return of the repressed"). Freud, in places, presumes that memory traces cannot be extinguished (1895d, p. 351), and, consequently, repression does not destroy the targeted mental content. Instead, the targeted idea forms a second psychical group, separate from consciousness: "the memory trace of the repressed idea has, after all, not been dissolved; from now on, it forms the nucleus of a second psychical group" (Freud, 1894a, p. 49).

> The idea is not annihilated by a repudiation of this kind [repression], but merely repressed into the unconscious . . . What he wanted was to do away with an idea, as though it had never appeared, but all he succeeds in doing is to isolate it psychically. [Breuer & Freud, 1895d, p. 123]

In spite of the fact that the idea component is now unconscious (or incapable of association) it persists as an active influence on behaviour, generating neurotic symptoms: "Thanks to the abundant causal connections, every pathogenic idea which has not yet been got rid of operates as a motive for the whole of the products of the neurosis..." (Breuer & Freud, 1895d, p. 299). The repressed persists as an active influence upon behaviour (i.e., it is responsible for symptoms) and, thus, Freud must provide an account for explaining how repression is maintained.

Maintaining repression: affect/idea dissociation

Rather than targeting immediate perception of the "external world", the primary targets of repression are mnemic mental content (i.e., memories) and thought processes. Freud here, like many authors, considers "thought" to be distinct from "perception", writing that repression "cannot be employed against perceptions, for these are able to compel attention (as is evidenced by their consciousness); it only comes in question against memories and thought" (Draft K, in Masson, 1985, p. 163). Freud refers to *Vorstellungen* ("presentations"), which was commonly used in German psychological and philosophical writing at the time (e.g., Brentano (1874, p. 5) and Freud's editor, Strachey, translates *Vorstellung* as "idea", covering the English terms "idea", "image", and "presentation" (in Freud, 1915e, p. 174).

Freud's philosophical position concerning memories and thought ("ideas") appears influenced by the Austrian philosopher Franz Brentano (1838–1917), whom Freud knew personally and whose lectures he had attended at the University of Vienna (Frampton, 1991; Jones, 1953; Merlan, 1945; Wollheim, 1991). While it is also true—as MacIntyre (1958) notes—that Freud's notion of "idea" has parallels with the British empiricist tradition's atomic view (e.g., Locke, 1690, p. 34), it is fair to say that both positions are present in Freud's account.[2] However, Brentano provides a discussion of psychological processes which is helpful for understanding both Freud's thought and cognition generally (even if Brentano denied the possibility of unconscious mentality). Brentano distinguishes mentality from physical objects through the notion of *intentionality*:

> Every mental phenomenon includes something as an object within itself, although they do not do so in the same way. In presentation something is presented, in judgement something is affirmed or denied, in love loved, in hate hated, in desire desired and so on . . . No physical object exhibits anything like it. We can, therefore, define mental phenomena by saying that they are those which contain an object intentionally within themselves. [Brentano, 1874, pp. 88–89]

That is, all mental acts such as judgements and emotions take (or *intend*) objects and Freud generally refers to "ideas" as the *object* of the mental act (McIntosh, 1986; Wollheim, 1991).

At the same time, however, the role of affects was paramount in this stage of Freud's theorizing and although no consistent articulation of their precise nature was given, they were generally conceptualized as the experienced dimension of the hypothesized excitations or psychical energy (Freud, 1894a, pp. 48–49):

> in mental functioning something is to be distinguished—a quota of affect or sum of excitation—which possesses all the characteristics of a quantity (though we have no means of measuring it), which is capable of increase, diminution, displacement and discharge, and which is spread over the memory-traces of ideas somewhat as an electric charge is spread over the surface of a body. [Freud, 1894a, p. 60]

Some authors appear to take this concept of "excitation" literally (e.g., Kaplan-Solms & Solms, 2000; Solms, 1997b), where, for instance,

Solms (1997b) sees psychic energy, cathexis, and discharge as "conceptually equivalent to the particles, waves, energies, and forces of the physicists" (p. 688). However, a simple problem with taking Freud concretely here is that it is difficult to see how Freud's account can be reconciled with what we know about nervous system functioning (Linke, 1998). Instead, these physicalist terms might be better understood as metaphors describing subjective experience where the "quantity of psychic energy" refers descriptively to the "intensity" of investment directed at the intended object of a mental act. McIntosh accordingly notes, "Motivation admits of degrees of magnitude . . . urges are more or less strong, desires more or less intense. The term 'psychic energy' means simply 'magnitude of urge or desire'" (McIntosh, 1986, p. 431; cf. Lewin & Kubie, in Kubie, 1947; Horowitz, 1977; Rosenblatt & Thickstun, 1977; Schwartz, 1987; Wallerstein, 1977; Zepf, 2001).

However, there are problems with Freud's explanation of repression in terms of ideas and affects. Freud proposes that it is the economic feature of affects that gives ideas their strength or intensity and influences their position in associative thinking. As he writes, "the part played in association by an idea increases in proportion to the amount of its affect" (Breuer & Freud, 1895d, p. 165). At this time, too, Freud also notes that the relation between affects and ideas could be one of attachment and detachment, whereby the affect associated with one idea could be displaced to another, in much the same way as anger could be displaced from one person to another. This provides Freud with a description of some psychopathological states involving a "false connection" between the affect and what it is directed at in both Freud's early (e.g., Breuer & Freud, 1895d, p. 67; Freud, 1894a, pp. 52–53) and later work (e.g., Freud, 1909d, pp. 175–176, 1915d, pp. 152–153).

At this stage, both Breuer and Freud believe that only ideas with sufficient affective intensity can become conscious. For an idea to become conscious, it must have a certain intensity (or be "quantitatively" strong enough): "As a rule, when the intensity of an unconscious idea increases it enters consciousness *ipso facto*. Only when its intensity is slight does it remain unconscious" (Breuer, in Breuer & Freud, 1895d, p. 223). Repression is said to dissociate the affect from the idea so that it becomes "weak" and thereafter it is incapable of becoming conscious:

Both the memory and the affect attached to the ideas are there once and for all and cannot be eradicated. But it amounts to an approximate fulfilment of the task [of repression] if the ego succeeds in *turning this powerful idea into a weak one*, in robbing it of the affect—the sum of excitation—with which it is loaded. The weak idea will then have virtually no demands to make on the work of association. [Freud, 1894a, pp. 48–49, his italics]

. . . we can infer in what the process of defence consisted: it consisted in turning a strong idea into a weak one, in robbing it of its affect. [Breuer & Freud, 1895d, p. 280]

That is, repression operates via robbing the offending idea of its affect/excitation so that it is weak and incapable of becoming known. As a result, the idea (now robbed of its intensity) remains unconscious and "excluded from association" (Breuer & Freud, 1895d, p. 11) whereas the affect (or sum of excitation) follows a different course in line with Freud's hypothesized functioning of the nervous system. Usually, after any experience, the emotional attachment and intensity connected with the memory fades due to *abreaction* (discharging the corresponding affect) or through a gradual "wearing away" by the normal processes of thought and association (Freud, in Breuer & Freud, 1895d, p. 116; cf. Freud, 1893a). Dissociating the affect and ideas through repression prevents these processes occurring: ideas remaining unconscious and excluded from association cannot "work off" the affect attached to them, and so the affect never achieves adequate discharge. As Rosenblatt (1985, p. 94) observes, Freud presents a "toxic" theory of affects: repression operates by robbing ideas of their affect (amounting to "de-powering" the ideas) and rechannelling the affect elsewhere into substitutes and symptoms.

Problems with the affect–idea dissociation account

There is a major problem with trying to explain repression via affect–idea dissociation. As I have argued elsewhere (Boag, 2007a), if it is accepted that repression operates via severing the affect from the idea and rechannelling the affect elsewhere, then a repressed idea should remain unconscious simply due to the fact that it is incapable of becoming conscious. Furthermore, the affect–idea dissociation explanation of the formation of unconscious ideas is self-contradictory with respect to explaining symptom formation, since there should be no problem after repression since the unconscious ideas are simply too weak to act as a nuisance to conscious awareness. Breuer, in fact, was aware of the problem with the claim, then, that unconscious ideas actively persist and exert a powerful effect upon behaviour: "What seems hard to understand is how an idea can be sufficiently intense to provoke a lively motor act, for instance, and at the same time not intense enough to become conscious" (Breuer, in Breuer & Freud, 1895d, p. 223).

In fact, Breuer even comes to contradict the claim that unconscious ideas lack intensity: "Ideas such as these which, though current, are unconscious, not because of their relatively small degree of liveliness, but in spite of their great intensity, may be described as ideas that are 'inadmissible to consciousness'" (Breuer, in Breuer & Freud, 1895d, p. 225).

In other words, the particular problem in this account of maintaining repression is that Breuer and Freud's theory is premised on the understanding that unconscious ideas remain powerfully operative, producing symptoms, and so should, accordingly, be capable of becoming conscious. However, since the repressed ideas are both powerful and do not become conscious, then some further explanation of why this is so is required to explain how ideas remain unconscious after repression.

The clinical phenomenon of resistance

Another problem with the affect–idea dissociation account is that it does not explain the clinical phenomenon of resistance. The first mention of resistance to treatment occurs in the case of Fräulein Elisabeth von R, who, during treatment, fell silent or suffered failures of associative thinking. Freud concluded that this was not accidental, but resulted from the same forces that initiated the original repression:

> At the time when I started her treatment the group of ideas relating to her love had already been separated from her knowledge . . . The resistance with which she had repeatedly met the reproduction of scenes

which operated traumatically corresponded in fact to the energy with which the incompatible idea had been forced out of her associations. [Freud, in Breuer & Freud, 1895d, p. 157]

. . . by means of my psychical work I had to overcome a psychical force in the patients which was opposed to the pathogenic ideas becoming conscious (being remembered). A new understanding seemed to open before my eyes when it occurred to me that this must no doubt be the same psychical force that had played a part in the generating of the hysterical symptom and had at that time prevented the pathogenic idea from becoming conscious. [Freud, in Breuer & Freud, 1895d, p. 268]

The failures of association and other forms of resistance result from the unpleasurable task of becoming aware of painful material that had been repressed (Breuer & Freud, 1895d, p. 282), and this activity, too, is attributed to the ego: "Thus a psychical force, aversion on the part of the ego, had originally driven the pathogenic idea out of association and was now opposing its return to memory" (Breuer & Freud, 1895d, p. 269; cf. p. 278).

Laplanche and Pontalis (1973) note, however, that Freud provides two explanations of resistance: "According to one, the resistance is governed by its distance from the repressed; according to the other, it is equivalent to a defensive function" (p. 395). The first appears to explain resistance in terms of mental "distance" and "storage", stating simply that resistance increases as distance to the repressed decreases. In other words, the amount of resistance produced is said to result as a function of the associational proximity of ideas to the repressed material, a position found also in Freud's later account of repression (Freud, 1915d, p. 150). To explain this, Freud writes that the repressed psychical material is "stratified in at least three different ways" around a central repressed nucleus (Freud, 1895d, p. 288):

To begin with there is a nucleus consisting in memories of events or trains of thought in which the traumatic factor has culminated or the pathogenic idea has found its purest manifestation. Round this nucleus we find what is often an incredibly profuse amount of other mnemic material which has to be worked through in the analysis and which is . . . arranged in a threefold order. [Breuer & Freud, 1895d, p. 288]

In this account, memories are ordered *chronologically, thematically,* and in relation to the *degree of consciousness* within the three separate layers. Ideas belonging to the external stratum remain in the ego's possession, while deeper material is unknown to the ego, or, if brought to its attention, appears "alien". Each stratum has a corresponding degree of resistance, increasing as attention moves from the peripheral strata towards the nucleus:

> The contents of each particular stratum are characterised by an equal degree of resistance, and that degree increases in proportion as the strata are nearer to the nucleus . . . The most peripheral strata contain the memories (or files), which, belonging to different themes, are easily remembered and have always been clearly conscious. The deeper we go the more difficult it becomes for the emerging memories to be recognised, till near the nucleus we come upon memories which the patient disavows even in reproducing them. [Breuer & Freud, 1895d, p. 289; cf. p. 300]

Geisler (1985) compares Freud's strategy here with a modern cognitive storage model:

> The way an item is stored depends on the degree of relatedness to the original traumatic memory, and this in turn is what affects the degree of difficulty in retrieving the item . . . Thus the degree of repression (i.e., the difficulty in retrieval) of an item can be thought of as depending on the way it is encoded and stored. Another way of conceptualising the above model is that memories which are associated with the original painful memory are encoded with a negative affective component. The strength of this component varies according to the closeness of the association. Thus, difficulty in retrieval will depend on the strength of the negative affective component associated with memory. [Geisler, 1985, pp. 277–278]

However, this encoding/storage metaphor is at best misleading, since, as Geisler suggests, the "difficulty in retrieval" is dynamic, arising from an affective basis (the strength of the negative affective component). That is, accounting for this negative affective component is required, and, as we have seen, this appears to require an evaluation by the ego of the target being "incompatible" (e.g., Breuer & Freud, 1895d, p. 167). Accordingly, if resistance has an affective basis (i.e., results from unpleasure), as Freud generally maintains, then any resistance produced cannot merely result from a certain idea p being located at a particular point in relation to the repressed core q, since there also needs to be an explanation as to how the unpleasure is generated. Instead, since resistance has an affective basis (as with repression), then it should be motivated by unpleasure based on conflict, which, as already noted, involves a subject cognizing the repressed as "incompatible" (a "traumatic moment") and, consequently, creating unpleasure. What must occur with resistance is that p is recognized as distressing or as having some relation to q, either of which *causes* distress and resistance. However, if it is the case that the ego does not know what material is repressed, then it is difficult to see how the ego could resist, as it appears to require one part of the person knowing what must be resisted and another part remaining ignorant of the material. In fact, it is from the concept of "resistance" that Sartre (1956) launches his well-known attack on Freudian repression in relationship to what "part" of the mind could possibly resist. Thus, Freud's early account of repression and repression remains incomplete, and the possibility of both knowing and not knowing an event still requires elaboration.

Notes

1. A slightly different version is found in Draft K (Masson, 1985, p. 164), where the seduction itself could be traumatic leading to repression.
2. It should also be pointed out that this atomist position is especially problematic (see McMullen, 1996a).

CHAPTER TWO

Repression in the topographic model

Rejection of the seduction hypothesis

F reud retracted his seduction hypothesis as early as 1897, in a letter to Fliess dated 21 September (Masson, 1985), although, as Frampton (1991) observes, public denouncement did not occur until 1906 (Freud, 1906a). The retraction is associated with a shift in Freud's thinking that was to underlie the later developments in Freud's psychoanalytic theory. Rather than repression simply targeting memories of sexual abuse, such memories were seen as imaginative falsifications or "screen memories" (Freud, 1899a). Here, the appreciation of the ubiquity of motivational factors contributing to psychic life becomes of paramount importance to Freud. As he writes in a letter to Fliess dated 2 May 1897, memory is not simply about recall and retrieval, but rather a motivated activity related to impulses: "[An] important piece of insight tells me that the psychical structures which, in hysteria, are affected by repression are not in reality memories—since no one indulges in mnemic activity without a motive—but *impulses* . . ." (Masson, 1985, p. 239, Freud's italics). Hence, although "memories" were targeted or distorted by defence, it was their association with motivational states (desires, impulses, and phantasies of gratification) that was the deciding factor in repression. Reflecting this, Freud begins to discuss the "repression of impulses" (in letters dated 31 May and 7 July 1897, in Masson, 1985, pp. 252, 255), which, to some extent, simply extends one line of Freud's early thinking in the *Studies* where he discusses the notion of conflicting "motive forces" (Breuer & Freud, 1895d, p. 270).

The emerging view of mind, then, in Freud's thinking was an active and dynamic one which recognizes the central role of endogenous motivational factors in both thought and behaviour. The mind becomes viewed as an economy of competing impulses attempting to cancel one another out, with the effect of a "Darwinian struggle in the mind" (Young-Bruehl & Bethelard, 1999, p. 825):

> When I have reconstructed the dream-thoughts, I habitually find the most intense psychical impulses in them striving to make themselves felt and struggling as a rule against others that are sharply opposed to them. [Freud, 1900a, p. 467]

> An impulse or urge is present which seeks to release pleasure from a particular source and, if it were allowed free play, would release it. Besides this, another urge is present which works against the generation of pleasure—inhibits it, that is, or suppresses it. [Freud, 1905c, p. 135]

Repression here involves one impulse inhibiting another and the dynamics of psychoneurotic psychopathology are described as a "volition . . . opposed by a counter-volition" (Freud, 1900a, p. 337) or a conflict "between two mental currents" (Freud, 1906a, pp. 276–277), "opposing tendencies" (Freud, 1909d, p. 192, 1905a, p. 267), or "two opposing impulses" (Freud, 1909d, p. 192). This "complication of motives" (Freud, 1905e, p. 60) leads to motivational disequilibrium, and one which Freud explains in terms of the relative strength of the impulses and their ability to dominate one another: "The suppressing current must, as the outcome shows, be a certain amount stronger than the suppressed one, which, however, is not on that account abolished" (Freud, 1905c, p. 135). Similarly, "Whether the struggle ends in health, in neurosis, or in a countervailing superiority of achievement, depends on *quantitative* considerations, on the relative strength of the conflicting forces" (Freud, 1910a, p. 50, his italics).

This greater explicit appreciation of motivational dynamics addresses the explanatory limitation from the early period by accounting for the "upward drive" of the repressed. Unlike the early period, the repressed is explicitly intense and active, attempting to "break through" into conscious thinking (Freud, 1907a, p. 48, 1910a, pp. 26–27, 1915d, p. 149): "The unconscious—that is to say, the 'repressed' . . . has no other endeavour than to break through the pressure weighing down on it and force its way either to consciousness or to a discharge through some real action" (Freud, 1920g, p. 19).

Thus, Freud's greater explicit appreciation for motivational factors accounts for one difficulty of the early period, although an account of maintaining repression is still required. However, during this phase in Freud's thinking, we also see the formal emergence of Freud's system theory of mind, which has major implications with respect to understanding repression.

Development of the systematic position

The publication of *The Interpretation of Dreams* (1900a) marks a major turning-point with the emergence of a theory of mind that has come to be known as the topographic model. Freud had earlier developed a systems account of the mind in the *Project*, but, unlike the neurological focus therein, the post-1900 account presents a psychological approach where mental processes possess particular qualities and operate according to certain laws pertaining to their respective system. Each system is primarily defined through their respective relation to consciousness, whereby Freud proposes that mental processes are either unconscious, preconscious, or conscious, depending upon whether they belong to the system *Unconscious* (*Ucs.*), *Preconscious* (*Pcs.*) or *Conscious* (*Cs.*). As suggested by their nomenclature, *Cs.* processes are *descriptively* conscious (i.e., presently in awareness), whereas *Ucs.* processes are *descriptively* unconscious (i.e., not known), and either inaccessible to conscious thinking or only becoming known with difficulty. On the other hand, *Pcs.* processes are *descriptively* unconscious (i.e., not presently in awareness), but capable of becoming conscious. Here, we see an account of unconscious mental processes that differs from other accounts which existed prior to Freud in the work of authors such as Theodor Lipps (see Jones, 1953; Whyte, 1962):

Both of them [systems *Ucs.* and *Pcs.*] are unconscious in the sense used by psychology; but in our sense one of them, which we term the *Ucs.* is also *inadmissible to consciousness*, while we term the other the *Pcs.* because its excitations . . . are able to reach consciousness. [Freud, 1900a, pp. 614–615, his italics; cf. Freud, 1915e, p. 173]

The system *Ucs.* is notable here as "a particular realm of the mind with its own wishful impulses, its own mode of expression and its peculiar mental mechanisms which are not in force elsewhere" (Freud, 1916–1917, p. 212; cf. Freud, 1912g, p. 266; 1915e, p. 186). Character-istics peculiar to it include *primary process* mentation, *exemption from mutual contradiction, timelessness,* and *replacement of external by psychical reality* (Freud, 1915e, p. 187). Primary process psychical energy is *highly mobile,* pressing for immediate discharge, and operating via the "pleasure principle": "As a result of the unpleasure principle, then, the first ψ-system [*Ucs.*] is totally incapable of bringing anything disagreeable into the context of its thoughts. It is unable to do anything but wish" (Freud, 1900a, p. 600).

However, though the one aim of wishes is discharge, primary process mobility means that wishes are subject to *condensation* and *displacement*:

The cathectic intensities [in the *Ucs.*] are much more mobile. By the process of *displacement* one idea may surrender to another its whole quota of cathexis; by the process of *condensation* it may appropriate the whole cathexis of several other ideas. I have proposed to regard these two processes as distinguishing marks of the so-called *primary psychical process.* [Freud, 1915e, p. 186, his italics]

With displacement, the object of a desire might shift to another, while with condensation, several desires may converge on a single object. Both these processes, and the pressure for immediate dis-charge, is said to give the *Ucs.* processes an *irrational* character, since the meaning and relation of ideas to reality is neglected:

The chief characteristic of these processes is that the whole stress is laid upon making the cathecting energy mobile and capable of discharge; the content and the proper meaning of the psychical elements to which the cathexes are attached are treated as of little consequence. [Freud, 1900a, p. 597; cf. Freud, 1915e, p. 187]

Hence, Freud depicts the system *Ucs.*'s operations as governing all that is *irrational* and *illogical* in the mind:

> The governing rules of logic carry no weight in the unconscious; it might be called the realm of the Illogical. Urges with contrary aims exist side by side in the unconscious without any need arising for any adjustment between them. Either they have no influence whatever on each other, or if they have, no decision is reached, but a compromise comes about which is nonsensical since it embraces mutually incompatible details. [Freud, 1940a[1938], pp. 168–169; cf. Freud, 1900a, p. 598, 1905e, p. 61, 1915e, p. 186]

The primary process is said to come first developmentally, and, initially, the infant's helplessness and inability to tolerate frustration in the face of an unsatisfied need creates a primary process hallucinatory reinvestment of experiences of satisfaction (Freud, 1900a, p. 598). This temporarily silences the need, but is insufficient to put a lasting end to the source of stimulation, since a *real* object or event is required for any actual gratification. The apparatus learns to inhibit reinvesting the mnemic idea to the point of hallucinatory perception. Accordingly, the infant learns to discern veridical from non-veridical experience through awareness of "indications of reality", which determine whether the wished for object and situation is, in fact, real or not: "A new principle of mental functioning was thus introduced; what was presented in the mind was no longer what was agreeable but what was real, even if it happened to be disagreeable (Freud, 1911b, p. 219).

This introduces the "reality" principle, a reality-tempered modification of the primitive pleasure principle, where actual conditions of satisfaction and frustration are taken into account before initiating action:

> Under the influence of the ego's instincts of self-preservation, the pleasure principle is replaced by the *reality principle*. This latter principle does not abandon the intention of ultimately obtaining pleasure, but it nevertheless demands and carries into effect the postponement of satisfaction, the abandonment of a number of possibilities of gaining satisfaction and the temporary toleration of unpleasure as a step on the long indirect road to pleasure. [Freud, 1920g, p. 10, his italics; cf. 1900a, p. 601, 1915c, p. 120, 1925i, p. 127).

A consequence is the development of the system *Pcs.* where the more reality-orientated *secondary* processes gradually replace or cover the earlier, primitive, primary processes. The secondary processes prevent the free discharge of excitations into hallucinations, delaying discharge until the required conditions for satisfaction are present (Freud, 1900a, p. 599, 1915e, p. 188).

The ego and the system Cs.

The system *Cs.* is presented as the *knower* responsible for attending to *qualities*,[1] comparable to a "sense-organ" receiving excitation from both the exterior (the perceptual system or *Pcpt.*) and interior (*Pcs.*) systems of the apparatus (Freud, 1900a, pp. 574, 615–616; cf. Freud, 1920g, p. 24, 1923b, p. 19, 1933a, p. 75). Freud, in several places, remarks that only a single knower exists within the person; there is no splitting up of consciousness such that there is a consciousness unknown to another consciousness within the one mind or person:

> We have no right to extend the meaning of this word [conscious] so far as to make it include a consciousness of which its owner himself is not aware. If philosophers find difficulty in accepting the existence of unconscious ideas, the existence of an unconscious consciousness seems to me even more objectionable. [Freud, 1912g, p. 263; cf. 1915e, p. 170]

As several authors note, the system *Cs.* and *Pcs.* together are comparable to the "ego" of the early period (Gill, 1963; McIntosh, 1986), with the *Cs.* situated metaphorically in the *Pcs.* system. Here, Freud likens the systems *Ucs.* and *Pcs.* to *two rooms*, with "consciousness as a spectator at the end of the second room" (Freud, 1916–1917, p. 296):

> The crudest idea of these systems is the most convenient for us—a spatial one. Let us therefore compare the system of the unconscious to a large entrance hall in which the mental impulses jostle one another like separate individuals. Adjoining this entrance hall there is a second, narrower room—a kind of drawing room—in which consciousness, too, resides . . . We are therefore justified in calling the second room the system of the *preconscious*. [Freud, 1916–1917, pp. 295–296]

The spatial metaphor of the systems account is epitomized by Jones (1949), where he proposes that "the mind could in many respects be likened to a series of water-tight compartments" (p. 10), and although such metaphors are crude and concrete, even "incorrect", says Freud, he acknowledges that they "must nevertheless be very far-reaching approximations to the real facts" (Freud, 1916–1917, p. 296). Repression subsequently involves the repressed remaining within the system *Ucs.* and prevented from entering the *Pcs.* (Freud, 1900a, pp. 177, 553, 617, 1915d, p. 153, 1915e, pp. 173, 191–194, 1916–1917, p. 295, 1917d, p. 225).

However, Freud also indicates that being "within" a system need not necessarily mean being located simply spatially, and another way of conceptualizing these systems is *temporally*:

> there is no need for the hypothesis that the psychical systems are actually arranged in a *spatial* order. It would be sufficient if a fixed order were established by the fact that in a given psychical process the excitation passes through the systems in a particular *temporal* sequence. [Freud, 1900a, p. 537, his italics]

That is, each psychical process passes through each system in sequence (*Ucs.–Pcs.–Cs.*) and repression here consists of preventing the target from entering the second phase of development:

> In the first phase the psychical act is unconscious and belongs to the system *Ucs.*; if, on testing, it is rejected by the censorship, it is not allowed to pass into the second phase; it is then said to be 'repressed' and must remain unconscious. If, however, it passes this testing, it enters the second phase and thenceforth belongs to the second system, which we shall call the system *Pcs.* [Freud, 1915e, p. 173]

One result of this is that the repressed is isolated from the remaining personality and consequently fails to develop:

> In the course of things it happens again and again that individual instincts or parts of instincts turn out to be incompatible in their aims or demands with the remaining ones, which are able to combine into the inclusive unity of the ego. The former are then split off from this unity by the process of repression, held back at lower levels of psychical development and cut off, to begin with, from the possibility of satisfaction. [Freud, 1920g, p. 11]

Both spatial and phasic accounts postulate repression, preventing targeted impulses from transition between unconscious to conscious thinking and, thus, repression "is essentially a process affecting ideas on the border between the systems *Ucs.* and *Pcs.* (*Cs.*)" (Freud, 1915e, p. 180). However, the issue of "incompatibility" still requires a psychological explanation and, thus, what Freud's account of repression must address is the notion of "testing" and the maintenance of repression.

Repression and the flight reflex

As in the early period, Freud proposes that "psychical activity draws back from any event which might arouse unpleasure" (Freud, 1911b, p. 219), and he claims that the prototype of repression is identical with "turning away" from unpleasurable perceptions:

> Let us suppose that the primitive apparatus is impinged upon by a perceptual stimulus which is a source of painful excitation. Unco-ordinated motor manifestations will follow until one of them withdraws the apparatus from the perception and at the same time from the pain. If the perception re-appears, the movement will at once be repeated (a movement of flight, it may be) till the perception has disappeared once more. In this case, no inclination will remain to recathect the perception of the source of pain, either hallucinatorily or in any other way. On the contrary, there will be an inclination in the primitive apparatus to drop the distressing memory-picture immediately, if anything happens to revive it, for the very reason that if its excitation were to overflow into perception it would provoke unpleasure (or, more precisely, would *begin* to provoke it) ... This effortless and regular avoidance by the psychical process of the memory of anything that had once been distressing affords us the prototype and first example of *psychical repression*. [Freud, 1900a, p. 600, his italics]

Here, the earliest defensive efforts are movements away from painful stimuli (see also Sperling, 1958, p. 27; Spitz, 1961, p. 642), whether via motor or psychical means, and here repression is comparable to a "flight-reflex in the presence of painful stimuli" (Freud, 1901b, p. 147):

> We consider these to be the older, primary processes, the residues of a phase of development in which they were the only kind of mental

process. The governing purpose obeyed by the primary process is easy to recognise; it is described as the pleasure–unpleasure [*Lust–Unlust*] principle, or more shortly, the pleasure principle. These processes strive towards gaining pleasure; psychical activity draws back from any event which might arouse unpleasure. (Here we have repression.) [Freud, 1911b, p. 219]

Hence, repression, or its prototype, is comparable to a "turning away" from painful stimuli. Freud's earlier reference to "effortless and regular avoidance" (Freud, 1900a, p. 600) appears to be further suggesting that after the initial act of repression, the defence could then occur "automatically", triggered simply by the beginning of unpleasure.[2] Nevertheless, any generation of unpleasure would presumably be based on an assessment of "incompatability", and Freud writes that although the primary response of the organism is away from unpleasure,

> a beginning of it must be allowed, since that is what informs the second system of the nature of the memory concerned and of its possible unsuitability for the purpose which the thought-process has in view. [Freud, 1900a, p. 601]

That is, to judge certain targets as unpleasurable requires knowing them to the extent that at least the beginning of unpleasure can occur.

At its simplest, then, repression involves the *Cs.*/*Pcs.* turning away and directing attention elsewhere: "repression can only consist in withdrawing from the idea the (pre) conscious cathexis which belongs to the system *Pcs.*" (Freud, 1915e, p. 180):

> We believe that, starting from a purposive idea, a given amount of excitation, which we term 'cathectic energy', is displaced along the associative paths selected by that purposive idea. A train of thought which is 'neglected' is one which has *not received* this cathexis [*Besetzung*]; a train of thought which is 'suppressed' or 'repudiated' is one from which this cathexis has been *withdrawn*. [Freud, 1900a, p. 594, his italics]

The term "cathexis" would be better translated as "occupied with" or "attending to" (cf. *Besetzung*) and so Freud is simply stating here that whatever is not attended to is unconscious, whereas other mental content becomes unconscious after first becoming known by the *Cs./Pcs.*, generating unpleasure, and subsequently having attention withdrawn from them. A similar view is proposed much more straightforwardly in a letter to Fliess (dated 14 November 1897), where Freud writes that "in the same manner as we turn away our sense organ (the head and nose) in disgust, the preconscious and the sense of consciousness turn away from memory. This is *repression*" (Masson, 1985, p. 280, Freud's italics). Within the systematic framework, this can be understood to mean that formal repression requires the development of the *Cs./Pcs.* that repudiates mental content based on unpleasure (Freud, 1900a, p. 580). This "second agency" (*Cs./Pcs.*) determines what can or cannot become conscious: "[This] second agency controls access to consciousness and can bar the first agency [the *Ucs.*] from any such access" (Freud, 1901a, p. 677).

However, while this "second agency" (*Cs./Pcs.*) appears to be equivalent with the "ego", the topographic theory also sees the development of a censor model (personified as a "watchman") preventing wishes in the *Ucs.* from accessing the *Pcs.*, within which consciousness resides:

> The unconscious wishful impulses clearly try to make themselves effective in daytime as well, and the fact of transference, as well as the psychoses, show us that they endeavour to force their way by way of the preconscious system into consciousness and to obtain control of the power of movement. Thus the censorship between the *Ucs.* and the *Pcs.*, the assumption of whose existence is positively forced upon us by dreams, deserves to be recognised and respected as the watchman of our mental health. (Freud, 1900a, p. 567]

The feasibility of explaining repression via a censor will be discussed in greater detail in Chapter Nine, and suffice it here to say that Freud's position on the censor is complex.

Primal repression and repression proper

The nature of unpleasure motivating repression can be viewed within the context of primary and secondary repression, a distinction that first appears in a letter from Freud to Ferenczi dated 6 December 1910 (in Jones, 1955, p. 499) and formerly published in the Schreber case study (Freud, 1911c). Freud proposes an account of repression which continues the earlier theme of repression found in the earlier seduction theory, whereby repression and symptom formation can be conceptualized in terms of three stages: *fixation, repression proper* (or after-pressure), and the *return of the repressed*. A similar account is later developed in the metapsychological paper "Repression" (1915d, p. 148), but with the first phase described as *primal repression*. In both accounts, *fixation/primal repression* results in the formation of a nucleus of unconscious ideas. *Repression proper*, on the other hand, targets either mental derivatives of the primary repressed material, or those sharing associative connection with it. The *return of the repressed* reflects the failure of repression and the onset of neurosis, and, along the lines of the seduction theory, an infantile repression is a necessary condition for adult neuroses (e.g., Freud, 1896b, p. 166; cf. Brenner, 1957; Madison, 1961; Laplanche & Pontalis, 1973):

> All repressions take place in early childhood; they are primitive defensive measures taken by the immature, feeble ego. In later years no fresh repressions are carried out; but the old ones persist, and their services continue to be made use of by the ego for mastering the instincts. New conflicts are disposed of by what we call 'after-repression'. [Freud, 1937c, p. 227]

Freud appears to have posited two accounts for the motivation of primal repression here, extending his earlier dual trauma theory (cf. Krystal, 1978). Freud's "primary" account refers to instinctual impulses that are too intense and threaten to overwhelm the organism: "It is highly probable that the immediate precipitating causes of primal repressions are quantitative factors such as an excessive degree of excitation and the breaking through of the protective shield against stimuli" (Freud, 1926d, p. 94; cf. 1933a, p. 94).

Although this account is accepted by many (e.g., Madison, 1961; Frank & Muslin, 1967; Jaffe, 1991), it has certain explanatory limitations and is contradicted by Freud himself. If repression results from "overstimulation" and non-gratification, then it is difficult to comprehend why broadly defined "sexual" impulses are typically targeted (e.g., Freud, 1926f, p. 267, 1940a[1938], p. 186) and not other needs such as hunger. Freud appears to even contradict the claim that tension accumulating through non-gratification as motivating repression when he writes, "repression does not arise in cases where the tension produced by lack of satisfaction of an instinctual impulse is raised to an unbearable degree" (Freud, 1915d, p. 147).

On the other hand, Freud's alternative account states that *psychical conflict* and the anticipation of danger is the motivating factor for primal repression. Repression occurs when the satisfaction of an impulse would "cause pleasure in one place and unpleasure in another. It has consequently become a condition for repression that the motive force of unpleasure shall have acquired more strength than the pleasure obtained from satisfaction" (Freud, 1915d, p. 147; cf. Freud, 1939a, pp. 116–117). That is, while gratifying an impulse is generally pleasurable, the anticipated consequences of its gratification might be believed to be unpleasurable enough to counter the anticipated pleasure and trigger repression.

The unpleasure leading to repression is typically also related to parental injunctions and the fear of punishment:

> [Repression] can almost never be achieved without the additional help of upbringing, of parental influence . . . which restricts the ego's activity by prohibitions and punishments, and encourages or compels the setting-up of repression. [Freud, 1940a[1938], p. 185]

Similarly, Freud (1914c) writes that "repression develops out of a prohibition or obstacle that came in the first instance from without" (p. 96). The Oedipus complex provides an illustration of this variety, whereby the young boy believes possessing his mother would be gratifying, but the threat of external punishment and anticipated mutilation (castration) outweighs this, motivating repression of the libidinal desire (Freud, 1908c, 1909b, 1924d). Thus, instinctual demands judged to have punishing real-world consequences are repressed, and, as Freud writes, "the instinctual situation which is feared goes back ultimately to an external danger situation" (Freud, 1933a, p. 89; cf. 1940e[1938], p. 275). Rather, then, than repression prompted by the non-gratification and overstimulation of needs, an instinctual demand is only dangerous if its satisfaction is believed to lead to actual real-world danger: "an instinctual demand is, after all, not dangerous in itself; it only becomes so inasmuch as it entails a real external danger . . ." (Freud, 1926d, p. 126).

The strength of this latter account is that Freud provides a specific explanation for the selective nature for why some impulses are targeted and not others. The account also has significant implications since it suggests that repression is more than simply a reflex response to physical pain, but instead requires a degree of cognitive sophistication for perceiving the social consequences of acting upon one's desires which conflict with parental injunctions. Hence, rather than simply responding to painful stimuli, as with reflex-defence (such as occurs when a hand is put on a hot stove), repression involves a cognitive appraisal and anticipation of future punishing consequences.

Rejection of Freud's claim that the primary repressed is never known

If repression involves anticipating that acting on a desire will lead to unpleasurable consequences, then this would mean that the target must be known (reflected upon) in the first instance, as with Freud's early view (Breuer & Freud, 1895d, p. 167). However, Freud was later to claim that the target of primal repression might never become the object of awareness:

> We have reason to assume that there is a *primal repression*, a first phase of repression, which consists in the psychical (ideational) representative of the instinct being denied entrance into the conscious. [Freud, 1915d, p. 148, his italics]

> ... when it comes to describing *primal* repression ... we are dealing with an unconscious idea which has as yet received no cathexis from the *Pcs.* and therefore cannot have that cathexis withdrawn from it. [Freud, 1915e, pp. 180–181, his italics]

That is, the target of primal repression does not have attention withdrawn from it (a withdrawal of cathexis), and instead the target of repression is never known and turned away from.

The view that repression can occur without any initial awareness of the repressed has subsequently been endorsed by many. For instance, Talvitie and Ihanus (2002) refer to "repressed contents that have never become conscious" (p. 1312) and write that this position is standard psychoanalytic theory (p. 1314). The problem here, however, that Maze and Henry (1996) note, is that if the target of repression is never in fact known, it is difficult to see how it could be evaluated as a threat prompting repression: "How can the infant mind defend itself

against impulses if it has never been aware of their existence or consequences?" (Maze & Henry, 1996, p. 1093). Indeed, if impulses are
targeted due to their imagined consequences, then they must be both
known and evaluated and Freud's account of repression in the early
work acknowledged that the repressed must have been in awareness
on at least one occasion (Breuer & Freud, 1895d, p. 167; Draft K, in
Masson, 1985, pp. 164–165). Furthermore, Freud, at times, indicates
that the primary repressed target *is* in fact known and cognized as a
threat: "The ego drew back, as it were, on its first collision with the
objectionable instinctual impulse" (Freud, 1925d, pp. 29–30). Thus,
Maze and Henry rightly conclude:

> Freud's assertion that in primal repression the repressed material has
> never been conscious is quite incompatible with his view of the
> dynamics of repression, is given no theoretical justification and should
> be abandoned. The term 'repression' would then be reserved for the
> impulses whose gratification, it is believed, would bring disastrous
> retribution. [Maze & Henry, 1996, p. 1094]

Accordingly, the preferred account of primal repression accepted
here proposes that repression must involve evaluation by the *Cs./Pcs.*
of mental content and a *judgement* that certain frustrating consequences follow from that content, and the benefit of this account is
that it explains why certain mental content are repressed (based on
evaluation of threat) and why others are not.

Can repression explain infantile amnesia?

Infantile amnesia is the pervasive phenomenon where all knowledge
before the age of four or five cannot be remembered (see Bruce, Dolan,
& Phillips-Grant, 2000; Weiskrantz, 1997), and although the point is
not a major one in Freud's thinking, Freud did believe that infantile
amnesia could be explained via primal repression in terms of motivated ignorance:

> It is impossible to avoid a suspicion that the beginnings of sexual life
> which are included in that period [before infantile amnesia] have
> provided the motive for its being forgotten-that this forgetting, in fact,
> is an outcome of repression. [Freud, 1916–1917, p. 326; cf. Freud,
> 1919e, p. 183, 1940a[1938], p. 153]

Aside from questions concerning whether it is or is not possible to remember events before the onset of infantile amnesia, there are good reasons for rejecting Freud's explanation here. Just as the preferred account of primal repression has explanatory power since it indicates why some and not other impulses are targeted, for that reason it cannot explain general forgetting. As Billig (1999) writes,

> [Freud] does not account for the fact that virtually everything which happens in the first years of life is lost to later recall. If shameful desires need to be repressed, then this does not account for the fact that 'innocent' memories too are swept along with the general forgetting. [Billig, 1999, p. 153]

Hence, the claim that repression is responsible for infantile amnesia should be rejected and it is probably safe to equate the offset of infantile amnesia being, at least in part, due to factors associated with biological maturation. For instance, there is some indication that infantile amnesia is associated with maturation of the hippocampal system (Rudy & Morledge, 1994; Weiskrantz, 1997; Zola, 1998).

Secondary repression and the persistence of the repressed

After primal repression, the primary repressed target is not destroyed, but, due to repression, the repressed forms compromised substitutive aims via association, which in turn might also require repressing: "repression does not hinder the instinctual representative from continuing to exist in the unconscious, from organizing itself further, putting out derivatives and establishing connections" (Freud, 1915d, p. 149). Here, the repressed becomes effective through transferring its intensity to *Pcs.* thoughts that are capable of becoming conscious:

> an unconscious idea is as such quite incapable of entering the preconscious and . . . it can only exercise any effect there by establishing a connection with an idea which already belongs to the preconscious, by transferring its intensity on to it and by getting itself 'covered' by it. [Freud, 1900a, p. 562; cf. Freud, 1898b, pp. 293–295]

These substitutes all serve as substitutive satisfactions, and though the expressions of these substitutes could vary, they typically take the form of substitutive *phantasies*:

[Phantasies] are substitutes for and derivatives of repressed memories which a resistance will not allow to enter consciousness unaltered, but which can purchase the possibility of becoming conscious by taking account, by means of changes and distortions, of the resistance's censorship. When this compromise has been accomplished, the memories have turned into phantasies, which can easily be misunderstood by the conscious personality—that is, understood so as to fit in with the dominant psychical current. [Freud, 1907a, p. 58]

These substitutive aims form the targets of repression proper (*eigentliche Verdrängung*) or 'after-pressure' (*Nachdrängen*):

The second stage of repression, *repression proper*, affects mental derivatives of the repressed representative, or such trains of thought as, originating elsewhere, have come into associative connection with it. On account of this association, these ideas experience the same fate as what was primally repressed. Repression proper, therefore, is actually an after-pressure. [Freud, 1915d, p. 148]

The important factor that Freud needs to account for here is to provide a workable account of how these derivatives are targeted based upon association. Given the role of perception and affect, association appears to require a cognizing subject first evaluating similarities between the primary repressed and the substitutes, and then anticipating that frustration can be expected given similarities between the derivative and the primary repressed, (i.e., a substitute aim y must be judged sufficiently like the primary repressed aim x, believed to lead to distress, and, subsequently, y is believed to lead to distress).

Repression from the repressed

One direction that Freud employs to explain secondary repression indicates that the primary repressed itself is active in secondary repression (Freud, 1911c, p. 67, 1900a, p. 547n, added 1914, 1905d, p. 176n, added 1915):

Hysterical amnesia, which occurs at the bidding of repression, is only explicable by the fact that the subject is already in possession of a store of memory-traces which have been withdrawn from conscious disposal, and which are now, by an associative link, attracting to themselves the material which the forces of repression are engaged in repelling from consciousness. [Freud, 1905d, p. 175]

... it is a mistake to emphasize only the repulsion which operates from the direction of the conscious upon what is to be repressed; quite as important is the attraction exercised by what was primally repressed upon everything with which it can establish a connection. Probably the trend towards repression would fail in its purpose if these two forces did not co-operate, if there were not something previously repressed ready to receive what is repelled by the conscious. [Freud, 1915d, p. 148]

What Freud precisely means here is unclear and might have led some authors on repression to ignore it altogether (e.g., Madison, 1961). However, since Freud writes that the primary repressed exerts the attraction, some authors suggest that the repressed somehow pulls the material down. For instance, Shevrin writes,

Presumably, the initially avoided idea is drawn in more closely within the sphere of more deeply repressed material once attention is withdrawn from it. We see in this latter point another important factor in repression—the pull from underneath—from the direction of the repressed wishes. [Shevrin, 1990, p. 104]

Brenner (1957) goes so far as to say, "Indeed, although there was no clear statement to this effect, the reader of these [Freud's] papers has the impression that at least in some cases the attraction exerted by the repressed might be the more important factor" (p. 32). However, the problem with asserting a "pull from underneath" is that there is no theoretical justification for why the repressed should draw material to itself. In fact, quite the opposite would be expected, since the repressed actively attempts to become conscious. Furthermore, Freud at other times equates this "pull from underneath" with the repressing forces:

In order to liberate it [the repressed libido], this attraction of the unconscious has to be overcome; that is, the repression of the unconscious instincts and of their productions, which has meanwhile been set up in the subject, must be removed. [Freud, 1912b, p. 103]

In this view, the "pull from underneath" is a result of mental content becoming associated with the primary repressed targets and subsequently becoming targeted by the repressing aspects of the personality. Hence, the preferred account of secondary repression—and which is generally consistent with Freud's dynamic picture—suggests that after primary repression (where a desire is repressed by the *Cs./Pcs.* (or ego) due to threat), the unsatisfied initial desire invests substitutive aims, which might further conflict with the aims of the *Cs./Pcs.* and lead to secondary repression (repression proper). This, however, appears to require the *Cs./Pcs.* knowing the secondary aims associated with the primary aims and that these threaten unpleasure. However, before evaluating this account in detail, it is necessary to discuss the next stage in Freud's thinking related to the theory of id, ego, and superego before discussing some of the intricacies in Freud's thinking that require further consideration.

Notes

1.   Freud writes in the *Project*: "Consciousness gives us what are called *qualities*—sensations which are different in a great multiplicity of ways and whose *difference* is distinguished according to its relations with the external world" (Freud, 1950[1895], p. 308, his italics).

2.   This is possibly what Freud means in an obscure reference: "It is not sufficient to take into account the repression between the preconscious and the unconscious; we must also consider the normal repression within the system of the unconscious itself. Very significant, but still very obscure" (Draft M, dated May 25 1897, in Masson, 1985, p. 248).

CHAPTER THREE

The structural theory and repression

Limitations of the topographic theory

F reud appears to have formulated what has become known as the "structural theory" in response to the limitations to, and difficulties with, dividing the mental apparatus into systems based on accessibility to consciousness. In particular, equating the repressed with the system *Ucs.* and the repressing forces with the *Cs.* and *Pcs.* was problematic, since aspects of the repressing forces, particularly the defences, were themselves unconscious in the systematic sense (Freud, 1923b, p. 18): "The truth is that it is not only the psychically repressed that remains alien to consciousness, but also some of the impulses which dominate our ego—something, therefore, that forms the strongest functional antithesis to the repressed" (Freud, 1925j, pp. 192–193).

The three main structures, or agencies, proposed instead are the id, ego, and superego. Although some claim that this new "structural" theory can be superimposed on the topographic theory (e.g., A. Freud, 1968; Gardner, 1993; Gill, 1963; Sandler, 1974; Sandler & Sandler, 1983), others see them as radically incompatible (e.g., Arlow & Brenner, 1964; Brenner, 1957). What is clear is that, with the structural theory, Freud made specific additions to the theory of repression, including reference to the "unconscious ego", formalizing the role of morality in repression (the "superego"), and subsequently revising the role of anxiety in repression.

The id and the development of the ego

The id (*das Es*) consists of all the impersonal forces within the person-ality and, as Bettelheim (1983, p. 57) notes, reference to "the It" conveys a better sense of Freud's meaning, since he states that his choice of terminology arose because "this impersonal pronoun seems particularly well suited for expressing the main characteristic of this province of the mind—the fact of its being alien to the ego" (Freud, 1933a, p. 72). The id can be conceptualized as the "pool" of instinctual desires primarily concerned with gratification, without regard to external constraints or possible consequences: "No such purpose as that of keeping itself alive or of protecting itself from dangers by means of anxiety can be attributed to the id" (Freud, 1940a[1938], p. 148). This, however, is not always adaptive: "The one and only urge of these instincts is towards satisfaction ... But immediate and unheeding satisfaction of the instincts, such as the id demands, would often lead to perilous conflicts with the external world and to extinc-tion" (Freud, 1940a[1938], pp. 197–198).

Hence, the id represents the primitive, impersonal instinctual forces within the personality pressing for immediate gratification and without considering the possible consequences of acting on impulses. The agency that develops to control the id is the *ego*, which, like the *Cs./Pcs.*, and in contradistinction to the unstructured id, imposes structure and organization upon mental events:

> in each individual there is a coherent organization of mental processes; and we call this his *ego*. It is to this ego that consciousness is attached; the ego controls the approaches to motility ... it is the mental agency which supervises all its own constituent processes ... [Freud, 1923b, p. 17, his italics]

Unlike the id, the ego is concerned with taking reality into account and safety: "Just as the id is directed exclusively to obtaining pleasure, so the ego is governed by considerations of safety. The ego has set itself the task of self-preservation, which the id appears to neglect" (Freud, 1940a[1938], p. 199).

While Freud also writes that "[t]he ego is not sharply separated from the id; its lower portion merges into it" (1923b, p. 24; cf. 1925i, p. 133), the ego also appears to assume the role of an *executive agent*, attempting to satisfy instinctual desires through activity in the world: "As a frontier-creature, the ego tries to mediate between the world and the id, to make the id pliable to the world and, by means of its muscular activity, to make the world fall in with the wishes of the id" (Freud, 1923b, p. 56; cf. Freud, 1924c, p. 167, 1933a, p. 75). To achieve this, the ego performs cognitive functions of perceiving stimuli, assessing them for potential danger through anticipating consequences, and then instituting or postponing action:

> its [the ego's] constructive function consists in interpolating, between the demand made by an instinct and the action that satisfies it, the activity of thought which, after taking its bearings in the present and assessing earlier experiences, endeavours by means of experimental actions to calculate the consequences of the course of action proposed. In this way the ego comes to a decision on whether the attempt to obtain satisfaction is to be carried out or postponed or whether it may not be necessary for the demand by the instinct to be suppressed altogether as being dangerous. [Freud, 1940a[1938], p. 199]

The ego's role in postponing behaviour is consonant with its role as the repressing agency. Repression is still considered to be a development of the "flight-reflex" (Freud, 1923b, p. 57), and also comparable to behaviour inhibition: "From this ego proceeds the repressions, too, by means of which it is sought to exclude certain trends in the mind not merely from consciousness but also from other forms of effectiveness and activity" (Freud, 1923b, p. 17; cf. Freud, 1932c, p. 221). Furthermore, a particular contribution here is that the structural revision makes explicit the view that repression is an *unconscious* activity of the ego (the "unconscious ego") (Freud, 1923b, p. 18, 1925j, pp. 192–193). The repressive act, including resistance, occurs unconsciously, and could only become known by the ego with difficulty, if at all.

Morality and the superego

The structural theory also formalizes the role of morality within the personality in terms of the "super-ego", possibly better translated as "over-I" or "Upper-I", given the German *Über-Ich* (Bettelheim, 1983, p. 58). Freud writes that the superego is "the representative . . . of every moral restriction, the advocate of a striving towards perfection" (Freud, 1933a, p. 67), playing a major part in instinctual conflict and repression: "[w]e know that as a rule the ego carries out repressions in the service and at the behest of its super-ego" (Freud, 1923b, p. 52). The super-ego develops out of both *biological* and *psychological* factors (Freud, 1933a, p. 66). The biological factor is the child's long dependence on its parents, a dependence that ensures the child's anxiety at the prospect of their loss. On the other hand, the psychological factor occurs with the Oedipus complex. Here, the young child's libidinal attraction towards its parents threatens loss of love and mutilation from the rival caregiver (typically the father):

> Children are protected against the dangers that threaten them from the external world by the solicitude of their parents; they pay for this security by a fear of *loss of love* which would deliver them over helpless to the external world. This factor exerts a decisive influence on the outcome of the conflict when a boy finds himself in the situation of the Oedipus complex in which the threat to his narcissism, by the danger of castration . . . takes possession of him . . . the child embarks on his attempts at defence—repressions. [Freud, 1940a[1938], p. 200, his italics]

This conflict situation is the grounds for the development of the superego. Due to anxiety at the prospect of mutilation, the young ego identifies with the offended rival and internalizes their prohibitions:

> The child's parents, and especially his father, were perceived as the obstacle to a realization of his Oedipus wishes; so his infantile ego fortified itself for the carrying out of the repression by erecting this same obstacle within itself. [Freud, 1923b, p. 34]

> . . . here we have that higher nature, in this ego ideal or super-ego, the representative of our relation to our parents. When we were little children we knew these higher natures, we admired them and feared them; and later we took them into ourselves" (Freud, 1923b, p. 36).

Identification here, according to Freud, involves *imitation*:

> The basis of the process is what is called 'identification'—that is to say, the assimilation of one ego to another one, as a result of which the first

ego behaves like the second in certain respects, imitates it and in a sense takes it up into itself. [Freud, 1933a, p. 63]

The consequence is the formation of the superego: "the ego ideal [super-ego] had the task of repressing the Oedipus complex; indeed, it is to that revolutionary event that it owes its existence" (Freud, 1923b, p. 34). The important implication here is that morality has a social basis, ultimately based upon a fear of punishment from social sources. This internalization of social values subsequently guides the ego as a type of constant reminder that certain actions lead to unfavourable consequences: "the ego is at bottom following the commands of its super-ego—commands which, in their turn, originate from influences in the external world that have found representation in the super-ego" (Freud, 1924b, p. 150).

After the superego develops, violations of moral beliefs, and the unconscious fear of punishment provide the incentive for repression (Freud, 1924b, p. 151). While many authors since Freud believe that the superego develops prior to the Oedipus complex (e.g., Brenner, 1982; Frank, 1999; Klein, 1928, 1933; Westen, 1986), and there has been an increasing trend in contemporary psychoanalysis to view the mother as the first source of prohibitions (see Frank, 1999), nevertheless, viewing the source of guilt primarily in terms of social interactions provides a workable developmental context for understanding morality and the motivation for repression.

Implications for primal and secondary repression

The role of the superego here contributes a new dimension to the earlier topographical account of primary and secondary repression. This can be viewed in terms of a distinction between pre- and post-superego repression:

> There is a danger of over-estimating the part played in repression by the super-ego. We cannot at present say whether it is perhaps the emergence of the super-ego which provides the line of demarcation between primal repression and after-pressure. At any rate, the earliest outbreaks of anxiety, which are of a very intense kind, occur before the super-ego has become differentiated. [Freud, 1926d, p. 94]

Pre-superego (external threat) repression constitutes primary repression, and post-superego secondary repression follows from the internalized fear of punishment acting as a standard guiding behaviour. This supports the theme that repression is located on a "defence" continuum, and Freud brings this all together in the following:

> If the id in a human being gives rise to an instinctual demand of an erotic or aggressive nature, the simplest and most natural thing is that the ego, which has the apparatus of thought and the muscular apparatus at its disposal, should satisfy the demand by an action. This satisfaction of the instinct is felt by the ego as pleasure, just as its non-satisfaction would undoubtedly have become a source of unpleasure. Now a case may arise in which the ego abstains from satisfying the instinct in view of external obstacles—namely, if it perceives that the action in question would provoke a serious danger to the ego. . . . Instinctual renunciation can, however, also be imposed for other reasons, which we correctly describe as *internal*. In the course of an individual's development a portion of the inhibiting forces in the external world are internalized and an agency is constructed in the ego which confronts the rest of the ego in an observing, criticizing and prohibiting sense. We call this new agency the *super-ego*. Thenceforward the ego, before putting to work the instinctual satisfaction demanded by the id, has to take into account not merely the dangers of the external world but also the objections of the super-ego, and it will have all the more grounds for abstaining from satisfying the instinct. [Freud, 1939a, pp. 116–117, his italics]

From this, the following picture emerges in the structural account of repression: (i) the ego anticipates danger resulting from socially proscribed desires; (ii) this fear motivates repression of the offending desires (primary repression); (iii) this is achieved, in part, through internalizing/identifying with the punishing source; (iv) this establishes an internalization of the external fear, motivating secondary repression of associated offending material.

The anxiety reformulation

What the structural account further highlights is the role of anxiety and fear in repression. However, Freud originally believed that *neurotic* anxiety was consequent on repression: "The anxiety in anxiety-dreams, like neurotic anxiety in general, corresponds to sexual affects, a libidinal feeling, and arises out of libido by the process of repression" (Freud, 1907a, p. 61). In this view, after repression, libido was transformed or discharged in anxiety (Draft E, in Masson, 1985; Freud, 1895b,f, 1898a, 1900a, 1916–1917), and neurotic anxiety represented an economic rechannelling of the libido and substitute discharge. This position was a continuation of Freud's early view of the quantitative account of affects, and it appears that all affects could be transformed into anxiety after repression (Freud, 1909b, p. 35, 1915e, p. 179, 1916–1917, pp. 403–404). This transformation could be contrasted with *realistic* or objective fear, a response appropriate to the evaluation of threat:

> [Fear] strikes us as something very rational and intelligible. We may say of it that it is a reaction to the perception of an external danger— that is, of an injury which is expected and foreseen. It is connected with the flight reflex and it may be regarded as a manifestation of the self-preservative instinct. [Freud, 1916–1917, pp. 393–394]

However, as Compton notes, the prominent role of "castration anxiety" as a motive for repression (e.g., Freud, 1918b, p. 113) led to a theoretical tension in terms of circularity, whereby anxiety was both cause and effect of itself (see Compton, 1972a, p. 26, 1972b, p. 379). Then, as if to resolve this issue, in *Inhibitions, Symptoms and Anxiety* (1926d) Freud introduces a new theory of anxiety reflecting a significant shift in the theory of repression. Anxiety is no longer seen as the *effect* of repression, but now as its *motive* (Freud, 1926d, pp. 108–109, 1933a, p. 86): "[it is] the ego's attitude of anxiety which is the primary thing and which sets repression going" (1926d, p. 109). This meant an entire recanting of Freud's earlier view: "It was not the repression that created anxiety; the anxiety was there earlier; it was anxiety that made the repression" (Freud, 1933a, p. 86). In this new formulation, Freud distinguishes *automatic* and *signal* anxiety, discernible through their relation to a *traumatic* situation. Automatic anxiety (*automatische Angst*) is a spontaneous reaction to a *traumatic* event, an event defined in a similar economic fashion to Freud's early account: an event is traumatic if it creates an accumulation of excitation that cannot be mastered or discharged (Freud, 1933a, p. 94; cf. Breuer & Freud, 1895d, p. 68). Psychologically, this is a "situation of helplessness": "physical helplessness if the danger is real and psychical helplessness if it is instinctual" (Freud, 1926d, p. 166).

The original trauma generating automatic anxiety is the birth situation, and all later danger situations are modelled upon that original experience (Draft E, in Masson, 1985; Freud, 1900a, pp. 236–237, 1910h, p. 173, 1916–1917, pp. 396–397): "[The] essential thing about birth, as about every situation of danger, is that it calls up in mental experience a state of highly tense excitation, which is felt as unpleasure and which one is not able to master by discharging it" (Freud, 1933a, p. 92).

Signal anxiety (*Angstsignal*) emerges if an event similar to the original traumatic one threatens a re-occurrence of the original state of helplessness (cf. Freud, 1950[1895], pp. 359, 382). Rather than a response to an immediate danger (as with automatic anxiety), signal anxiety involves an *expectation* or *anticipation* of a *situation of danger*: "A danger-situation is a recognised, remembered, expected situation of helplessness" (Freud, 1926d, p. 166). All situations of danger are similar in that they threaten an accumulation of excitation that cannot be mastered. However, specific dangers generally arise with specific developmental periods. After birth, the first danger is "non-satisfaction" of needs (Freud, 1926d, p. 137), and then the loss of the caregivers, associated with meeting needs, extends this as a situation of danger signalling helplessness (Freud, 1926d, pp. 137–138). With the development of the Oedipus complex, the next situation of danger corresponds to "castration", and then, subsequently, its heir, the superego (Freud, 1926d, pp. 146–147).

Implication of the anxiety reformulation

What Freud's new theory of anxiety means is that both neurotic anxiety and realistic anxiety constitute a reaction to the perception and evaluation of a threat (Freud, 1926d, pp. 108–109, 1933a, p. 85). What distinguishes these types of anxiety is their relation to the object of fear. Realistic anxiety is a response to a *known* danger, whereas neurotic anxiety occurs when the object of fear "remains unconscious and only becomes conscious in the form of the distortion" (Freud, 1926d, p. 126). Invariably, the unknown or distorted danger is instinctual in origin:

Real danger is a danger that is known, and realistic anxiety is anxiety about a known danger of this sort. Neurotic anxiety is anxiety about an unknown danger. Neurotic danger is thus a danger that has still to be discovered. Analysis has shown that it is an instinctual danger. By bringing this danger which is not known to the ego into consciousness, the analyst makes neurotic anxiety no different from realistic anxiety, so that it can be dealt with in the same way. [Freud, 1926d, p. 165]

What is specifically feared in neurotic anxiety is "the strength of the passions in the id" (Freud, 1933a, p. 78) and fear of external consequences. The threatening instinctual impulses might also give rise to a third form of anxiety, whereby transgression of the superego gives rise to *moral anxiety* as an extension of the external threat:

if we ask ourselves what it is that the ego fears from the super-ego, we cannot but think that the punishment threatened by the latter must be an extension of the punishment of castration. Just as the father has become depersonalised in the shape of the super-ego, so has the fear of castration at his hands become transformed into an undefined social or moral anxiety. [Freud, 1926d, p. 128; cf. 1933a, p. 78]

Hence, both neurotic and moral anxieties indicate that an instinctual impulse is feared, but neurotic anxiety occurs when an instinctual impulse is perceived to be threatening, but is replaced in conscious awareness with a substitute, whereas moral anxiety occurs where an instinctual desire is known and believed to violate superego values, prompting an unconscious fear of punishment.

Anthropomorphism and the structural theory

Although the structural account has received various criticisms in terms of ill-defined terms (e.g., Boesky, 1995; Gillett, 1997; Hayman, 1969; Macmillan, 1991; Slap & Saykin, 1984), and not reflecting the clinical data (Sandler, 1974), one particularly important theoretical issue concerns the articulation of the theory in terms of anthropomorphic metaphors. As Laplanche and Pontalis comment, "[the structural theory] is shot through with anthropomorphism" (Laplanche & Pontalis, 1973, p. 452; cf. Grossman & Simon, 1969), and Wiedeman writes that "anthropomorphisation of the concepts ego, id, and superego has been rampant in analytic writing" (Wiedeman, 1972, p. 310). The specific issue here concerns populating the mind with little people (homunculi), a problem that coincides with reification of the concepts into concrete entities (Beres, 1965; Hayman, 1969). Furthermore, as noted earlier, explaining behaviour in terms of multiple "persons" simply defers explanation, since further multiple explanation of each person's activity is required (without resorting to postulating further homunculi).

Nevertheless, as others note, the development of the superego through identification with actual people would lead the superego to be represented by personal forms (Beres, 1965; Gardner, 1993; Hopkins, 1995b), and, consequently, as Jones writes of the superego: "It is like an inner voice saying, 'Check those forbidden impulses, else I shall punish you severely'" (Jones, 1948, p. 161). The problem then is discerning what is meant descriptively and what is actually purporting to explain repression, and this is particularly so with respect to the ego as the instigator of repression and the relationship between the ego and anxiety. Freud describes the ego as both the subject generating anxiety (". . . the source of anxiety") and the subject experiencing it (". . . the sole seat of anxiety") (Freud, 1926d, p. 161; cf. Freud, 1933a, p. 85). In a similar fashion to the ego set out in the *Project* (Freud, 1950 [1895], p. 359), part of the ego's function is to inhibit the full production of anxiety, allowing only an amount necessary to generate a signal that a danger situation is impending (Freud, 1926d, p. 166, 1926e, p. 202; 1933, p. 82). Here, Freud describes the ego's behaviour in purposive and teleological terms: the ego anticipates a danger situation and generates an anxiety signal *in order to* trigger defence and prevent the danger from occurring: "The ego, which experienced the trauma passively, now repeats it actively in a weakened version, in the hope of being able to direct its course" (Freud, 1926d, p. 167). Freud further describes the ego's use of anxiety as "intentional", involving a transition "from the automatic and involuntary fresh appearance of anxiety to the intentional reproduction of anxiety as a signal of danger" (Freud, 1926d, p. 138). Similarly, the ego instigates "purposefully":

> the ego subjects itself to anxiety as a sort of inoculation, submitting to a slight attack of the illness in order to escape its full strength. It vividly imagines the danger situation, as it were, with the unmistakeable purpose of restricting that distressing experience to a mere indication, a signal. [Freud, 1926d, p. 162]

The signal announces: "I am expecting a situation of helplessness to set in", or: "The present situation reminds me of one of the traumatic experiences I have had before. Therefore I will anticipate the trauma and behave as though it had already come, while there is yet time to turn aside" (Freud, 1926d, p. 166).

Freud's thesis of signal anxiety appears to receive broad acceptance and subsequent discussion has debated whether other affects can act as signals (e.g., "signal guilt", Schur, 1969; "signal depression", Brenner, 1975, 1981; see also Shill, 2004 for relevant discussion). However, Freud's account here of the ego's use of anxiety as a signal has been rightly criticized for both its teleological and anthropomorphic character (e.g., Compton, 1972a,b; Schur, 1953, 1969) and, instead, a workable non-teleological account of signal anxiety needs to be provided which elucidates the specific meaning of "signal".

The problem of "signal" anxiety

Gillett (1990) notes that there are two general meanings of the term; one as a "sign" intended to communicate something other than itself (such as a warning, direction, or information) and the other as an "exciting cause". The former involves a ternary relation between a cognizing subject interpreting the relation between the signifier (anxiety), and the signified (the danger situation),[1] and this communicative sense of signal is seen in the following from Freud: "The signal announces; 'I am expecting a situation of helplessness to set in', or; 'The present situation reminds me of one of those traumatic experiences I have had before'" (Freud, 1926d, p. 166). In this sense, the signal is a warning of danger and this sense has been incorporated into more recent accounts. For instance:

> in adulthood, the anxiety is, generally speaking, reduced to signal anxiety, i.e., a much smaller quantity which serves as a warning signal to the ego to actively defend against the emergence into consciousness of material associated with the conflict. [Geisler, 1985, p. 288]

Here, anxiety warns the ego of a threatening impulse, and so signals the ego to initiate repression. However, as Gillett (1990) notes, if anxiety is a sign conveying a warning of danger, then it should cause an expectation of danger, but, as he points out, Freud also states that anxiety arises from an expectation of danger. Consequently, if the ego anxiously evaluates a situation as dangerous—and responds anxiously—then there is no need to refer to a signal of anxiety *informing* the ego because the ego already knows the threatening situation.

On the other hand, if the meaning of "signal" is restricted to an "exciting cause", then the issue is clearer. In this view, anxiety is simply involved in the anticipation of danger and sufficient as a cause and initiator of defence (cf. Gillett, 1990; Schur, 1953). Subsequently, Gillett calls for the rejection of the term "signal": "it would be clearer to speak of affect as a cause rather than as a signal" (Gillett, 1990, p. 562), a not unjustified conclusion, since it would help to avoid confusion arising from the ambiguous nature of the term "signal". Furthermore, the immediate advantage of an "exciting cause" account is that it does not require an anthropomorphized agent "deciding" whether to repress or not. However, care is needed to avoid oversimplifying the situation; it must be stressed that an "exciting cause" still requires the ego anxiously knowing the target of repression. Here, Shill (2004) warns against attempting to reduce signal anxiety to non-psychological (biological) processes "devoid of psychic content" (p. 122): "Merely describing signal anxiety as triggering defense does not convey the complexity of the phenomena involved and also obscures their metapsychological and technical implications" (p. 118). Instead, he rightly claims that appraisal is a necessary component of signal anxiety, where the ego anticipates that a situation will arouse unpleasurable affect, which subsequently causes distress and prompts repression. Thus, the preferred account (anxiety as an "exciting cause") requires that anxiety is consequent on the perception and evaluation of some threat, based on the recognition that a present scenario threatens to revive the helplessness of an earlier scenario. Again, the ego is implicated and Freud's account of neurotic and moral anxiety appears to require the ego knowing and evaluating the target of repression.

Note

1. Compare Petocz' (1999) discussion of "symbols" as ternary relations between the symbol, the symbolized, and a cognizing subject.

CHAPTER FOUR

The apparent paradox of Freudian repression

Repression and the indestructibility of the repressed

What emerges in Freud's account of repression is that the ego must know the target of repression—at least on one occasion—for repression to occur. If this were the end of the matter, then there would be no particular difficulty in attempting to explain repression. However, as Maze and Henry (1996) note, one factor that makes Freud's account of repression both so interesting and difficult to comprehend is Freud's claim that repression does not do away with the repressed: instead, the repressed remains causally active, pressing towards conscious thinking, and generating symptoms as substitute satisfactions (e.g., Freud, 1900a, p. 577, 1915e, p. 166, 1919g, p. 260, 1933a, p. 68, 1939a, p. 95). As Freud writes,

> The unconscious—that is to say, the 'repressed' ... has no other endeavour than to break through the pressure weighing down on it and force its way either to consciousness or to a discharge through some real action. [Freud, 1920g, p. 19]

> ... the unconscious ... has a natural "upward drive" and desires nothing better than to press forward across its settled frontiers into the ego and so to consciousness. [Freud, 1940a[1938], p. 179]

In Freud's early account, there was no theoretical justification for this upward drive, since affect/idea dissociation meant that the repressed idea could not become conscious simply because it lacked sufficient intensity (Breuer & Freud, 1895d, p. 280). As already argued, however, this position is problematic, since it contradicts the basic mechanism of symptom-formation as well as Breuer and Freud's (1895d) clinical experience. On the other hand, the developing appreciation of endogenous motivational stimuli in Freud's thinking allowed him to account for the repressed content's upward drive and subsequent symptom formation, whereby, and in contradistinction to the early affect/idea dissociation account, the repressed remains explicitly intense: "The mark of something repressed is precisely that in spite of its intensity it is unable to enter consciousness" (Freud, 1907a, p. 48). In fact, the relatively *continuous* character of the instinctual drives, which, without gratification, provide a "constant" source of activation to the repressed desires (Freud, 1915c, pp. 118–119; 1933a, p. 96), results in the unconscious ideas having even greater than normal intensity due to "the damming-up consequent on frustrated satisfaction" (Freud, 1915d, p. 149). Explaining the impetus for psychoneurotic symptoms then follows from repression preventing adequate satisfaction (i.e., the repressed drives remain in a state of frustration), which, in conjunction with their lack of integration and development, results in the repressed aim's "insatiability, unyielding rigidity and the lack of ability to adapt to real circumstances" (Freud, 1910c, p. 133). This subsequently allows Freud to explain both dreams and psychoneurotic symptoms in terms of substitutive aims after the original impulse is repressed (e.g., Freud, 1926f, p. 267, 1939a, p. 127).

While Freud now has a theoretically justifiable account of the upward drive of the repressed, he now needs to provide some explanation of the type of preventative measure which stops the repressed from becoming known in thought and behaviour. Otherwise, the ego, or consciousness, would face continual intrusions of the repressed, which Freud portrays as analogous to a person expelled from a lecture and now angrily intruding, clamouring at the doors of consciousness:

> If you come to think of it, the removal of the interrupter and the posting of the guardians at the door may not mean the end of the story. It may very well be that the individual who has been expelled, and who has now become embittered and reckless, will cause us further

trouble. It is true that he is no longer among us: we are free from his presence, from his insulting laughter and his *sotto voce* comments. But in some respects, nevertheless, the repression has been unsuccessful: for now he is making an intolerable exhibition of himself outside the room, and his shouting and banging on the door with his fists interfere with my lecture even more than his bad behaviour did before. [Freud, 1910a, pp. 26–27]

Madison notes the result:

if the repressed impulse was conceived as exerting a constant pressure toward expression in consciousness and behaviour, that impulse ought to keep appearing and thus repression would have to be repeated constantly—the impulse would be like a jack-in-the box that endlessly popped up and had to be repeatedly pressed down. [Madison, 1961, pp. 46–47]

The *dynamic* view of repression itself proposes a mind perpetually in conflict, where the repressed wish is continuously attempting to find expression while being actively blocked by the repressing forces: "The process of repression . . . may thus be compared to an unending conflict; fresh psychical efforts are continuously required to counterbalance the forward pressure of the instinct" (Freud, 1907b, p. 124). Similarly,

'Repressed' is a dynamic expression, which takes account of the interplay of mental forces: it implies that there is a force present which is seeking to bring about all kinds of psychical effects, including that of becoming conscious, but that there is an opposing force which is able to obstruct some of these psychical effects, once more including that of becoming conscious. [Freud, 1907a, p. 48]

Successful repression subsequently involves a psychical stalemate where "both the prohibition [repression] and the instinct persist: the instinct because it has only been repressed and not abolished, and the prohibition because, if it ceased, the instinct would force its way through into consciousness and into actual operation" (Freud, 1912–1913, p. 29). The end result is a continuous expenditure of energy for maintaining repression. Therapy, in part, aims "to save the mental energy which he [the neurotic] is expending upon internal conflicts" (Freud, 1923a, p. 251; cf. Freud, 1926e, p. 256):

An important element in the theory of repression is the view that repression is not an event that occurs once but that it requires a permanent expenditure [of energy]. If this expenditure were to cease, the repressed impulse, which is being fed all the time from its sources, would on the next occasion flow along the channels from which it would have been forced away, and the repression would either fail in its purpose or would have to be repressed an indefinite number of times. [Freud, 1926d, p. 157; cf. Freud, 1910d, p. 146, 1915d, p. 151, 1925d, p. 30, 1940a[1938], pp. 172–173]

Post-Freudian account of repression

The ongoing interplay between the repressed and the repressing forces is not restricted to Freud's writings and constitutes a basis for similar accounts of repression in post-Freudian thinking. For example, Sandler and Sandler (1997) note that "[repression] is a mechanism *that has continually to be reapplied* as the threatening content arises . . . The relevant content is repressed over and over again as it is pushed forward towards consciousness" (p. 177, their italics). Similarly, Gillett (2001) writes that "repression is not an all-or-none matter. Once a putatively dangerous content has been repressed, the struggle continues between the content pressing toward consciousness and the defence opposing this pressure" (p. 276). In fact, as Weinberger (2003) points out, it is precisely this continuous interplay that contributes to the distinctive hallmark of psychoanalytic theory:

> For a content to be repressed, it must arouse anxiety that then motivates the person to keep it from reaching consciousness. It then must continually strive for expression. This then leads to all of the vicissitudes of the unconscious that are so unique to psychoanalytic theory. [Weinberger, 2003, p. 152]

Furthermore, this continuous, active nature of the repressed shows that repression is more that simply ignoring unpleasant situations, as for instance, Bower (1990) believes:

> [Repression] does not imply a "continual effort to suppress" thinking about it, as Freud suggested, any more than the fact that I get absorbed in a movie means that I am working hard to avoid doing my income

taxes at home. Activities can simply be absorbing in themselves, and doing one activity need not involve "effortful suppression" of others. [Bower, 1990, p. 219]

While the existence of such selective inattention is indisputable (and can be seen within a spectrum of repressive activities, as Erdelyi, 1993, 2006 suggests), if repression was reducible to such everyday cases, then there would be no theoretical framework for understanding how neurotic symptoms could arise. Similarly, while much of psychoanalytic thinking still emphasizes the repression of memories (e.g., Blum, 2003a; Erdelyi, 1990, 2006; Hutterer & Liss, 2006), one question here is why an unconscious memory should both be pathogenic and press towards conscious awareness. Here, Hutterer and Liss invoke Freud's concept of "fixation" and "repetition compulsion" ("the unconscious tendency to keep repeating past traumatic experiences", p. 293) but, as others rightly note, "fixation" and "repetition compulsion" are, at best, non-explanatory descriptive terms (Laplanche & Pontalis, 1973), and similarly so with "tendency" (Boag, 2011a). Even proponents of the common "motivated forgetting" view, such as Erdelyi (1990), note that repression should not require persistent effort if the targets are merely memories of distressing episodes. Rather, as Erdelyi (1990) notes, the "typical situation—a recurring internal impulse, conflict, or thought" requires persistent repression "because the 'stimulus' is continually being re-presented endogenously" (Erdelyi, 1990, p. 16). Thus, the persistence of the repressed allows Freud to explain the upward drive of the repressed and symptom formation while also creating an explanatory challenge with respect to how this dynamic interplay occurs entirely independent of the subject's knowing. If it is the case, as Nesse (1990) writes, that "[a]t every moment, a barrage of primitive impulses struggle for expression without our least awareness" (Nesse, 1990, p. 269), then some mechanism must explain how the targets of repression are prevented from becoming known.

Secondary repression and resistance

The complexity of the situation is exacerbated by Freud's postulation that repression also actively target derivatives (substitutes) for the primary targets impulses (Freud, 1915d, p. 149). As Freud writes, "Repression has not only descended upon the unconscious complexes, but it is continually attacking their derivatives as well, and even prevents the patient from becoming aware of the products of the disease itself" (Freud, 1909b, p. 124).

> The instinctual desire is constantly shifting in order to escape from the *impasse* and endeavours to find substitutes—substitute objects and substitute acts—in place of the prohibited ones. In consequence of this, the prohibition itself shifts about as well, and extends to any new aims which the forbidden impulse may adopt. Any fresh advance made by the repressed libido is answered by a fresh sharpening of the prohibition. [Freud, 1912–1913, p. 30]

This indicates that secondary repression is actively cognitive (though that same activity is not necessarily conscious), and the secondary aims must either be perceived as threatening in their own right (and, as such, constituting a target of primal repression), or perceived to be similar enough to the primary repressed aim to be evaluated as threatening. This extends also into post-Freudian accounts, where repression proper is described as a "finely tuned selective process . . . in which ideas more or less closely related to the originally repressed wish or the super-ego prohibition are also repressed" (Geisler, 1985, p. 260).

The clinical phenomenon of resistance raises similar questions concerning explanations of repression and since, as Auld, Hyman, and Rudzinski (2005) write, "[r]esistance is ubiquitous in analytic therapy and is inherent in every aspect of the client's participation" (p. 120), providing a coherent explanation of resistance is not an insignificant issue for psychoanalytic theorizing. Freud's own characterization of resistance highlights the seemingly paradoxical nature of resistance, since it is the ego that both resists and remains ignorant of the repressed. On the one hand, Freud writes that "[t]he resistance can only be a manifestation of the ego, which originally put the repression into force and now wishes to maintain it. That, moreover, is the view we always took" (Freud, 1933a, pp. 68–69; cf. Freud, 1923b, p. 17, Freud, 1926d, pp. 159–160). On the other hand, since resistance is motivated by the perception of threat and anxiety, it requires that the ego knows that a threat is emerging: "If the ego during the early period has set up a repression out of fear, then the fear still persists and manifests itself as a resistance if the ego approaches the repressed material" (Freud, 1926e, p. 224). On top of this, the ego is also ignorant of its own resisting: "The first step in overcoming the resistances is made, as we know, by the analyst's uncovering the resistance, which is never recognised by the patient, and acquainting him with it" (Freud, 1914g, p. 155).

we find during analysis that, when we put certain tasks before the patient, he gets into difficulties: his associations fail when they should be coming near the repressed. We then tell him that he is dominated by a resistance: but he is quite unaware of the fact, and, even if he guesses from his unpleasurable feelings that a resistance is now at work in him, he does not know what it is or how to describe it. [Freud, 1923b, p. 17]

... the patient who puts up a resistance is so often unaware of that resistance. Not only the fact of the resistance is unconscious to him, however, but its motives as well. [Freud, 1933a, p. 108]

As a manifestation of the repressive dynamic interplay, resistance shows that the conflicted individual both struggles to know and not know the repressed:

In the patient under treatment two forces were in operation against each other: on the one hand, his conscious endeavour to bring into consciousness the forgotten idea in his unconscious, and on the other hand, the resistance ... which was striving to prevent what was repressed or its derivatives from thus becoming conscious. [Freud, 1910a, p. 30; cf. Freud, 1912b, p. 103]

Paradoxically, while unconsciously resisting the person is also consciously attempting to discover what is unconscious, leading Freud to write, "[i]n psycho-analysis the patient assists with his conscious efforts to combat his resistance, because he expects to gain something from the investigation, namely, his recovery" (Freud, 1906c, p. 112. cf. Freud, 1913c, p. 143). The same state of affairs is also noticeable in post-Freudian accounts:

A paradoxical phenomenon regularly encountered in the course of insight-oriented psychotherapy ... The patient, who has sought professional help to uncover neurotic problems, opposes the process in a variety of ways that would serve to defeat the objective of change. [Moore & Fine, 1990, p. 168]

[Therapy is] characterised by a paradoxical phenomenon. While the patient consciously wishes to work with the analyst to get the job done and is more or less determined to say everything that comes to mind, sooner or later he will find that he is no longer able or willing to do so. The patient, sometimes knowingly but more often not, will begin "resisting" the fundamental rule . . . The explanation is perhaps obvious. We have asked the patient to free-associate in order to discover those feelings that are causing his emotional problems. But *he is unaware of these feelings*, precisely because they cause him so much distress, and *because he does not want to be aware of them*. From the beginning, then, free association is an impossible task. At the same time that the patient is working with us, he is resisting us. [Pulver, 1995, pp. 84–85, italics added]

. . . the desire to reveal one's unconscious feelings and thoughts to oneself and one's therapist is countered by an equally strong desire to keep those feelings and thoughts out of awareness and away from the therapist's attention. Thus every client struggles to reveal and to conceal, to express and repress. [Auld, Hyman, & Rudzinski, 2005, p. 111]

This would appear to require both knowing that the repressed is being approached and yet also not knowing the same state of affairs. This paradoxical nature of resistance is illustrated in Shill's (2004) statement that "[t]he ego triggers unconscious resistance when a danger situation is detected by the ego. This danger constitutes a threat to the ego, which responds with signal anxiety. This is intolerable, and the ego proceeds with defense (resistance)" (p. 126). Here the ego detects the danger (i.e., knows it), and yet resistance is also said to be unconscious.

On the other hand, reducing "resistance" to accidental ignorance, as some propose (e.g., Schafer, 1973), neither adequately captures Freud's account nor provides any explanation for why simply educating the analysand is ineffective. As Freud writes, resistance needs to be removed if therapy is to be successful:

It is a long superseded idea, and one derived from superficial appearances, that the patient suffers from a sort of ignorance, and that if one removes this ignorance by giving him information (about the causal connection of his illness with his life, about his experiences in childhood, and so on) he is bound to recover. The pathological factor is not his ignorance in itself, but the root of this ignorance in his *inner resistances*; it was they that first called this ignorance into being, and they still maintain it now. The task of the treatment lies in combating these resistances . . . If knowledge about the unconscious were as important for the patient as people inexperienced in psycho-analysis imagine, listening to lectures or reading books would be enough to cure him. Such measures, however, have as much influence on the symptoms of nervous illness as a distribution of menu-cards in a time of famine has upon hunger. [Freud, 1910k, p. 225, his italics; cf. Freud, 1913c, pp. 141–142, 1919a, p. 159, 1937d, p. 257).

Without removing the resistances the subject is not in a position to lift the repression and remove the pathology. Instead, Freud writes concerning resistance: "The patient wants to be cured—but he also wants not to be. His ego has lost its unity, and for that reason his will has no unity either. If that were not so, he would be no neurotic" (Freud, 1926e, p. 221; cf. Freud, 1928b, p. 179).

The problem of the ego

This supposed unity of the ego requires careful consideration and Gill (1963) suggests that the paradoxical nature of resistance and the ego led Freud, in part, to develop the structural theory in place of the topographic theory. Freud does, in fact, write that it was "resistance" that led him to "revise the relation between the ego and the unconscious" (Freud, 1933a, p. 108) and that unconscious aspects of the ego are held responsible for resistance: "Now these resistances, although they belong to the ego, are nevertheless unconscious and in some way separated off within the ego" (Freud, 1937c, pp. 238–239). Similarly,

since, however, there can be no question but that this resistance emanates from his ego and belongs to it, we find ourselves in an unforeseen situation. We have come upon something in the ego itself which is also unconscious, which behaves exactly like the repressed— that is, which produces powerful effects without itself being conscious and which requires special work before it can be made conscious. [Freud, 1923b, p. 17]

That being said, although resisting behaviour could occur uncon-sciously (as will be discussed), explaining resistance still requires an evaluation of threat, generating anxiety, and instituting resistances. Accordingly, what makes repression potentially problematic is Freud's insistence that the ego—which remains unaware of the repressed—is also the instigator of repression and resistance (Breuer & Freud, 1895d, pp. 269, 278; Freud, 1940a[1938], pp. 179–180). How-ever, as Anna Freud writes, "[a]s a rule, the ego knows nothing of the rejection of the impulses" (A. Freud, 1968, p. 9). Subsequently, repres-sion appears to be an impossible task, since it appears to require the repressing subject (the ego) re-knowing the target in order not to know it. Thus, as Maze (1983) notes, the difficulty is "explaining how the ego contrives not to know something when the contriving requires that it does know it . . ." (p. 149).

A brief side-step: repression and anosognosia

While Freud discusses repression within the context of unsatisfied impulses forcing themselves into consciousness, the problem involv-ing a subject both knowing and not knowing a given state of affairs is found in cases of anosognosia, where, after physical trauma to the right hemisphere, a person might be left with a physical deficit (e.g., paralysis) but be incapable of acknowledging this. A particularly interesting case of anosognosia is reported by Ramachandran (1994) of a seventy-six-year-old woman (BM) who, after a right hemisphere stroke "had complete paralysis of the left side of her body" (p. 319), nevertheless maintained that she was not paralysed, despite all evidence to the contrary. Ramachandran found that caloric stimu-lation (via administering ice-cold water into the left ear of the patient) led to a remarkable undoing of the anosognosia where, after a brief interview, she was both cognizant of the deficit and that the deficit had been present for some time. Commenting on this, Rama-chadran (1994) writes, "we may conclude that at some deeper level she does indeed have knowledge about the paralysis" (p. 324). In other words, it appears that BM knew all along that she was paralysed but was somehow prevented from acknowledging this: "uncon-sciously these patients do perceive and remember that they are para-lysed, notwithstanding the facts that they are unable to direct their conscious attention to these facts" (Kaplan-Solms & Solms, 2000, p. 159).

A similar reported case example involving comparable theoretical complexity is reported by Kaplan-Solms and Solms (2000) of a woman (Mrs A) who, after an accident, was simultaneously suicidally depressed about her physical deficit *and* yet simultaneously unaware of her physical symptoms. Kaplan-Solms and Solms note here the apparent paradox:

> How could it be that Mrs A was suicidally depressed about the loss of independence (as she called it) and yet, simultaneously, *consciously unaware* of the immediate physical basis if that loss? . . . *Mrs A herself was completely unaware of the fact that she was hemiplegic, and hemianopic, and so forth.* We are thus faced with a paradoxical situation in which Mrs A was depressed about the very events that she simultaneously denied had ever happened in the first place. [pp. 176–177, their italics]

These authors then rightly conclude that

> the concept of unconscious knowledge is indispensable to us. This concept allows us to say that Mrs A's depression was a reaction to a loss of which she was *unconsciously* aware; it was a reaction to *knowledge that she was defending herself against.* [p. 177, their italics]

That is, Mrs A both knows the deficit (and reacts with suicidal depression) and yet is also ignorant of that same state of affairs, as is said to occur with repression, and, in fact, Kaplan-Solms and Solms (2000) believe that repression (motivated ignorance) is a contributing factor: "these patients are unconsciously aware of the damaged state of their bodies. They know perfectly well what has happened to their bodies, but they do not *want* to know" (p. 172, their italics). Thus, the examples above parallel the Freudian example of repression, entailing both knowing and not knowing a given situation, and even maintaining denial or ignorance in face of evidence to the contrary. In fact, the situation is even more complex, since Kaplan-Solms and Solms (2000) describe anosognosia in terms avoiding the knowledge of the cause of distress: "these patients are indeed positively *avoiding* their unconscious knowledge of the paralysed state of their bodies, because this knowledge is a source of intolerable distress to them" (p. 160, their italics). Other authors similarly describe repression in terms of *avoiding* the repressed, which suggests some knowledge of what situations to avoid. For example, Slap and Saykin write, "The ego, having repressed the pathological schema, continues to avoid, in so far as it can, any recognition of its content" (Slap & Saykin, 1984, p. 122). However, to avoid knowledge of something would appear to require knowledge of the situations to be avoided, which is precisely what is said to be prevented by repression.

Repression and the paradox of self-deception

The discussion of repression, above, draws some parallel with problems associated with the paradox of self-deception. Repression is, at times, described as a form of self-deception (e.g., Baumeister, Dale & Sommer, 1998; Johnson, 1998; Neu, 1988; Nesse, 1990; Slavin, 1985, 1990; Slavin & Grief, 1995), although some dispute exists concerning the exact relation between self-deception and repression (see Bach, 1998; Erwin, 1988; Gardner, 1993; Pataki, 1997; Schafer, 1973). While accounts of self-deception are diverse, self-deception is typically modelled on *interpersonal* deception, whereby person *A* deceives person *B* into believing that *p*, when person *A* believes that not-*p*. Subsequently, self-deception is viewed in terms of a person believing that *p*, and yet deceiving him or herself that not-*p* is the case. If repression is viewed similarly, then the theoretical difficulties of accounting for self-deception hold also for repression. Here, Neu (1988) writes,

> Paradox seems inevitable if we attempt to understand self-deception on the model of other-deception. Other-deception, as in the ordinary case of lying, requires that the deceiver know the truth while keeping the deceived from knowing it. But in the case of self-deception, the two parties are collapsed into a single person, and the problem arises of how one person can simultaneously know (as he must, if he is to be a deceiver) and not know (as he must, if he is to be deceived) a single thing. [p. 82]

Accordingly, as Johnson (1998) notes, if "repression" is "a kind of self-deception in which people hide painful information about themselves from themselves" (p. 300), then this raises the difficult question: "how does a self hide knowledge of itself from itself?" (p. 305). Nevertheless, Freud discusses repression in precisely such terms:

I must draw an analogy between the criminal and the hysteric. In both we are concerned with a secret, with something hidden . . . In the case of the criminal it is a secret which he knows and hides from you, whereas in the case of the hysteric it is a secret which he himself does not know either, which is hidden even from himself. [Freud, 1906c, p. 108]

In addition to the issue of the apparent knowing–not-knowing paradox, if self-deception is modelled in terms of intentional behaviour (whereby the subject has desires and beliefs relevant to achieving self-deception), then this, too, is seen to raise difficulties. As Neu (1988) writes,

For if one were intentionally to decide to deceive oneself, to deny what one knows to be true, that would presuppose that one does already know what one knows to be true . . . Similarly, how can one intentionally forget? It would seem to require following a rule under conditions which do not allow one to knowingly follow it. [Neu, 1988, p. 81]

However, several authors note that posing repression in terms of purposive activity might itself be the source of the problem (Bach, 1998; Gardner, 1993; Jones, 1993), and if repression is explicable without reference to intentional activity, then the theoretical problem with "intentional repression" is subverted:

It seems to me that the difficulties for some in the concept of the dynamic unconscious come in its description as an *active* and *purposeful* process carried out by a separate and distinct part of the mind. Freud early on rejected the notion of repression as a conscious act, and even much later, when he referred to repression as a defensive manoeuvre carried out by the ego, it seems clear to me that he was speaking metaphorically. [Jones, 1993, p. 89, her italics]

For example, repression could occur non- or sub-intentionally, through non-rational motivating factors, as described earlier in the case of anxiety, acting as an "exciting cause" (Gillett, 1990). In such an account, repression could be triggered by intense anxiety, without involving an agency intentionally repressing and without any "rational" decision to repress (although some plausible mechanism is still required for how this precisely occurs).

However, in contradistinction to Jones (1993) above (and developed in detail later), such accounts still require knowing the target of repression simply because evaluating a target as a threat requires an evaluation that cannot be reduced to non-psychological activities. Maze and Henry (1996) accordingly summarize the apparent paradox: "The question remains, how can the knowing entity continually deny the existence of something while continually maintaining a watch against it?" (p. 1094). This is indeed a complex question, and one that would make repression appear to be impossible. However, it will be shown that it is possible to provide a coherent account of repression that does Freud's account justice. None the less, before addressing this it is necessary to clarify some of the basic elements that constitute the building blocks of repression.

PART II

MAKING SENSE OF REPRESSION

CHAPTER FIVE

Unconscious mental processes and the nature of the repressed

Repression and the unconscious

Freud writes that the *"the essence of repression lies simply in turning something away, and keeping it at a distance, from the conscious"* (Freud, 1915d, p. 147, his italics), and psychoanalytic therapy "aims at . . . nothing other than the uncovering of what is unconscious in mental life" (Freud, 1916–1917, p. 389). (Freud qualifies this position with respect to overcoming resistances (1910k, p. 225, 1913c, pp. 141–142, 1919a, p. 159, 1937d, p. 257).) However, Freud also indicates that repression (and its offshoot, resistance) shaped his understanding of unconscious mentality, writing that "we obtain our concept of the unconscious from the theory of repression. The repressed is the prototype of the unconscious for us" (Freud, 1923b, p. 15). The relation between repression and unconscious mental processes thus requires careful articulation, particularly so given that recent discussions cast doubt upon the possibility of unconscious mentality altogether (e.g., Searle, 1992; Talvitie, 2009; Talvitie & Tiitinen, 2006). Freud's account, however, is further complicated by his *descriptive, dynamic,* and *systematic* accounts of unconscious mental processes (Freud, 1912g, 1915e), a point not always recognized by critics of Freudian theory (e.g., Rofé,

2008). The aim of the present chapter is to articulate an account of unconscious mental processes as a basis for understanding Freud's theory of repression.

Freud's justification of unconscious mental processes

For Freud, unconscious processes were justified in the explanation of both normal and pathological behaviour. Behaviour that appeared inexplicable in terms of conscious intentions could be accounted for by interpolating unconscious mental processes:

> If the chain of ideas . . . seems inexplicable by psychological determi-
> nants alone, we have already found out the reason for this and we can
> attribute it to *the existence of hidden unconscious motives*. We may thus
> suspect the presence of such secret motives wherever a breach of this
> kind in the train of thought is apparent or when the force ascribed by
> the patient to his motives goes far beyond the normal. [Breuer &
> Freud, 1895d, p. 293, Freud's italics]

> . . . the data of consciousness have a very large number of gaps in
> them: both in healthy and in sick people psychical acts often occur
> which can be explained only by presupposing other acts, of which,
> nevertheless, consciousness affords no evidence. [Freud, 1915e, p. 166]

Boudreaux (1977) calls this the "argument from the continuum": unconscious mental acts may be inferred from analogous cases that are ordinarily considered to involve conscious mental acts. It is in this sense, according to Wollheim (1991, 1993), that Freud *deepened* the ordinary (folk-psychological) desire/belief model of explaining human behaviour through inserting unconscious beliefs and desires (cf. Cavell, 1993; Gardner, 1993; Hopkins, 1995a,b; Mackay, 1996). If human action generally is to be explained through ascriptions of desires and beliefs, then neurotic behaviours, no less than ordinary actions, presuppose beliefs and desires that might not be known to the individual.

Freud further notes that "consciousness is in general a highly fugi-tive state. What is conscious is conscious only for a moment" (Freud, 1940a[1938], p. 159). Our awareness turns from one event to another, and so what is actually conscious at any time is small in comparison to everything that is known to the individual. In this respect, Freud proposes that becoming conscious is determined by the psychical function of *attention* (Freud, 1900a, pp. 593–594), whereby whatever we turn our attention to can be described as conscious (i.e., to be conscious of x is to attend to, or be currently aware of, x). Consequently, whatever we are currently unaware of can be described as unconscious:

> Now let us call 'conscious' the conception which is present to our consciousness and of which we are aware, and let this be the only meaning of the term 'conscious'. As for latent conceptions, if we have any reason to suppose that they exist in the mind—as we had in the case of memory—let them be denoted by the term 'unconscious'. [Freud, 1912g, p. 260]

In other words, for p to be conscious is simply for p to be currently known (such that S currently knows p), and for p to be unconscious means simply for p not to be currently known. Freud describes this *descriptive* view of mentality (i.e., describing mental processes with respect to whether they are known or unknown) as the "oldest and best" meaning for the term "unconscious":

> The oldest and best meaning of the word 'unconscious' is the descriptive one: we call a psychical process unconscious whose existence we are obliged to assume—for some such reason as that we infer from its effects—but of which we know nothing. [Freud, 1933a, p. 70]

By implication, then, comparing the totality of a person's beliefs with whatever he or she is currently aware of at any given moment provides evidence for the existence of unconscious beliefs. As Weintraub (1987) points out, since "very few thoughts (perhaps only one) are consciously present in our minds at one and the same time" most of our beliefs are unconscious at any given moment (p. 424), a position Freud maintained throughout his work:

> in support of there being an unconscious psychical state, that at any given moment consciousness includes only a small content, so that the greater part of what we call conscious knowledge must in any case be for very considerable periods of time in a state of latency, that is to say, of being psychically unconscious. When all our latent memories are taken into consideration it becomes totally incomprehensible how the

existence of the unconscious can be denied. [Freud, 1915e, p. 167; cf. Freud, 1912g, p. 260, 1933a, p. 70, 1939a, p. 95).

Simply put, at any given moment we have an indefinite number of beliefs which, for the most part, we are not currently aware of, and so these can be described as unconscious beliefs. Such unconscious beliefs might, nevertheless, influence our behaviour. For instance, when driving on "autopilot", one might be currently aware of matters quite unrelated to driving (listening to the radio, holding a conversation, etc.) and yet still be guided by beliefs of laws and safety (Boag, 2008b, 2010a). In fact, if any activity required all the relevant beliefs to come to mind, then undertaking any activity would be unendurably laborious (see Boag, 2008b).

Making sense of the descriptive/epistemic view of mental processes

The descriptive view above proposes a distinction between conscious and unconscious states in terms of whether something is currently the *object* of attention. In this sense, to attend to something is to enter into a certain relation with the object of attention, and it is this notion of "relation" that has far-reaching implications for understanding mentality generally and repression specifically. Cognition generally refers to acts of *knowing*, such as believing, thinking, remembering, wishing, and desiring, which might either be veridical or non-veridical: "psychological processes are . . . typified by a kind of relation not to be found in merely physical interactions, and that is the relation of *knowing about* or *referring to*" (Maze, 1983, p. 83, his italics; cf. Maze & Henry, 1996, p. 1089). This *of*-ness or aboutness of mental states is explicit within Brentano's (1874) concept of *intentionality* discussed earlier, whereby terms such as "consciousness" and "awareness" imply that we are conscious *of* or aware *of* some state of affairs. Consequently, cognitive acts (e.g., beliefs *of* x or perceptions of y) involve *relations* between a cognizing *subject* (a knower) and the object or event (including mental events) cognized.

The concept of relation is one of the more neglected concepts within psychology, and so a short word on the matter is in order. Anything that exists stands in an indefinite amount of relations, whether it be to parents or strangers, spatial relations (such as near, far, above, below), temporal relations (past, present, and future), causal relations (causes and effects), legal relations, etc. The common facet of all relations is that they involve at least two or more distinct *terms*, where "term" means not some linguistic entity, but rather whatever is said to be standing in relation to other things. To say that the terms of any relation must be distinct is to say that they must have their own intrinsic properties (i.e., exist independently of the relation) to speak sensibly about what stands in the relation:

> Anything that can stand . . . in any relation at all, must have at least some intrinsic properties. If that were not the case . . . then we could not understand what it was that was said to have those relationships. A relation can only hold between two or more terms, and a part of what is involved in seeing those terms as related is being able to see them as distinct, that is, as each having its own intrinsic properties, so that we can say what the terms *are* that are related. This means that each term of the relation must be able in principle to be described without the need to include any reference to its relation to the other. [Maze, 1983, p. 24, his italics; cf. Maze, 1954, p. 231; Michell, 1988, p. 234]

For instance, to say that John is *different* from Mike means that both John and Mike must exist (i.e., have properties) in order to enable such a comparison to be made. Relations, however, should not to be taken as either things or properties of the terms, since a relationship cannot be reduced to either of the terms of the relationship (i.e., relations refer to how the various things stand with respect to one another and are not reducible to either). So, to say that John is different from Mike is to note a relation between John and Mike and is not referring to a property of either (i.e., "difference" cannot be reduced to either John or Mike). However, again, this is not to say that that John and Mike do not have characteristics that they differ in; only that the relation is *between* those properties rather than constituting a property itself. For instance, if we say that the cup is on table, then the relation of on-ness is not a third entity or quality existing independently of the cup and the table (see also Boag, 2011b).

With respect to cognition, the relation of knowing involves a knowing *subject S*, the something known (*p*), and *S*'s knowing *p* cannot be reduced to either the knower or the known alone:

> Knowledge being taken as a relation, it is thus asserted that, when I know this paper, 'I know' in no way constitutes this paper, nor does 'know this paper' in any way constitute me, nor does 'know' constitute either me or this paper. [Anderson, 1927, p. 27]

Any account of cognition thus requires stipulating the subject term (the knower) and object term (the known) involved. In this respect, the subject S must be capable of description independently of both p and the cognitive relation with p (i.e., S must have its own intrinsic qualities). Similarly, the object of cognition must also be logically independent of the knower and the cognitive relation, which is not to say that the object must necessarily be located externally to the knower's body. Since the knower (a term that will be discussed later) may be taken to include the subject's nervous system, then the object of cognition could be located within the body, yet still external to the nervous system (Boag, 2008a; Michell, 1988). Indeed, since the nervous system is complex, one part of the nervous system could know another part of that same system.

Accordingly, as a relation, "consciousness" (or, better, *to be conscious of*) is not a thing or a property of things, and so to describe something as conscious or unconscious is only to say that it is known or unknown (i.e., has entered into a certain relation). An important implication from this relational view is that in coming to know something (or coming to be ignorant of it), there is no change in the object of knowing (or ignorance). Thus, I might attend to x and not y, and then attend to y and not x, and neither x nor y are changed by my entering or exiting that attended-to relation. Thus, if we consider Freud's comment,

> [s]ome processes become conscious easily; they may then cease to be conscious, but can become conscious once more without any trouble ... This reminds us that consciousness is in general a highly fugitive state. What is conscious is conscious only for a moment. [Freud, 1940a[1938], p. 159]

Any object or event that becomes known, slips into unconsciousness, and then back into consciousness is simply to note relations of attention rather than changes in the object of attention. Of course, once I am aware of some situation I might be in a position to act on it, but this is a further action independent of the act of awareness.

A further important consideration to keep in mind is that relations cannot be reduced to the terms of the relations (i.e., relations should not be reified as properties), and neither should they be treated as any type of independently existing substantive entity. Given that relations cannot be reduced to terms in the relation, then mental processes (as relations) cannot be reduced to neural processes. Neural processes (and other physical and biological processes) are, of course, involved in cognizing, but these are what stand in the relation and are not the cognitive relation itself. While the knower consists of physical properties and processes (e.g., neural processes), the cognitive relation cannot be reduced to those same physical properties and processes any more than the relation of marriage can be reduced to either the husband or wife. Thus, although neurological processes may constitute one (or part of the) subject term of the cognizing relation (i.e., knower), such processes are insufficient to constitute the knowing relation. Similarly, Petocz (1999) has recently demonstrated that "meaning" and symbolism cannot be reduced to anything less than a *ternary* relation between a cognizing subject, signifier, and signified, and thus Blass and Carmeli (2007) are correct when they write that "meaning" cannot be reduced to neural states (p. 30). However, while "meaning" cannot be reduced to neural events, this is not to say that neural events are not involved (or that such neural states are not the legitimate object of scientific enquiry).

The relational view of cognition discussed here is not novel and has antecedents in Aristotelian thinking (see Petocz, 1999), medieval scholasticism (see Pasnau, 1997), the American new realists (e.g., Holt—Holt et al., 1912), British Realists (e.g., Moore, Laird, and Alexander; see Michell, 1988), and, more recently, in a school of realism associated with the Scottish-born philosopher John Anderson (see Anderson, 1927, 1930; Baker, 1986).[1] Recognizing that we are speaking about cognition as a relation and not a property of events allows asking relevant questions about the terms involved in the relation. With respect to cognition specifically as a relation, we can ask questions concerning *what* is doing the knowing (the cognizing *subject* or knower) and *what* is cognized (the object of cognition) (Anderson, 1927; Boag, 2008b; Maze, 1983; Michell, 1988). Furthermore, we can also recognize a distinction between knowing something and knowing that we know it.

Knowing our own mental processes

While we can sensibly talk of being conscious of events, it is also important to make a clear distinction between *knowing* something and *knowing that it is known*, since the former does not necessitate the latter: we can be aware of *x*, without being aware of being aware of *x*. However, confusing awareness with self-awareness has a long tradition, notably in Descartes's treatment of mentality, but also by Freud's contemporaries (e.g., Brentano, 1874), as well as some later critics of Freudian theory (e.g., Sartre, 1956; Thornton, 1999). Descartes, for instance, writes,

> As to the fact that there can be nothing in the mind, in so far as it is a thinking thing, of which it is not aware, this seems to me self-evident. For there is nothing that we can understand to be in the mind, regarded in this way, that is not a thought or dependent on a thought. If it were not a thought or dependent on a thought it would not belong to the mind *qua* thinking thing; and we cannot have any thought of which we are not aware at the very moment when it is in us. [Descartes, 1641, p. 171; cf. Descartes, 1648, p. 357]

What is being asserted here by Descartes is that when subject *S* knows *p*, he or she is also conscious of the fact that he or she knows *p* (i.e., he or she also knows that that *p* is known). If this were indeed true, then the concept of "unconscious mental processes" would be a contradiction in terms, a point not lost on Freud (e.g., Freud, 1925e, p. 216; 1940a[1938], pp. 157–158), and an argument posed at times to dismiss the possibility of unconscious mentality (e.g., Thornton, 1999, p. 7). Recently, Talvitie and Ihanus (2005) write, "[w]e are directly conscious of our contents of consciousness—both present and past: I am conscious of gazing at the computer now, and I am conscious of having listened to Stevie Ray Vaughan's guitar playing yesterday . . ." (Talvitie & Ihanus, 2005, p. 665). While, in some respects, it is, of course, true that in attending to something (say, gazing at a computer) that what is attended to is known, it is not the case that knowledge of attending to that situation is known. The confusion results from failing to articulate clearly *what* is, in fact, conscious when we say that we are conscious of something (i.e., the object term). While watching a film, we might say that we are "conscious of watching the film", and, of course, that is correct in so far as there is awareness of the film.

However, whether we also *know* that we are watching a film is another matter: I can be watching a film, engrossed in the storyline, without reflecting on the fact of watching a film (and, presumably, a good film is one which does not prompt such reflection).

Logically, it cannot be the case that knowing involves knowing that that knowing is known, since it would entail an infinite regress of knowing acts. That is, if knowing *p* involves also necessarily knowing that I know it, then I would need to know that, too, *ad infinitum* (see Maze, 1983, p. 90; Michell, 1988, p. 236). Instead, if we consider for the moment Freud's comment that "there are mental things in a man which he knows without knowing that he knows" (Freud, 1916–1917, p. 101), it appears clear that coming to know what we know requires a second mental act where we turn our attention to (or reflect upon) our own mental acts. For instance, if someone asks me "what do you think about *x*", then I might be prompted to engage in the mental act of considering what I think on the matter. In the relational view, then, when *S* knows (or wishes, etc.) that *p*, the relation of knowing (or wishing, etc.) (SRp), is itself unconscious and does not become conscious unless it becomes the object of a second mental act such that *S* knows SRp. Hence, knowing our own cognitive acts must involve a second mental act (independent of the one known), and the notion of unconscious mental processes is perfectly legitimate and theoretically justified.

Of course, we should also ask what it means to become conscious of one's own mental processes, and, in the relational view, to know one's own cognition requires perceiving the cognitive relation, which requires knowing the terms of the relationship (but not necessarily everything about those terms) and the connection between them. As Michell (1988) writes,

> To know cognition is to know a relation between two terms and whether our own cognitions or those of others, what is known in observing cognition must be the same kind of situation: a connection between a person and the environment. [Michell, 1988, p. 236]

However, Freud further discerns that it is possible to have direct and indirect knowledge of one's own mental acts, noting that "[t]o have heard something and to have experienced something are in their psychological nature two quite different things, even though the content of both is the same" (Freud, 1915e, p. 176), a distinction that relates to a distinction sometimes described between emotional and intellectual insight (Richfield, 1954). For instance, a person might be conscious of having a desire that p (e.g., through the analyst's interpretation) without consciously desiring that p, a distinction that Finkelstein (1999) draws attention to:

> it's one thing to say that someone's fear or jealousy is conscious rather than unconscious (i.e., that he is consciously afraid or consciously jealous), and quite another thing to say that someone is conscious of (i.e., aware of) his own fear and jealousy. [Finkelstein, 1999, p. 83]

A person, for instance, might be conscious of his belief that p without consciously believing p, or even while consciously believing that not-p. Finkelstein here suggests that the distinction hinges upon the manner in which the person becomes conscious:

> If my knowledge that I believe p is based only upon the testimony of my therapist, then—while I may be said to be conscious of my belief that p—I cannot be said to consciously believe p . . . What it means for me to consciously believe that p (or to be consciously hopeful or afraid, etc.) is that I know my mental state via a *particular* cognitive mechanism—the mechanism by which I ordinarily find out about my own states of mind. It is tempting to refer to this mechanism as 'inner sense,' but perhaps we should just call it 'mechanism M.' What it means for one of mental states to be conscious (i.e., for me to be consciously angry, sad, or whatever) is that I'm aware of it *via mechanism M*. What it means for one of mental states to be unconscious is that—although I may be aware of it—I am not aware of it via mechanism M. [Finkelstein, 1999, p. 80]

In this fashion, Michell proposes that awareness of our cognitive activity could sometimes result from *inference* rather than direct perception of the cognitive relation. For example, an analyst's interpretation of the analysand's utterances might allow the analysand to infer, say, a belief or emotion that he or she was previously unaware of, and so, in some sense, the analysand can be said to be conscious of that belief or emotion without directly knowing it (i.e., S knows S believes p via q), in much the same way that I might know about events on the other side of the world via a newspaper, which is distinct from directly experiencing one's own mental act (where S knows S feels x).

The distinction between knowing and knowing that one knows is not a new position and is either explicit or implicit in various accounts of first- and second-order knowledge (e.g., Brakel, 2010) and metacognition (Metcalfe & Shimamura, 1994). However, there are important implications of this distinction that are much less recognized, including giving substance to Freud's claim that no mental act can be conscious without first having been unconscious. Freud, in fact, writes that "we see the process of a thing becoming conscious as a specific psychical act, distinct from and independent of the process of the formation of a presentation or idea" (Freud, 1900a, p. 144). That is, any mental act must first be unconscious because it exists logically prior to any reflection upon it. Furthermore, when Freud says that all "mental processes are in themselves unconscious" (1916–1917, p. 143), it is best not to understand this to mean that the features of the world (including mental events) are fundamentally unknowable, as Solms (1997b, 2003) suggests (a position which simply obscures the ontology of unconscious mental processes and creates an untenable dualism). Instead, Freud is simply drawing attention to the fact that "consciousness" (or, better, the relation of knowing) is not a quality of mental processes and that although mental processes involve knowing, they are not themselves automatically known. This is clear from repeated instances in Freud's work: "Everything conscious has an unconscious preliminary stage: whereas what is unconscious may remain at that stage and nevertheless claim to be regarded as having the full value of a psychical process" (Freud, 1900a, pp. 612–613). Similarly, "every psychical act begins as an unconscious one, and it may either remain so or go developing into consciousness" (Freud, 1912g, p. 264; Freud, 1916–1917, p. 295). This clearly indicates that *psychical acts* exist unconsciously until attention is turned to them and they become known. As Freud writes, coming to know our own mental acts involves turning our attention to them (coming to know what we know):

> In psycho-analysis there is no choice for us but to assert that mental processes are in themselves unconscious, and to like the perception of them by means of consciousness to the perception of the external world by means of the sense-organs. [Freud, 1915e, p. 171; cf. Freud, 1924f, p. 198, 1940a[1938], p. 160]

More formally, if a subject S becomes aware that p, and then at a later time is prompted to pay attention to the fact that they had become aware that p (i.e., S knows that S knows p), then that awareness of p can now be called conscious, whereas previously it had been an unconscious mental act (descriptively unconscious). Furthermore, there is no necessity that any given mental act should become known if the necessary causal antecedents fail to occur. An unconscious process might never become the object of attention, and so might remain unconscious, and so it is possible for S to wish that p and never become conscious of that wish. Here, certain neural machinery can be posited to allow self-reflection, and in the case with non-human species without such nervous system properties, it could be said that all of their mental acts remain unconscious.

Applying the distinction between knowing and knowing that one knows

The distinction between knowing and knowing that one knows can be applied to a great variety of phenomena that are relevant both to psychoanalysis and general psychology. For instance, "tip-of-the-tongue" experiences (Brennen, Vikan, & Dybdahl, 2007) demonstrate that it is possible to know something (say, a name), and yet not be able to reflect upon it. Similarly, the distinction between knowing and "knowing that one knows" also allows us to make sense of subliminal perception, sometimes referred to as "knowing without knowing" (Masling, 1992, p. 259). In such cases, we can surmise that the individual perceiving subliminally actually perceives the stimulus but is prevented from perceiving that first act of perception. Similarly, the distinction is also relevant for the concept of "unconscious attention", which, for some authors, appears to be a self-contradictory concept, even if necessary for psychoanalytic explanation. For instance, Kaplan-Solms and Solms (2000) write,

> We take it that it is now generally accepted that human perceptual and memory functions are largely unconscious. It is, however, more questionable whether there is such a thing as unconscious attention. Many people—Freud included—would say that it is precisely the function of attention which renders unconscious mental processing conscious,

that it is attention that raises perceptions and memories above the threshold of awareness. [Kaplan-Solms & Solms, 2000, p. 159]

However, there is only a problem with '"unconscious attention" if there is no clear distinction between the act of attention and the object of the act. While an act of attention is necessary for coming to know the object of cognition (where S attends to p), since the act of attending itself is unconscious in the first instance (i.e., S is unaware that S attends to p) until it is itself also attended to, it is, thus, perfectly intelligible to speak of "unconscious attention", since in attending to p, S attends to p, but there is no necessity that S further attends to attending to p. That is, p is known, but not the act of attention itself (i.e., not the *relation* between S and p—SRp). Thus, in the case of the quote above, turning attention to one's mental process makes the mental process known, but the *act* itself is unconscious, until the act itself is attended to (such that S attends to S *attending to* p).

Unconscious processes and the nature of the repressed

With respect to understanding repression and unconscious mentality, Talvitie and colleagues (e.g., Talvitie, 2009; Talvitie & Ihanus, 2003a,b, 2005; Talvitie & Tiitinen, 2006) believe that there is a fundamental problem with psychoanalytic conceptions of unconscious processes, writing that "no one has ever said what those unconscious contents are actually like, and where and how they exist" (Talvitie, 2009, p. 91). This issue poses a fundamental challenge for psychoanalytic theory: "All in all, unconscious fantasies are a cornerstone of psychoanalysis, but it seems impossible to say why we should believe that they exist" (Talvitie & Ihanus, 2005, p. 665). In response to this difficulty, some authors propose instead that unconscious processes must actually be neural, non-conscious, or non-psychological (or non-intentional processes). Gillett (1988), for instance, proposes a reductionist stance, claiming that

terms referring to unconscious mental events actually refer to neural events, and to postulate the existence of a psychical unconscious in the sense of something non-physical distinct from neural events commits one to an untenable dualism on the unconscious level. [p. 570]

Similarly, Cavell (1991, 1993) interprets Freud himself as proposing a reductionist stance, writing concerning

> Freud's interesting but strange claims 'that everything conscious has an unconscious preliminary stage' ... and that 'mental processes are in themselves unconscious': Presumably Freud intends both conscious and unconscious to refer to orders of the mental. But what can the content of these passages be other than a reductivist thesis that mental processes are 'really' merely organic, or neurophysiological? [Cavell, 1993, p. 48; cf. Cavell, 1991, p. 146]

The reductionist position has found prominence in Searle's (1992, 1995) work and been recently discussed extensively by Talvitie (2009) and Talvitie and Ihanus (2003a, 2005). Searle (1995) criticizes Freud's view that unconscious processes are mental: "The naïve notion of the unconscious that we have inherited from Freud is that unconscious mental states are just the same as conscious mental states only minus the consciousness" (p. 332). The problem with this, says Searle, is that conceptualizing unconscious mentality is inconceivable. Instead, Searle (1992) distinguishes "nonconscious" states involving non-mental physical properties (although these might become the object of cognition) from conscious states involving intentionality in Brentano's sense (e.g., where S believes that p). A belief, says Searle, has intentionality (intrinsic mentality), which qualifies it as a mental state, and since unconscious processes, by definition, do not involve awareness, says Searle, then we have a paradox:

> Once one adopts the view that mental states are both *in themselves* mental and *in themselves* unconscious, then it is not going to be easy to explain how consciousness fits into the picture. It looks as if the view that mental states are unconscious in themselves has the consequence that consciousness is totally extrinsic, not an essential part of any conscious state or event. [Searle, 1992, p. 170, his italics]

Searle concludes that since unconscious processes are non-intentional (i.e., without objects) at best, they must be brain states.

Rather than unconscious mentality, then, Searle proposes a "dispositional unconscious", whereby unconscious states are, in fact, neural states that are mental only by virtue of their power to bring about conscious mental states: "Unconscious beliefs are indeed dispositional states of the brain, but they are dispositions to produce conscious thoughts and conscious behaviour" (Searle, 1992, p. 161). Talvitie (2009) has recently extended Searle's argument to attack what he calls the traditional psychoanalytic three-sphere framework that proposes the existence of: (i) consciousness, (ii) a mental unconscious, and (iii) neural processes, arguing that (ii) cannot be coherently formulated. The argument for this follows Searle's:

(a)   mental states, *by definition*, involve awareness;
(b)   unconscious states, *by definition*, do not involve awareness;
(c)   therefore unconscious states are not mental.

Talvitie (2009) instead proposes a "two-sphere" psychoanalytic approach, proposing only conscious (mental) states and neural processes and dispensing with unconscious mentality altogether: "the unconscious is only the brain and its neural processes" (p. 94). As a consequence, if unconscious states are simply non-intentional brain states, then it becomes difficult to conceptualize any account of repressed *mental* content:

> If repressed contents exist somewhere, they are in the brain. However, according to present-day views of neuroscience, we cannot even conceive of what these contents are like, or of the kind of equipment that would reveal their existence. Although the expression has been traditionally used in a different context, repressed fantasies (beliefs, etc.) could be said to appear from the cognitive viewpoint as "ghosts in the machine"—it is even hard to conceive of where and how such entities might exist. [Talvitie & Ihanus, 2003a, p. 138]

Instead, these authors conclude that since repressed ideas are not stored in the brain (since the brain simply consists of physical properties), "[t]he obvious logical conclusion is that when ideas are missing from consciousness, they are not "hiding" anywhere, but are prevented from being formed in the domain of consciousness" (p. 91).

Reductionism and cognitive neuroscience

The reductionist trend appears to also follow from the growing trend in psychoanalysis to embrace "cognitive (neuro)science" (e.g., Bucci,

1997; Davis, 2001; Gabbard & Westen, 2003; Mancia, 2006; Pugh, 2002; Westen & Gabbard, 2002) as well as a tendency to equate the repressed with implicit, procedural, and non-declarative processes. For instance, memory acquired "implicitly" is, at times, described as being "non-conscious" (e.g., Fonagy & Target, 2000, p. 414; Öhman, 2009, p. 135) and linked with Sandler and Joffe's (1969) "non-experiential" (non-psychological) realm. Fonagy (1999), for instance, writes that "fantasy may be thought to exist in the non-experiential realm of implicit memory" (p. 219), and Talvitie and Ihanus (2002) accordingly deduce, "if we treat repressed contents in terms of implicit knowledge, the idea of becoming conscious of the repressed should be abandoned" (Talvitie & Ihanus, 2002, p. 1312; cf. Talvitie, 2009, p. 1312). Alternatively, Mancia (2006) equates repression with "explicit" or "autobiographic memory" whereas pre-verbal and pre-symbolic experiences "are stored in the implicit memory and are not, therefore, susceptible to being repressed" (Mancia, 2006, p. 87), which, in turn, leads to the "unrepressed unconscious".

Need we reject the repressed mentality?

If the notion of repressed mental acts is indefensible, then a radical reconceptualization of Freud's theory of repression would be required. However, the conclusion that unconscious mentality is incoherent follows from a lack of clarity with respect to the distinction between knowing and knowing that one knows. As noted earlier, if we accept that "being known" or "unknown" is not a quality of processes, but rather a relation entered into, then we can conceptualize any mental process that is not currently known as unconscious. Of particular relevance to the psychoanalyst, however, is not so much that a mental process is unconscious, but rather the cases where knowing what is known is prevented. Here, Freud's distinction between descriptively unconscious and preconscious processes is relevant, since some mental processes become known easily. Freud writes, "Everything unconscious that . . . can thus easily exchange the unconscious state for the conscious one, is therefore preferably described as 'capable of becoming conscious' or as *preconscious*" (Freud, 1940a [1938], pp. 159–160). In contradistinction to preconscious processes, "the essence of the process of repression lies, not in putting an end to, in annihilating, the idea which represents an instinct, but in preventing it from becoming conscious" (Freud, 1915e, p. 166). That is, "[t]he essence of repression lies in its interference with one's ability to reflect on one's mental state" (Eagle, 2000b, p. 173), and, as Freud notes, for therapy to be effective requires removing this interference (Freud, 1910k, p. 225, 1913c, pp. 141–142, 1919a, p. 159, 1937d, p. 257). Viewing repression as a process that prevents reflection upon mental states provides an important answer to the question of locating the repressed: after repression there is no change in the location of the repressed. Simply being ignorant of the repressed does not imply any actual interference with the target of repression itself: it does not change location, it is simply no longer known. To illustrate this, consider the following example: imagine there is a locked box with a particular content. One person, Patrick, is aware of this content but another person, Arthur, is prevented from knowing what is inside. Obviously, the content is exactly the same whether it is known by Patrick or not known by Arthur, and if Patrick were even to forget the box's content, then the content remains unaffected with respect to being known or unknown. In other words, whether something is known or unknown is not a thing's property or location, and there is no reason why this crude example could not work for understanding the nature of the repressed: a person could desire that p, feel threatened by that desire and repress it, such that the desire exists exactly where it did in the first place, but simply is now no longer known. Thus, while it is legitimate to ask *where* the repressed content exists, given the relational view, there is no reason to locate the repressed anywhere different from any non-repressed mental content. Since repression prevents mental content from becoming the object of a second mental act, a repressed mental content can be conceptualized simply as any mental act which the individual is dynamically prevented (i.e., motivated) from reflecting on, such that S desires p but is incapable of knowing that S desires that p. That is, desires and wishes might exist unconsciously, but attention cannot be turned to them so as to make them conscious.

Searle (1992), in fact, does recognize that there is a distinction between knowing and knowing that one knows, and even comes to the sound logical conclusion that the act is itself unconscious until it becomes the object of a second mental act. However, he tentatively indicates that there might be the problem of an infinite regress here:

What about the act of perceiving—is this a mental phenomenon? If so, it must be "in itself" unconscious, and it would appear that for me to become conscious of that act, I would need some higher-level act of perceiving of my act of perceiving. I am not sure about this, but it looks like an infinite regress argument threatens. [Searle, 1992, p. 171]

However, Searle's concern here is unfounded. There is only the threat of an infinite regress if the first mental act by *necessity* entails a second, which is precisely the problem for the Cartesian position that knowing necessitates knowing that we know. If we accept that mental states involve awareness (of something), it does not logically follow that that same awareness is itself known. As argued earlier, knowledge of what is known requires a second mental act reflecting upon the first mental act, in much the same way as when someone asks me about what I believe on some matter, I might then reflect upon that mental act of believing (which involves a certain discovery of the what one believes).

It is interesting to note, similarly, that even Talvitie (2009), while rejecting the possibility of unconscious mentality, implicitly refers to the distinction between knowing and knowing that one knows when he discusses consciousness and self-consciousness:

There is also the distinction between consciousness and self-consciousness. A fish is conscious of another fish swimming in front of it, and an infant is conscious of the light being switched off. Fish and infants possess conscious states, but they are not self-conscious beings: they do not possess ideas on their personal characteristics (sex, age, unique life history, idiosyncratic ways of reacting to stimuli, etc.), do not know what their current feelings are compared to those they had yesterday, and they do not understand that their life is finite. [Talvitie, 2009, p. 96]

In saying that both fish and babies are *aware* of their environment (a point indisputable, as their bodily movements indicate) but lack self-consciousness, Talvitie appears to be implying a distinction between being aware of x and awareness of the awareness of x. That is, the self-consciousness that Talvitie refers to, while rather specific with respect to different matters that might or might not be known (e.g., that life in finite), entails reflection upon one's own mental processes, or, in other words, knowing that one knows. However, adults, too, are not necessarily aware of all the matters Talvitie mentions throughout their daily lives. For instance, how many of us spend our times reflecting upon life's finitude? However, it is perfectly reasonable to say that adults *generally* know that life is finite (etc.) without necessarily reflecting upon knowing this, in much the same way that we believe many things without necessarily being aware of everything (or anything) that we believe at any given moment. Thus, Talvitie's approach can be recast into relational terms, whereby, when *knowing* states of affairs (what Talvitie calls "consciousness"), such acts of knowing are not thereby themselves known (i.e., we can, thus, postulate unconscious knowing), and so "self-consciousness" in Talvitie's account refers to *knowing that one knows* (or being conscious of one's own mental acts). If this is the case, then there is merit to Talvitie's approach, but in contradistinction to Talvitie's claim, there is no reason to reject unconscious mentality and repressed mental acts.

Note

1. This position has been recently referred to as "situational realism" (Hibberd, 2009). Further discussion of this position can be found in Boag (2005, 2008a, 2010), Maze (1983), McMullen (1996a,b), Medlow (2008), Michell (1988), Petocz (1999), and Rantzen (1993). For discussion specific to conscious and unconscious processes see Boag (2008b, 2010b), and McIlwain (2001).

CHAPTER SIX

Repression and the system *Ucs.*

Systematic mentality in the topographic and structural theories

While Freud's descriptive view of unconscious mentality is logically defensible, it does not follow that other aspects of Freud's account of unconscious mentality are without problems. Notable here is Freud's systematic view of mentality, arising prominently with the topographic theory and carrying over into the structural theory. Here, Freud proposes that qualitatively distinct processes pertain to the different mental systems, and some view this as Freud's major contribution to a theory of unconscious processes. Macmillan (1991), for example, claims that Freud's innovation was the proposition that consciousness or unconscious was bound up with the topographic systems, and Jones (1953) believes that Freud's "revolutionary contribution to psychology" was "his proposition that there are two fundamentally different kinds of mental process, which he termed primary and secondary respectively, together with his description of them" (p. 436). This systematic view was not restricted to the topographic theory and, as many note (e.g., Boesky, 1995; Compton, 1972a, 1981; Matte-Blanco, 1975; Petocz; 1999; Wiedeman, 1972; Wollheim, 1991), there is considerable overlap between the topographic and structural theories and much of the difference between the models is in name only: "the criteria of *Ucs.* and *Pcs.* are the same as those of id and ego" (Gill, 1963, p. 53), and the primary and secondary process distinction carries over from the topographic theory to the structural one (Boudreaux, 1977; Petocz, 1999). However, some authors believe that psychoanalysis has, nevertheless, neglected the "unrepressed unconscious" (e.g., Fayek, 2005; Matte-Blanco, 1975), and others note that the systematic view has major implications for Freud's theory of repression (e.g., Petocz, 1999). The aim of the present chapter is to develop Freud's systematic distinction and its implications for repression.

The systematic distinction

As already noted, Freud proposes qualitatively distinct processes pertaining to different mental systems. Freud writes that the system *Ucs.* is "a particular realm of the mind with its own wishful impulses, its own mode of expression and its peculiar mental mechanisms which are not in force elsewhere" (Freud, 1916–1917, p. 212; cf. Freud, 1912g, p. 266; 1915e, p. 186), including *primary process* mentation, *exemption from mutual contradiction, timelessness,* and *replacement of external by psychical reality* (Freud, 1915e, p. 187). Freud depicts the system *Ucs.*'s operations as governing all that is *irrational* and *illogical* in the mind (Freud, 1900a, p. 598, 1905e, p. 61, 1915e, p. 186, 1940a[1938], pp. 168–169) whereas the development of the system *Pcs.* and the more reality-orientated *secondary* processes gradually replace or cover over the earlier, primitive, primary processes. The secondary processes prevent the free discharge of excitations into hallucinations, delaying discharge until the required conditions for satisfaction are present (Freud, 1900a, p. 599, 1915e, p. 188).

The precise nature of these systems is, however, open to interpretation. On the one hand, the *Ucs.* is, at times, treated metaphorically as a container or a location where unconscious processes reside (e.g., Freud, 1916–1917, p. 295), giving rise to the dungeon metaphor of "the unconscious". Taken literally, this spatial metaphor involves viewing unconscious mental processes as being *somewhere* different from consciousness and repression then entails "banishing" the repressed "to the unconscious" (see Matte-Blanco, 1975, p. 8, for a summary and critical discussion of the spatial metaphors in Freud's writing). As noted in the preceding chapter, locating the repressed in the unconscious is viewed as a major problem for the concept of repressed mentality, since the obvious question becomes precisely where such a location exists (e.g., Searle, 1992; Talvitie, 2009). However, the problem with treating unconscious mental processes as substantive entities is the same as treating conscious processes as substantive entities: a relation is reified into a substantive. In the relational account of mentality discussed here, any discussion of cognition in terms of substance, entity, location, or container must be rejected because relations cannot be reduced to "things" (entities with their own intrinsic properties). However, as noted earlier, Freud also proposes that the mental systems need not simply be conceptualized spatially, but instead can be temporally located (e.g., Freud, 1900a, p. 537), and subsequent authors such as Matte-Blanco (1975), while rejecting the *Ucs.* spatial metaphors, nevertheless accept the notion of the system *Ucs.* with respect to qualitatively distinct *processes* (e.g., *Ucs.* "symmetrical" (non-linear, timeless) logic and *Cs.* 'asymmetrical' Aristotelian logic processes, which he refers to as distinct "modes of being", p. 88). The question, then, is whether such accounts are defensible and what implications arise for understanding repression.

Logical implications of the systematic view for repression

According to Freud, with the development of the qualitatively distinct secondary processes, certain mental contents remain unconscious and are incapable of becoming known:

> In consequence of the belated appearance of the secondary processes, the core of our being, consisting of unconscious wishful impulses, remains inaccessible to the understanding and inhibition of the preconscious; the part played by the latter is restricted once and for all to directing along the most expedient paths the wishful impulses that arise from the unconscious. These unconscious wishes exercise a compelling force upon all later mental trends, a force which those trends are obliged to fall in with or which they may perhaps endeavour to divert and direct to higher aims. A further result of the belated appearance of the secondary process is that a wide sphere of mnemic material is inaccessible to preconscious cathexis. [Freud, 1900a, pp. 603–604]

Here, certain content remains unconscious, not due to motivated defence, but simply due to the development of the secondary process. In the Schreber analysis (Freud, 1911c), Freud describes a first phase of this process as *fixation*, acting as "the precursor and necessary condition of every 'repression'" (Freud, 1911c, p. 67). Freud describes this as "a passive lagging behind", whereas later repression (repression proper) is "an essentially active process" (Freud, 1911c, p. 67):

> Fixation can be described in this way. One instinct or instinctual component fails to accompany the rest along the anticipated normal path of development, and, in consequence of this inhibition in its development, it is left behind at a more infantile stage. [Freud, 1911c, p. 68]

Although the choice of the term "inhibition" suggests dynamic prevention, Freud has been interpreted here to mean a non-dynamic developmental delay (Brenner, 1957; Laplanche & Pontalis, 1973) and Brenner, in fact, writes that Freud believed "infantile repression occurred independently of experiential factors" (Brenner, 1957, p. 28). This interpretation has subsequently given rise to a view termed "passive" primal repression (Frank, 1969; Frank & Muslin, 1967), whereby mental contents prior to the secondary process remain unconscious simply because they lack the necessary characteristics for becoming conscious. Petocz (1999) notes the obvious implication:

> Rather than the unconscious being unconscious because it has been repressed, the repressed is repressed *because it is unconscious*. No censor, no blocking mechanism, no dynamic force is required to prevent the repressed from entering consciousness. It simply *cannot* become conscious because it lacks the attributes or qualities of conscious processes. [Petocz, 1999, p. 153, her italics]

At least one supporter of the passive account (Frank, 1969) says that "passive" primal "repression" would appear to be a misnomer, given that repression is a dynamic process (cf. Freud, 1907a, p. 48). Frank retorts, however, that the justification for calling this "repression" is that the same result obtains: the "higher segments of the mind are not in communication with the lower" (Frank, 1969, p. 52). However, defining "repression" simply in terms of such effects is an over-extension of the concept's meaning. The person suffering from a congenital brain disorder, such that he or she is incapable of conscious thought, would, in this passive view, be described as suffering from repression, a position Freud would reject, given his objection to Janet's explanation of the "splitting of consciousness" due to congenital degeneracy (Freud, 1894a, p.46; 1913m, p. 207).

Nevertheless, Frank's position is not unjustified, given Freud's systematic distinction, and as Petocz (1999) notes, although this systematic account of repression was not Freud's favoured account, it was, none the less, both present in his writings and a logical consequence of the systematic account of mentality. Furthermore, although this "failure of translation" does not preclude a dynamic account (cf. Masson, 1985, p. 208, Freud's letter to Fliess dated 6 December 1896), this systematic viewpoint allows Martindale (1975) to reject accounts of *dynamic* repression altogether, arguing that what is commonly mistaken as "defensive" activity is, in fact, activity related to Freud's primary and secondary process distinction, conceptualized as distinct "languages" differing in syntax, semantic base, and realization rules (p. 331). "Repression" is simply the result of failing to translate correctly between levels of representation:

> It is argued that the nature of the translation among levels of primary- and secondary-process sign systems itself adequately explains a number of phenomena treated by psychoanalytic theory as due to repression, defence, and unconscious thought processes. [Martindale, 1975, p. 331]

Here, Martindale proposes that the infant's concepts mature via different levels of organization, resulting in different "languages" of mental activity. Early levels of concept formation might be more generalized (e.g., the concept of "dog" applying to all four-legged animals), while later levels have a higher degree of specificity (e.g., specific species of dogs). Consequently, with regression from secondary to primary process thinking, the translation from a higher to a lower level

> will involve improper specification or concretization while the reverse translation will involve improper generalization. There is no need to invoke repression or other defenses, since the imprecisions result directly from the codes of the different languages. [Martindale, 1975, p. 344]

Martindale similarly claims that distortion in dreams results from a return to earlier levels of concept organizations (regression) and *not* motivated defence:

> The basic model is that there exists a continuum of "languages" from secondary process to primary process and that the grammar of thought and the apprehension of elements from the subjective lexicon varies systematically along this continuum. The dream has the form it has not because of purposeful or motivated defense but because of the "language of the level" at which it is conceived. Defenses may similarly be seen as due to the "language" of the regressed thought of the patient in whom they occur rather than as due to unconscious machinations; as manifestations of psychopathology as much as, or even rather than, purely mechanisms for avoiding psychopathology. [Martindale, 1975, p. 332]

Certain "higher" processes cannot be conceived of at "lower" levels, and so become incapable of conscious awareness. Alternatively, a "lower" level's representation might be incapable of "higher" representation:

> The phenomena usually ascribed to the defense of repression could result from two very different conditions. One could remain on a regressed level where the abstract concepts necessary for the avoided realization are unavailable. Thus if a patient avoided the conclusion 'I act toward my wife as I acted toward my mother', he could be on a level where the verb 'act' or the notion 'similar' are unavailable. In such a regressed state, the patient would be unable to see *any* analogous relations, not only the one specifically avoided. The idea that 'falling apples and the moon both obey the law of gravity' would be just as 'repressed' as the conclusion concerning wife and mother. The second condition would be to remain on an overabstract level. If repressed wishes are coded in a form inscrutable to the secondary process, then a wish such as the Oedipal one would not be coded in the form 'I desire sex with mother'. Rather what is desired would correspond to no exact secondary-process concept; further, the 'mother$_1$' of the wish would not correspond with the 'mother$_2$' of secondary-process cognition. [Martindale, 1975, pp. 344–355, his italics]

Thus, Martindale argues that there is no need for the concept of "defence" and instead, understanding the rules of translation is enough for explaining distortion. Hence, a consequence of Freud's own systematic account is that it is taken as justification for rejecting his preferred account of dynamic repression. Matte-Blanco (1975) reaches a similar conclusion:

> *there is no need for a dynamic process, because its very structure and the structure of consciousness prevent it from being conscious. There is an intrinsic impossibility of it entering directly into consciousness and this seems to be a point which has never been clear in psycho-analytic thinking.* [p. 84, his italics]

Criticism of Martindale's account and passive primal repression

Gay (1982) correctly points out that Martindale's use of "avoid" above is contradictory, since it is a *dynamic* reference; if Martindale is to be consistent, the person cannot conceive of the relation because he or she is in an altered state of consciousness, not because the relation is being "avoided". Developing this point, a specific problem for Martindale's account emerges, since he provides no adequate account for how repression is maintained. The only way to "avoid" knowing "repressed" material would be to remain in a mental state where certain relations could not be known. For instance, in Martindale's first example, above, the subject is said to be in a primitive state where he or she cannot cognize particular relationships and so cannot know a certain sophisticated mental content. Repression, here, is simply explained in terms of mental regression and the implication is that if the subject progresses to a state sufficient for knowing that relation, then nothing would prevent such relations from becoming known. However, since Freud's case studies (e.g., Breuer & Freud, 1895d; Freud, 1905e) demonstrate that the individuals suffering from repression were capable of a sufficient degree of intellectual competence for cognizing relations necessary for knowing the repressed, they should, on Martindale's thesis, be able to become aware of the repressed without difficulty. Freud's cases indicate the opposite, however, and Martindale fails to account for this. Similarly, the second proposed mechanism of "remaining on an overabstract level", where primitive wishes are undecipherable to the secondary processes, is open to exactly the same criticism. If regression occurs, then there is no prevention of knowing the repressed. To then argue that the person is *prevented* from regressing (or progressing) introduces dynamic considerations, which Martindale's strategy denies.

A further problem with this systematic passive account of repression is that it cannot explain why Freud's clinical studies reveal that only specific mental relations, usually involving sexual or aggressive impulses, are targeted by repression (i.e., as with the issue of infantile amnesia, there is no explanation for differential targeting found with repression). Cohen and Kinston (1983) note accordingly that Freud's account of "fixation" lacks explanatory power:

> The notion that primal repression is inherent in normal development does not explain why some children and not others develop particular fixations and why neurosis, psychosis and other disturbances occur in the later life of one person and not another. [p. 414; cf. Cohen, 1985, p. 177]

Furthermore, even if a passive lagging behind does occur, as Freud suggests, then secondary repression becomes redundant. If the primary repressed is literally inaccessible to consciousness, then defending against emanations of the primary repressed (secondary repression) is unnecessary, since, by definition, the primary repressed remains unconscious. Alternatively, if the primary repressed transfers its "energy" to preconscious thoughts, then the problem emerges concerning how these transference thoughts could be selected for repression, since the primary repressed is never known to conscious thinking (Maze & Henry, 1996). The result would be that either *nothing* would be targeted, or *everything* could be subjected to secondary repression.

Language and repression

Passive accounts of "repression" also follow from the perceived connection between the development of language and symbolic thinking. This can be tied to the systematic distinction proposed by Freud with respect to thing-presentations (*Dingvorstellung / Sachvorstellung*) (or visual mnemic content) and word-presentations (*Wortvorstellung*) (or auditory mnemic content):

the real difference between a *Ucs.* and *Pcs.* idea (thought) consists in this: that the former is carried out on some material which remains unknown, whereas the latter (the *Pcs.*) is in addition brought into connection with word-presentations. This is the first attempt to indicate distinguishing marks for the two systems, the *Pcs.* and the *Ucs.*, other than their relation to consciousness.[Freud, 1923b, p. 20; cf. Freud, 1915e, pp. 201–202).

Thing-presentations are "sensory images" and impressions (Freud, 1916–1917, pp. 180–181), whereas *word-presentations* involve either auditory or visual verbal residues and can be thought of in the broad sense as any linguistic symbolization (Freud, 1923b, pp. 20–21). Freud believes that perception of the external world are automatically conscious, whereas mental processes lack sufficient "quality" necessary for consciousness (see Freud, 1900a, pp. 574, 617, 1915e, p. 202, 1923b, p. 19, 1940a[1938], p. 162). In order for a mental process to become conscious, it must first be linked to verbal residues to gain sufficient quality, and, thereby, become an object of perception and hence capable of conscious awareness:

> Thought-processes are in themselves without quality, except for the pleasurable and unpleasurable excitations which accompany them, and which, in view of their possible disturbing effect upon thinking, must be kept within bounds. In order that thought-processes may acquire quality, they are associated in human beings with verbal memories, whose residues of quality are sufficient to draw the attention of consciousness to them and to endow the process of thinking with a new mobile cathexis from consciousness. [Freud, 1900a, p. 617; cf. letter to Fliess dated May 1896, Masson, 1985, p. 189; letter to Fliess dated 6 December 1896, Masson, 1985, p. 208; Freud, 1950[1895], p. 366; 1911b, p. 221, 1915e, p. 201, 1923b, p. 23, 1940a[1938], p. 162]

Thus, Freud proposes that *Ucs.* ideas must become connected with word-presentations if they are to become known: "The question, 'How does a thing become conscious?' would thus be more advantageously stated: 'How does a thing become preconscious?' And the answer would be: 'Through becoming connected with the word-presentations corresponding to it'" (Freud, 1923b, p. 20; cf. Freud, 1915e, pp. 202–203, 1939a, p. 97, 1940a[1938], p. 162).

Freud's position here that verbal representations are necessary for consciousness is commonly accepted (e.g., Beres, 1962; Bower, 1990;

Davies, 1996; Diamond, 1997; Dollard & Miller, 1950; Jones, 1993; Kaplan-Solms & Solms, 2000; Kendall & Speedwell, 1999; McIntosh, 1986; Morley, 2000; Schafer, 1968) and appears similar to Fingarette's (1969) proposal that "spelling-out" is necessary for becoming "explicitly conscious". That is, to become conscious of a desire (e.g., a desire that p) requires some verbalization to the effect of "I desire that p".

Implications for repression

A major implication of the claim that language is necessary for consciousness is that since all preverbal experience is incapable of consciousness, all preverbal experience necessarily falls victim to primal repression:

> It is clear in the context of concurrent psycho-analytic psychology that the development of the system preconscious and of the secondary process is intimately associated with verbal mnemic symbols. Hence, the onset of the process which leaves the primally repressed in their wake is initiated by the acquisition of the mnemic residues of speech. [Frank & Muslin, 1967, p. 73]

> In infants and toddlers, before the development of language, experiences, feelings, and wishes are encoded in nonverbal form not henceforth accessible to verbal, that is, conscious recall. [Jones, 1993, p. 86]

Thus, passive primal repression consequently affects all mental content that occurs prior to language acquisition (see also Dollard & Miller, 1950, p. 198). Accordingly, "excavating" this portion of the past would be impossible and here one finds parallels with accounts of "implicit memory", whereby a person's behaviour reflects past experience of which the person is incapable of knowing, leading to a non-dynamic unconscious (e.g., Fonagy, 1999). Mancia (2006), for instance, writes that pre-verbal and pre-symbolic experiences "are stored in the implicit memory and are not, therefore, susceptible to being repressed" (Mancia, 2006, p. 87), which, in turn, leads to leads to the "unrepressed unconscious": "implicit memory of experiences, phantasies and defences . . . belong to the presymbolic and preverbal stage of development and cannot therefore be remembered. Nevertheless, they can condition the affective, emotional, cognitive and sexual life even of the adult" (p. 89).

However, even after the child has developed the skill of language, he or she may still be prevented from knowing certain mental content if the child lacks the appropriate words to become conscious of an experience. Jones (1993) calls this *postverbal infantile repression*:

> The classic example of this type of repression concerns an experience for which a linguistically competent child simply has no words. If no one verbalized the experience for the child or helps the child to verbalize it, the experience may simply not be accessible later to verbal, or conscious, recall. [Jones, 1993, pp. 86–87]

Furthermore, repression could operate by preventing unconscious thing-presentations from becoming associated with word-presentations:

> we are in a position to state precisely what it is that repression denies to the rejected presentation in the transference neuroses: what it denies to the presentation is translation into words which shall remain attached to the object. A presentation which is not put into words, or a psychical act which is not hypercathected, remains thereafter in the *Ucs.* in a state of repression. [Freud, 1915e, p. 202]

Freud's position here has been taken up into contemporary psychoanalytic thinking to suggest a possible mechanism for repression. For instance, Kaplan-Solms and Solms (2000) write that conscious awareness requires establishing associative links between *Ucs.* processes and audio-verbal (*Pcpt.*) traces; subsequently, "once this link is withdrawn, the thought processes at issue are no longer capable of becoming conscious—that is, they are *repressed*" (p. 110, their italics). Gardner (1993) similarly proposes that repression operates by breaking down the propositional structure of a mental process into pre-propositional mental states (what he refers to as the "destruction of propositional form"—Gardner, 1993, p. 105). Gardner associates propositionality with linguistic structure and writes, "Consciousness is bound up with the predominantly *propositional* character of its contents, so a good way of accounting for the impossibility of something's becoming conscious is to suppose that it is prevented from assuming a propositional form" (Gardner, 1993, p. 104, his italics). Repression, consequently, involves disintegrating the linguistic structure: "What happens in repression is that a propositional mental state disintegrates into more primitive, *pre-propositional components*; these are blocked from recombining in a propositional form and being manifested in consciousness" (Gardner, 1993, p. 104).

Once achieved, these repressed states are left unable to communicate with the propositional network constituting the ego.

"Verbal images" and the role of language

A potential advantage of all the accounts above is that since (according to these theories) non-verbal mental processes cannot become conscious, then no account of maintaining repression is required. However, there are reasons for rejecting the view that word associations are necessary for knowing our own mental processes. A primary difficulty with the claim is that acquiring language of mental processes (i.e., associating verbal labels with mental processes) requires conscious awareness of one's own mental states prior to associating verbal labels (words) to "things". That is, to associate x (say, the word "anger") with y (the actual experience of anger) requires knowing x and y independently first in order to be able to make the association. For instance, when the care-giver says to an angry child that what the child is experiencing is "anger", for the child to know that this refers to the state of anger and not, say, some item of clothing, smell in the air, an aspect of the social interaction, or any other variety of possible referents, requires that the child knows the actual state of anger *prior* to any association with the word "anger". Consequently, the child must be capable of reflecting upon his or her own mental processes prior to language acquisition and so it cannot possibly be the case that language is necessary for conscious awareness (see Boag, 2008c for further discussion). This is not to dispute the claim that language might help to acquaint us with our own cognitive states, but, as Michell (1988) points out, language is not the mental state itself, and simply provides a prompt that might sometimes direct our attention to what we know:

> Now this process of implicit verbalisation cannot by itself be sufficient for us to know our own cognitions. The reason is that in selectively attending to past utterances we are not attending to any cognitive acts [directly]. However, if I not only implicitly verbalise the sentence

"today is cold" but also perceive that today is cold, then I can observe the *sensitivity of my implicit verbalisation to the fact perceived* and so be aware of my cognition of this fact. Of course, it is through the overt verbalisations of others that I can see most clearly their sensitivity to various matters of fact and, so, see their cognition of these facts. Likewise, implicit verbalisations play the same role in observing our own cognitions. Despite their importance in our becoming aware of our own cognitions, they are not necessary. [Michell, 1988, p. 240, his italics]

In this respect, the verbalizations of the therapist do not act differently from one's own self-verbalizations, since both draw attention to mental states.

Hence, there is no good reason for believing that repression can be explained with reference to non-verbal mental content being incapable of becoming conscious, even if language may facilitate knowing our own mental processes and even allow a greater degree of sophistication and articulation of our thinking (Talvitie, 2009). Furthermore, Freud's word–thing dissociation actually presupposes an independent process of repression (e.g., selective inattention) to explain the dissociation between "word" and "thing". Consider, for example, Kaplan-Solms and Solms' (2000) statement that repression involves "withdrawing the link" between *Ucs.* processes and audio-verbal (*Pcpt.*) traces. What requires explanation is the "withdrawal" that leads to the *effect* of word–thing dissociation, which requires providing an account of withdrawal *independently* of the effect of word–thing dissociation (Boag, 2010b, 2011a). In other words, any dissociation between language and mental content should be seen as an effect of repression rather than as the mechanism: after repression, the individual cannot know his or her repressed mental content, and so, subsequently, cannot label the targeted material. Such an effect is comprehensible in terms of selective inattention: since to label x requires knowing x, if repression prevents x being known, then x will not be available for naming.

Indeed, if the preverbal material remains literally "inaccessible" as some maintain (e.g., Frank, 1969, p. 60), then it could have no practical usage in therapy, a point similarly noted by Talvitie (2009) with respect to the equation of the repressed with implicit memory. Similarly, Fayek's (2005) claim that the "nonrepressed unconscious is aconscious or consciousless (*Ucs.*)" (p. 531n) also appears to be irrelevant to therapy. However, clinical accounts of passive primal repression and implicit non-conscious memory contradict this position. For example, Frank reports a case of passive primal repression where the analysis led to "the translation of her primitive feelings into understandable verbal concepts" (Frank, 1969, p. 71). If so, then the inaccessibility is only apparent and not actual, since the person *could* come to know and understand what had been pre-verbal. In fact, writes Frank, therapy proceeds on the assumption that such states are both accessible and valuable therapeutically: "The re-experiencing, understanding, and translation of these primitive ego states by the more developed apparatuses of the adult ego are of particular therapeutic value" (Frank, 1969, p. 56). Similarly, while implicit memories are described as "non-conscious" (and so, presumably, to be taken to be non-psychological neurobiological states) it is difficult to reconcile this with their perceived role in therapy. For instance, the examples of implicit memories provided in Mancia's (2006) case study appear to be fully fledged psychological acts (e.g., hating) (p. 91), of which the analysand is capable of becoming conscious.

General problems with Freud's systematic account of mental processes

Aside from the problems discussed above, Freud's systematic account, premised on the notion of qualitatively distinct types of systems and processes, cannot be coherently sustained. The general problem is that the supposed peculiarities said to be exclusive to one system can be found across the others. As various authors have noted, each system in Freud's account is capable of containing or possessing thought processes antithetical to the system's proposed functioning (Arlow & Brenner, 1964; Gay, 1982; Gill, 1963; Macmillan, 1991; Petocz, 1999; Westen, 1999; Weintraub, 1987). Freud himself was aware that the systematic distinction was not invariant, noting that *Ucs.* processes could be retained in consciousness:

> certain modes of thought proper to the unconscious have also been retained by the conscious—for instance, some kinds of indirect representation, allusion, and so on—even though their conscious employment is subject to considerable restrictions. [Freud, 1905c, p. 204]

Conversely, Freud writes that the *Ucs.* at times operates in a manner more aligned with conscious processes:

> Among the derivatives of the *Ucs.* instinctual impulses . . . there are those which unite in themselves characters of an opposite kind. On the one hand, they are highly organised, free from self-contradiction, have made use of every acquisition of the system *Cs.* and would hardly be distinguished in our judgement from the formation of that system. On the other hand they are unconscious and are incapable of becoming conscious. Thus *qualitatively* they belong to the system *Pcs.*, but *factually* to the *Ucs.* [Freud, 1915e, p. 191, his italics]

For example, parapraxes, such as slips of the tongue, are said to be products of *Ucs.* processes (Freud, 1905c), but appear to be highly organized, syntactically valid structures, more indicative of secondary processes (Gay, 1982; Macmillan, 1991), and further contradicting the word-thing-presentation systematic distinction. Similarly, since dreams appear to show that the *Ucs.* contains highly structured, repressed fantasies that should be antithetical to the system *Ucs.*, this allows Macmillan (1991) to conclude that dreams thus require the existence of a class of fantasies that cannot exist, according to the systematic theory:

> Repressed fantasies cannot exist in the *Ucs.* and cannot therefore be incorporated into dreams. Dreams incorporating such fantasies disprove the theory. Further, because fantasies well enough structured to resemble real memories of childhood seduction cannot exist in *Ucs.* they cannot explain hysterical symptoms. [Macmillan, 1991, p. 271]

The systematic distinction also creates confusion for Freud's account, since the logical conclusion is that the organized repressed content must then somehow belong to the ego rather than the id:

> If we assume that the fantasy which is unconscious retains its organization, to whatever degree, we must grant the continued activity of ego functions. 'The ego is an organisation', Freud has said, 'and the id is not'. An 'id fantasy', then, is by definition a contradiction in terms, and to speak of a fantasy being 'repressed into the id' is, in my opinion, a complex of logical fallacies. [Beres, 1962, p. 324; cf. Slap & Saykin, 1984, p. 110]

Furthermore, Freud's claim that the *Ucs.* is the realm of the illogical and irrational, while the *Pcs./Cs.* is rational and logical (Freud, 1900a, p. 65, 1915e, p. 187), is similarly problematic. As others have noted, unconscious processes do not have exclusive rights to irrationality since (pre)conscious thought activity might also be illogical or irrational (Arlow & Brenner, 1964; Petocz, 1999; Weintraub, 1987). Similarly, "exemption from mutual contradiction" is not exclusive to the *Ucs.*, since contrary impulses and wishes can exist side by side consciously (Weintraub, 1987).

Taken together, these criticisms demonstrate that there appears to be no systematically or qualitatively distinct processes exclusive to particular systems, as Freud proposes. Following Petocz (1999), if there are no qualitatively distinct processes defining these systems (either in terms of "mechanisms", "characteristics" or "contents") then the systematic theory should be rejected. Consequently, the attempt to explain repression systematically should be rejected, as there is no reason to conclude that a repressed mental content differs qualitatively from conscious mental content; such qualitative differences have not been shown to exist. It might, however, be the case, as Mac-Intyre (1958) notes, that the unconscious characteristics Freud refers to may simply be general *descriptions* of dreams and symptoms, not characteristics of systems causing those same features: "timelessness, reconciliation of incompatibles, carelessness of contradiction: these terms describe the world of dreams, and not the inaccessible and the unknowable" (MacIntyre, 1958, p. 74; cf. Petocz, 1999, p. 177). If so, the explanation for this should not be sought in terms of the characteristics of particular systems. Thus, Freud's systematic distinction should be rejected on the basis that qualitatively distinct processes (either in terms of "mechanisms", "characteristics", or "contents") have not been shown to exist, a point particularly conspicuous in Freud's own account (Freud, 1905c, p. 204, 1915e, p. 191). Consequently, the attempt to explain repression systematically fails and all accounts of "repression" based on such a theory must be rejected.

CHAPTER SEVEN

A general model for situating repression

Situating memory within Freud's general theory

From the beginning of Freud's theory, memory has been associated with repression. Freud's early account explicitly equates repression with forgetting (Breuer & Freud, 1895d, p. 10) and "motivated forgetting", based on primary process thinking, is described as the prototype of repression (Freud, 1900a, p. 600). Freud further emphasizes the relationship between repression and memory when he attempts to clarify the relation between repression and defence, equating repression with hysterical *amnesia* (Freud, 1926d, p. 163). Nevertheless, this apparent association between repression and memory needs to be understood within a greater context. Freud's (1915d) metapsychological paper on repression makes no reference to memory at all, and Madison notes that while "[r]epression is tied up in our minds with forgetting . . . when we check with Freud's writings, we find that forgetting is apparently not a good criterion of repression" (Madison, 1956, p. 76). To appreciate this greater context requires recognizing the distinction between conflict-free *traumatic neuroses* and conflict-ridden psychoneuroses (Freud, 1919d, p. 209). The significance of this latter class of neuroses emerges with the abandonment of the seduction hypothesis and the emergence of a dynamic framework, picturing the mind as a society of conflicting motives. Within this framework, memories become repressed in so far as they are associated with desires and anxiety, and, given this broader picture, "memories" are not isolated cognitive units within some non-affective, computational apparatus, but rather intimately bound with drives and affects (Freud, 1907a, pp. 48–49). Freud's (1900a) account of the development of wishes links these to attending to memories of past satisfactions (p. 598), and Freud recognizes this complex relation between past and present, wishes and memory when he discusses the relation of wishes and memories to previous satisfactions:

> Mental work is linked to some current impression, some provoking occasion in the present which has been able to arouse one of the subject's major wishes. From there it harks back to a memory of an earlier experience (usually an infantile one) in which the wish was fulfilled; and it now creates a situation relating to the future which represents a fulfilment of the wish. [Freud, 1908e, p. 147; cf. Freud, 1942a[1905]]

Thus, to isolate "memory" when discussing repression does a disservice to the integrated person that emerges in the Freudian account. Instead, to appreciate repression requires enquiring into the nature of wishes and desires, their relation to memory and motivation, and to thus consider repression within the broader Freudian picture. The aim of the present chapter is to develop Freud's general model and provide a coherent basis for situating repression and clarifying the targets of repression.

Situating repression within the desire–belief model of behaviour

As noted by various authors (Cavell, 1991, 1993; Gardner, 1993; Hopkins, 1988, 1995b; Mackay, 1996, 1999; Petocz, 1999; Pataki, 2000; Wollheim, 1991, 1993), Freud's theory is both situated within, and interpreted as extending, the folk-psychological model of behaviour (i.e., behaviour explicable in terms of desires and beliefs). In this view, *intentional* action arises from a motivational state or "desire" component, guided by an instrumental cognitive or "belief" component. Here, when explaining person P's doing A, it is proposed that: (i) P

desires *B*; and (ii) *P* believes that doing *A* leads to *B*. The "belief" component includes knowledge, memory, and phantasy and specifies the known possible means of satisfaction (or for avoiding frustration). Beliefs, although necessary, are not sufficient for behaviour to occur, since they are policy neutral (simply about states of affairs) and cannot explain why, for any given belief, one person acts in one particular way and another differently (Maze, 1983, 1987; Mackay, 1994):

> Any information which can be put into the form X *leads to* Y can be used either in promoting Y or in avoiding it . . . The belief, for example, that a certain diet will increase body weight may lead one either to adopt that diet or to avoid it, depending on one's already existing motives or drive state; it may produce opposing behaviours in the same person at different times. Thus, as it is identically the same belief operating in each case, it cannot be said to imply either policy. Factual information in itself is policy-neutral; it can initiate behaviour only if it is perceived as relevant to one of the person's existing policies – that is, as relevant to the success of some action pattern specific to a currently active drive state. [Maze, 1987, p. 191]

The additional factor required is a motivational component (i.e., the "desire") to explain a given person's policy regarding how he or she acts on that belief, and, thus, Frank's (1996) assertion that "beliefs" are sufficient for explaining the motivating factor in human behaviour cannot be sustained.[1] What this means, further, is that any account of repression modelled within this framework must provide a satisfactory account of motivation.

Conceptualizing the "desire" component

Desires and wishes can be conceptualized as a species of *propositional attitudes*, attitudes towards propositions or states of affairs (e.g., *S* desires/wishes for *x*) (cf. Cavell, 1993; Gardner, 1993; Mackay, 1996; Pataki, 2000; Suppes & Warren, 1975). However, as Mackay (1996) notes, wishes might also have negative variants, such as a desire for something *not* to occur, the latter translated into fear and hate of the object (cf. Talvitie, 2009, p. 78). As such, desires are necessarily psychological (i.e., intending objects) (cf. Talvitie & Ihanus, 2002, p. 1313), which is not to say that they are necessarily conscious (such that *S* knows that S desires x). As discussed earlier, a person could desire p without knowing that he or she desires that p (knowledge of which would require a second mental act). Furthermore, although some authors claim that propositional attitudes "are like 'sentences in the head'" (Talvitie, 2009, p. 115; cf. Gardner, 1993), a distinction should be made between sentences and propositions. Although sentences *state* propositions, their independence is demonstrated by the fact that two sentences can express the same proposition, for example, "New York is larger than San Francisco" and "San Francisco is smaller than New York" (Hospers, 1959, p. 64): while these sentences differ in many respects, both refer to the same proposition. Furthermore, a pre-verbal infant's separation anxiety is propositional (S fears x), despite the infant having no words to express the proposition.

Desires as causal constructs

Accepting the traditional viewpoint, Talvitie and Ihanus (2002) write that "desire and fear cause striving and avoidance" (p. 1313) and this raises questions for conceptualizing desires as motivating states within the organism. If desires are defined in relation to their goal (such that S desires x), and we attempt to explain x-directed behaviour, then there are problems with invoking these as "antecedent entities" motivating behaviour without leading to a circular explanation (Boag, 2011a; Mackay, 1996; Maze, 1983). For example, we could explain why any person acts in a way that achieves x by claiming that S desires x or S wants x or S likes x (etc.) without being any clearer as to why S stands in that desiring (wanting/liking) relation. Similarly for wishes and intentions:

> wishes and beliefs are not *as they stand*, independently specified states of the person. Wishes, identified as wishes *for* some goal, as strivings towards some end, are defined in relation to those goals. That is, their very existence is as goal-directed somethings. They are, so to speak, intrinsically related to their objects, which is to say they have no intrinsic properties at all. And the explanations that such relationally defined processes enter into become teleological, which is to say that they are not explanations at all. [Mackay, 1996, p. 10, his italics]

In this latter respect, the relation between desires and teleological explanations of behaviour rest upon the premise that an end-state (an effect) is causally efficacious, so that, for example, *P* does *A in order to bring about B*, some future state of affairs. The main problem here is that effects become confused with causes. Borrowing an example from Maze (1983),

> it might be said in describing the 'emergency pattern' of physiologi-
> cal discharges that the adrenal glands secrete adrenaline in order
> to procure the release of red blood cells in order to provide for the
> more rapid distribution of oxygen (in case this should be required
> for the energetic use of the muscles in fighting or fleeing). . . .
> [However] [i]f the adrenaline *causes* the release of the red blood cells,
> then on any particular occasion (leaving aside the matter of the
> survival value of such a mechanism making it genetically more
> common over many generations) the consequences of the spleen's
> behaviour would be perfectly irrelevant to its occurrence. [p. 19,
> original italics]

In other words, the release of the red blood cells is an effect explicable in terms of the adrenaline, and the important conceptual point is that the effect is not the cause (even if past circumstances have helped to shape such a mechanism via natural selection). Thus, teleological thinking is incompatible with deterministic thinking, which explains behaviour in terms of antecedent conditions, and care is required not to confuse effects with causes. However, notable examples of teleo-logical arguments are found in the literature relating repression to "evolutionary functions" (e.g., Nesse, 1990; Slavin, 1985, 1990; Slavin & Grief, 1995), where repression is explained in terms of its effects and function, rather than due to antecedent conditions such as anxi-ety. For instance, Nesse (1990) writes that repression occurs "because it allows people to deceive themselves about their true motives, and thus better deceive others as they unconsciously pursue these covert selfish motives" (Nesse, 1990, p. 273; cf. Slavin, 1990, p. 321; Slavin & Grief, 1995, p. 154). That is, repression is said to occur because of the effects (deception) and no reference is made to causal antecedents (such as anxiety) that are generally considered necessary for instigat-ing repression. Instead, the "deception" should be seen as an effect of repression, since it occurs subsequently to the repressive act and the causes looked for in antecedent events.

The issue of teleology is also a potential source of paradox for understanding how repression and defence could reasonably operate.

For example, Bleichmar (2004) writes in the case of projection, "To protect his narcissism and not feel faulty or guilty, a patient criticizes other people, projecting his feelings of inadequacy on to others" (p. 1381). That is, the person criticizes other people in order to protect his narcissism, which makes projection sound like an intentional activity guided by desires and beliefs. However, if defence occurs because a person feels threatened, then the teleological account simply confuses matters. Indeed, teleological accounts propose an account of repression that is *purposive* and deliberate, not occurring due to unpleasure, but rather *in order to* achieve this end-state. Deterministically, however, if *every* event is caused by antecedent conditions, then the outcome or purpose is irrelevant to explanation (i.e., the outcome of purpose is the effect to be explained) (Maze, 1983). Teleological thinking provides only pseudo-explanations which potentially tempt us to believe that we know what brings a certain event about, when in fact we are confusing effects with causes.

Adopting a deterministic, non-teleological stance does not involve rejecting psychological processes as causes or saying that psychological states are thereby redundant in explanations of behaviour. There is no logical problem with viewing beliefs as antecedent conditions. However, if wishes (desires, and so on) are defined relationally and psychologically, then some motivational account must still be provided. Here, it is Freud's theory that proves to be substantive. Freud's theory of instinctual drives defined by their bodily source allows us to clarify the desire component and specify distinct systems from which desires, wishes, and behaviours arise.

Freud's theory of instinctual drives

Freud's theory of instinctual drives is arguably one of the most important contributions to a thorough-going theory of human behaviour, grounding the movement of all thoughts, behaviour, and affects in what are termed "instincts". Yet, for all this, Freud appreciated the difficulty in elucidating their specific nature: "Of all the slowly developed parts of analytic theory, the theory of the instincts is the one that has felt its way the most painfully forward and yet that theory was indispensable to the whole structure" (Freud, 1930b, p. 117). Similarly, they are "at once the most important and the most obscure element of psychological research" (Freud, 1920g, p. 34; cf. Freud, 1905d, p. 168, 1925d, pp. 56–57n). Freud even refers to them as his "mythology": "Instincts are mythical entities magnificent in their indefiniteness. In our work we cannot for a moment disregard them, yet we are never sure that we are seeing them clearly" (Freud, 1933a, p. 95).

The choice of the term "instinct" was chosen by Freud's editor, Strachey, as a translation for *Trieb*, which is not unproblematic, given that the English "instinct" commonly refers to unmodifiable or stereo-typed species-specific behaviour patterns (Laplanche & Pontalis, 1973; Mills, 2004; Ritvo & Solnit, 1995). *Trieb*, on the other hand, implies pressure (*treiben*: to push—Laplanche & Pontalis, 1973, p. 214) and Strachey himself footnotes in *Beyond the Pleasure Principle* (Freud, 1920g) that *Trieb* has a greater sense of urgency than the English "instinct" (p. 35n). While there is no single English equivalent for *Trieb*, the word "drive" provides a fair approximation, which for many is the preferred translation (e.g., Fulgencio, 2005; McIntosh, 1986; Solms & Turnbull, 2002; Zepf, 2001): "drive" provides a greater sense of an "impelling" factor, although such drives can be considered "instinctual", given their biological or innate foundation.

Freud, however, was not alone in developing a theory of "instincts", and in his book, *The History of Psychoanalysis*, Fine (1990) states that Freud's theory was merely in agreement with instinct theories of his day. What made Freud's theory novel, says Fine, was that "he had reduced all instincts to sexuality . . . hence Freud's real contribution lay not in instinct theory but in his elucidation of sexuality" (p. 201). Fine further notes that Freud also postulated non-sexual instincts, but believes that he did not take them seriously:

> Freud's initial position on instinct was taken from the instinct theory prevalent in his day, which, following Darwin, ascribed the major impetus in human behaviour to instinctual drive. The one momentous change introduced by Freud was a focus on sexuality as the only phys-iological instinct. (*Freud always paid lip service to the ego instincts but did not take them seriously.*) [Fine, 1990, p. 235, my italics]

However, Freud, on several occasions, rebutted this charge of "pan-sexualism" (e.g., 1905d, p. 134, 1917a, p. 138, 1925e, p. 218), and Fine's remark ignores the fact that Freud repeatedly stipulates that neuroses are a product of conflict between sexual *and non-sexual* repressing forces within the personality (Freud, 1910i, p. 223, 1913m, p. 209. 1913i, p. 326, 1913j, p. 181, 1917d, p. 138, 1923a, pp. 252, 257, 1925e, p. 218).

Instead, what really distinguishes Freud's theory from his contemporaries, notes Maze (1983) and Petocz (1999), is his approach to both the nature of drives and the specification of them. This is clear when comparing Freud with his contemporary, McDougall (1923), cited by Fine as both the leading instinct theorist in Freud's time and as testimony to Freud's lack of originality. For McDougall, instincts were defined by their *goals* or *aims*: "We must . . . define any instinct by the nature of the goal, the type of situation, that it seeks to bring about, as well as by the type of situation or object that brings it into activity" (McDougall, 1923, pp. 118–119).

Freud, however, recognized the peril in specifying instincts according to aims since, in principle, as many instincts could be postulated as there are distinct goals. To settle which of these were "primary" drives would then come down to arbitrary choice:

> What instincts should we suppose there are, and how many? There is obviously a wide opportunity here for arbitrary choice. No objection can be made to anyone's employing the concept of an instinct of play or of destruction or of gregariousness, when the subject-matter demands it and the limitations of psychological analysis allow of it. Nevertheless, we should not neglect to ask ourselves whether instinctual motives like these, which are so highly specialised on the one hand, do not admit of further dissection in accordance with the *sources* of the instinct, so that only primal instincts—those which cannot be further dissected—can lay claim to importance. [Freud, 1915c, pp. 123–124, his italics; cf. Freud, 1940a[1938], p. 148]

Moreover, to explain any given behaviour by attributing a drive responsible for it proposes a vacuous account of motivation, since the "evidence" for the drive is always available (Maze, 1983, 1993):

> Drives specified by aim can be postulated without check, because the 'evidence' for them is always available: the observed behaviour they were postulated to explain. Any commonly occurring behaviour can be 'explained' by saying there must be an instinct or drive behind it, but it is only a pseudo-explanation. [Maze, 1993, pp. 462–463; cf. Freud, 1933a, p. 95]

Furthermore, the problem with such an account is confounded by the fact that the goal of any given behaviour might not be transparent. For instance, behaviour that appears to be gratifying hunger might actually be in response to painful emotions. Thus,

> In consequence [of being defined by their aim], their specification rests entirely on the presumed intuitive power of the theorist to identify the true end goal of the behaviour in question simply from inspection of its course. Yet such intuition is always disputable because every behavioural event has consequences and further consequences, and so on indefinitely. Accordingly, it is always possible that the alleged consummation was not actually the gratifying event sought, but that its consequence, or some further consequence was. [Maze, 1993, pp. 462–463]

Subsequently, Freud's (1920g) life and death instinct account, defining instincts by their aims, contradicts his own criterion (Compton, 1981; Maze, 1983, 1993; Petocz, 1999) and should be rejected. Similarly, Rosenblatt and Thickstun's assertion that "[motivational] systems may be classified according to their goals" (Rosenblatt & Thickstun, 1977, p. 550; cf. Rosenblatt, 1985, p. 90) is problematic, since there are potentially as many drives as there are goals, and Peskin's (1997) attempt to identify drives in terms of perceived evolutionary adaptation introduces the opportunity for arbitrary specification in terms of what can be considered adaptive. Since "adaptivity" is a relationship between an organism and some specific set of circumstances (where *a* adapts to *b*), and any activity might be at one and same time both adaptive *and* maladaptive (for instance, being a workaholic might be adaptive financially, but maladaptive socially), consequently, judging whether any activity is adaptive rests upon some subjective interpretation on the part of the observer and, thus, does not serve as a basis for an objective identification of drives (see also Maze, 1987).

Freud's contribution to drive theory

In contradistinction to these accounts, Freud stipulates that instinctual drives must be identified by their somatic *source* to circumvent postulating instinctual drives *ad hoc* and *ad libitum*. Compared to the behaviours and cognitions emanating from the drives, "the source is relatively constant and is therefore the best qualified to serve as a basis for a classification of the instincts" (Bibring, 1969, p. 295; cf. Freud, 1933a, p. 97). Here, Freud's theory provides an in principle foundation for integrating psychoanalysis with psychobiological research, since he postulates a biological/somatic foundation for drives which provides (another) tangible avenue for empirical research. Thus, it is not the case, as Fulgencio (2005) claims, that drives are outside of empirical research enquiry (p. 106). Fulgencio's claim arises from treating the Freudian drives as disembodied forces, which ignores Freud's argument for the primacy of the body as the source of motivation. As Mills (2004) notes,

> The reason Freud logically situates the source of a drive within our biologically determined facticity is simply that we are embodied beings. We are thrown into a body a priori, and hence all internal activity must *originally* arise from within our corporeality mediated by internal dynamics. Here Freud is merely asserting an empirical fact grounded in a natural science framework. [p. 674, his italics]

While it is true that Freud chiefly speculated on the precise nature of the drives, this was not because drives are without real-world referents, but only because *psycho*analytic observations of behaviour are limited with respect to what can be inferred about the source of any drive (Freud, 1915c). That is, the drive's "source" means that drives must be identified through investigating the internal workings of the body and not through psychological (psychoanalytic) enquiry alone. Frank's (1996) claim that drives "cannot be proven" (p. 422) similarly misses Freud's point, since if the instinctual drives are defined physiologically, as Freud (1915c) proposes, then such structures are then, in principle, identifiable, and, hence, propositions concerning them are potentially falsifiable (i.e., they either do, or do not, exist).

Drives and propositional attitudes

Freud's approach to drives grounds them somatically but relates them intimately to motivational states, cognitive activity, and behaviour, and, thus, they would appear to be suitable candidates for understanding propositional attitudes. Brakel (2005), however, recently claims that "[d]rives do not fit well into the propositional-attitude psychology . . . to account for motivation and intention" (p. 77; cf. Brakel, 2009, p. 89). Here, Brakel understands drives to be "the mental representative of a physiologic need state" (p. 76; cf. Brakel, 2009, pp. 91ff) and she provides an example of a baby with a number of "oral drives", such as to suck and swallow. While this approach appears to ignore the drive's source, it is also not entirely clear why such "drives" would be incompatible with a desire–belief account (S desires to suck, swallow). Here, she attempts to propose a distinction between desires and drives based on their objects: the object of a *desire* is something determinate (e.g., a desire for a cool drink) whereas the object of a *drive* is somewhat indeterminate, since a specific object cannot be identified (e.g., general thirst-reduction). However, this is an unnecessary and unhelpful distinction, since it attempts to create a dualism between general and specific features of situations, when, rather, any specific object of the desire is simply an instantiation of the general aim. Accordingly, rather than saying that drives and desires involve different *relations*, it would be better to say that the drive is the somatic mechanism that generates desires (Brakel, in fact, also refers to "drives" driving "desire" (2005, p. 78)). Drives, then, are literally something like "biological engines" (Maze, 1983), which are analogous to the engine of a car that instigates driving behaviour, and necessary for accounting for any activity:

> Simply put, a mechanistic and deterministic account of any behaviour requires the postulation of a driving mechanism, for to say otherwise would be analogous to attempting to explain a car's operation in the absence of its having an engine. [Boag, 2007a, p. 379]

While the above analogy has obvious limitations with respect to determining the direction of behaviour, Freud's account of biological sources provides a manner for determining innate "biological priorities" that channel behaviour, even if these are open to learning, elaboration and distortion. Nevertheless, the concept of drive, for all of its explanatory value, remains a neglected concept within much of contemporary psychoanalytic theorizing. McIlwain (2007) comments that "[i]t is surprising . . . that so much current psychoanalytic theory is discussed without any explicit recognition that drives or (at times) even affects may play a part in the metapsychology" (p. 542). Solms and Turnbull (2002) similarly note the unfortunate consequences:

> The concept of drive seems to be unfashionable in psychoanalysis nowadays. It is unclear why this happened, but it has had the unfortunate result of divorcing psychoanalytic understanding of the human mind from knowledge derived from all other animals. We humans are not exempt from the evolutionary biological forces that shaped other creatures. It is therefore difficult to form an accurate picture of how the human mental apparatus really works without using a concept at least something like Freud's definition of "drive" . . . [p. 117]

Drives and motivational conflict

A particular point of relevance to psychoanalytic theorizing pertains to drive and motivational conflict, and Petocz (1999) writes that "[a]lthough we do not know exactly how many drives there are, still, in order to accommodate the facts of mental conflict, of a conflict of interests within a single mind, there must be a plurality of drives—at least two" (p. 221; cf. McIlwain, 2007, p. 535). The view that the human organism is composed of *multiple* motivational systems appears to receive broad support across a variety of relevant disciplines, including psychology, biology, and neurobiology, including evidence of drives related to thirst, hunger, sex, sleep, fear, power-dominance, pain reduction, and nurturance (Sewards & Sewards, 2002, 2003; Wagner, 1999). As Halliday (1995) argues, however, empirically disentangling distinct primary drives is not a simple task, given that interconnections between supposedly diverse drives occur. Furthermore, the relationship between drives and affects requires careful consideration, since it is not always clear what precisely is being proposed as the motivating structures. For instance, Panksepp and colleagues (e.g., Panksepp, 1999, 2001, 2005; Panksepp & Moskal, 2008) identify seven subcortical emotional systems (SEEKING, FEAR, RAGE, PANIC, LUST, CARE, and PLAY) that each appear to have motivational components but are distinct from "specific motivational systems, such as thirst, hunger, and thermoregulation . . ." (Liotti & Panksepp, 2004, p. 52). Panksepp (1999) further associates these emotional systems with the "basic id functions that are contained in the mammalian brain" (p. 18), describing them as "instinctual action systems" (Panksepp, 2005, p. 31), and writing that these "affective/emotional processes provide intrinsic values—organic 'pressures' and 'drives'—for the guidance of behaviour" (Panksepp, 2003, p. 6). However, these emotional id functions appear to also subserve the more basic drives of hunger, thirst, and sexuality (etc.). For instance, the SEEKING system, which Panksepp and Moskal (2008) refer to as a "general-purpose emotional-motivational SEEKING system" (p. 67), "can serve a large variety of distinct motivational urges (drives?)" (Panksepp, 1999, p. 23) and its output includes "an insistent urge to act in certain ways", which "increases an organic pressure to action" (Liotti & Panksepp, 2004, p. 53). Turnbull and Solms (2007) similarly refer to drives governing emotion systems (p. 1085) and take Panksepp's proposal to mean that "appetitive drives" such as hunger, thirst, and sex activate a SEEKING system, which motivates interest in sources of satisfaction (see Solms & Turnbull, 2002; cf. Colace, 2010). Accordingly, whether affects are primary sources of motivation is obscure. Nevertheless, that multiple sources of motivation exist is indisputable and provides a basis for understanding the motivational conflict underlying repression.

"Pressure" and the return of the repressed

Freud contrasts drives that operate as endogenous stimuli with stimulation from external sources. Whereas external stimuli come and go, the stimulation of drives requires an activity or action that removes the internal stimulus (Freud, 1950[1895], pp. 296–297, 1905d, p. 168, 1915c, p. 118–119):

> An instinct, then, is distinguished from a stimulus by the fact that it arises from sources of stimulation within the body, that it operates as a constant force and that the subject cannot avoid it by flight, as is possible with an external stimulus. [Freud, 1933a, p. 96]

Freud writes that drives are basically motivated to remove unpleasurable states of stimulation: "What, then, do these instincts want? Satisfaction—that is, the establishment of situations in which the bodily needs can be extinguished" (Freud, 1926e, p. 200). This incorporates the "pressure" component of drives:

by the pressure [*Drang*] of an instinct we understand its motor factor, the amount of force or the measure of the demand for which it represents. The characteristic of exercising pressure is common to all instincts: it is in fact their very essence. Every instinct is a piece of activity: if we speak loosely of passive instincts, we can only mean instincts whose *aim* is passive. [Freud, 1915c, p. 122, his italics; cf. Freud, 1909b, p. 141, 1933a, p. 96]

"Pressure", here, is best conceptualized in terms of repeatedly inducing or re-presenting cognitive–behavioural expressions of the drive (e.g., repeatedly thinking about states of satisfaction), and some authors have criticized Freud's drive theory here on the basis of the use of the term "constant". For example, Madison (1961) writes that since instinctual drives are continual sources of stimulation, "Freud's conception of instinct does not allow for . . . periods of inactivity" (p. 107). However, this ignores the fact that instinctual drives *might be satisfied*. As Freud writes in the *Project*, with instinctual drives (or, as he says there, "endogenous stimuli"), "the organism cannot withdraw as it does from external stimuli . . . They only cease subject to particular conditions which must be realised in the external world. (cf., for instance, the need for nourishment.)" (Freud, 1950[1895], pp. 296–297). Similarly, "A better term for an instinctual stimulus is a 'need'. What does away with a need is 'satisfaction'. This can be attained only by an appropriate ('adequate') alteration of the internal source of stimulation" (Freud, 1925e pp. 118–119). That is, instinctual drives can be satisfied if certain conditions obtain. One of these conditions, as Hopkins (1995b) notes, is the phenomenon of *wish-fulfilment*, which implies a distinction between drive *satiation* and *pacification*. In wish-fulfilment, a drive system might be *pacified* if the wished-for situation is believed to obtain (through illusory gratification). However, ultimately, the drive system is not *satiated*, the latter occurring after the necessary conditions obtain and the driving conditions cease to operate. Without this, the driving conditions persist as a "constant" activating force.

Satisfaction and the plasticity of aims

Although the ultimate aims of drives are satisfaction, the conditions and means necessary for satisfaction vary:

> The aim [*Ziel*] of an instinct is in every instance satisfaction, which can only be obtained by removing the state of stimulation at the source of the instinct. But although the ultimate aim of each instinct remains unchangeable, there may yet be different paths leading to the same ultimate aim: so that an instinct can be found to have various nearer or intermediate aims, which are combined or interchanged with one another. [Freud, 1915c, p. 122]

The aims that are believed to be the most direct route to satisfaction could be considered the *primary aims* or objects of the instinctual drive (cf. Petocz, 1999). However, since the methods of satisfaction are contingent upon environmental factors, and subject to distortion from intrapsychic conflict, this might lead to the formation of substitute secondary aims. Consequently, it is not always obvious from any given behaviour that it is, in fact, satisfying a biological source and, while the physiological drive factors are presumably relatively unchanging, the objects of the drives vary according to individual experiences of satisfaction and frustration. Accordingly, Westen's argument that drives are incapable of accommodating learned behaviour (that is, they are "primitive drives immune to experience") (1997, p. 542; cf. Westen, 1999, p. 1094) appears to confuse drives with the common meaning of "instinct". The modifiability of aims is similarly not appreciated when it is claimed that human behaviour is not "instinctual", given its ostensibly "non-biological character". For example, White, arguing against the notion that the ego is motivated by drives, writes that the "activities of the ego are clearly not instinctual" (White, 1963, p. 1). Similarly, Billig writes,

> The urge to shout out in a quiet, formal lecture theatre is not an instinctual desire, which is genetically transmitted from generation to generation. The temptation is created by the social conditions of restraint, as the existence of social rules itself provokes the possibility of shameful desire. [Billig, 1999, p. 76; cf. Billig, 1997, p. 151]

The problem here is that drives are mistakenly equated with the unmodifiable, species-specific behaviour pattern concept of instinct rather than recognizing the interaction of the biological structures and the shaping of their activities by environmental contingencies. While certain behaviours might appear "non-biological", to explain the policy of social rules in relation to undesirable activity requires an account ultimately rooted in biology (cf. Mills, 2004, p. 674; Petocz, 1999, pp. 263–264).

Sexuality and repression

With respect to the plasticity of aims, the sexual instincts are of particular interest in Freud's account of repression, but, as he points out, although the sexual drives are subjected to repression more than any other drives, this is an empirical rather than an *a priori* assertion:

> Theoretically there is no objection to supposing that any sort of instinctual demand might occasion the same repressions and their consequences: but our observation shows us invariably, so far as we can judge, that the excitations that play the pathogenic part arose from the component instincts of sexual life. [Freud, 1940a[1938], p. 186]

Thus, Bleichmar (2004) rightly notes that it is not inconceivable that sexuality could repress the aim of self-preservation (p. 1387). Furthermore, sexuality, in Freud's thinking, is not a unified drive, but rather comprises several component instincts (Freud, 1905d, 1908d) and two factors conspire to make sexuality prone to repression more than any other. The first factor is that sexuality conflicts with moral values and culture more than any other drive: "It must be borne in mind that in the course of cultural development no other function has been energetically and extensively repudiated as precisely the sexual one" (Freud, 1940a[1938], p. 186; cf. Freud, 1926f, p. 267). Consequently, due to external obstacles such as culture, the primary sexual aims become subject to repression, leading to the formation of compromised secondary aims. The second factor contributing to sexual repression involves the nature of sexuality itself. Unlike hunger and thirst, which require specified substances for satisfaction (and which, if not met, lead ultimately to the death of the organism), the sexual drives are highly plastic and modifiable, capable of achieving satisfaction through ostensibly non-sexual aims: "The sexual instincts are noticeable to us for their plasticity, their capacity of altering their aims, their replaceability, which admits of one instinctual satisfaction being replaced by another, and their readiness for being deferred . . ." (Freud, 1933a, p. 97).

The instinctual demands forced away from direct satisfaction are compelled to enter on new paths leading to substitutive satisfaction, and in the course of these *detours* they may become desexualised and their connection with their original instinctual aims may become looser. [Freud, 1940a[1938], p. 201]

That is, since the inhibition of sexuality is non-life threatening (see Ågmo & Ellingsen, 2003) and surrogate aims might achieve degrees of satisfaction, a sexual drive denied its primary aim might find substitutive satisfaction in outlets not affected by repression. Accordingly, the nature of sexuality allows a greater degree of both repression and substitution.

Repression and instinctual frustration

In Freud's mature theory of repression, the primary targets are wishes and desires representing the drives ("instinctual impulses" and "instinctual representatives") (Freud, 1915d). In the *Interpretation of Dreams*, Freud sets out a deterministic account for the development of wishes with respect to memories of satisfying experiences being reinvoked in times of need (Freud, 1900a, p. 598). Wishes, as such, are intimately connected with memory, and are instrumental to guiding action with respect to learnt sources of gratification and frustration (i.e., the guiding belief component which Freud sometimes also describes as the "idea"—e.g., Freud, 1915d, p. 157). Repression, thus, necessarily entails targeting memories, but memories related to the drives' wishful activities. However, while repression involves interference with reflection on such wishes, it does not prevent the endogenous source of stimulation: "the essence of the process of repression lies, not in putting an end to, in annihilating, the idea which represents an instinct, but in preventing it from becoming conscious" (Freud, 1915e, p. 166).

Consequently, a problem with repression is that it acts as a form of instinctual frustration, preventing drives from satiation. The frustrated drive remains in varying states of activation (Freud, 1915d, p. 151), in part mediated through substitute (secondary) satisfactions (Freud, 1912c, p. 236, 1939a, p. 116). However, in so far as drives are activated and the primary aim unobtainable, some secondary aim is necessitated. Gardner (1993) writes that a "desire held in check will be disposed to do *something*—almost anything—rather than remain idle" (p. 134, his italics), and if "desire" here is understood in terms of its source, then Gardner's claim that a "desire is plastic or 'object-hungry'" (Gardner, 1993, p. 135) means that a frustrated drive, denied its primary aim, will intend approximating aims based upon perceived similarity (cf. Gardner, 1993; Hopkins, 1995b; Petocz, 1999; Wollheim, 1993). These derivatives are distorted to a greater or lesser extent by secondary repression, and subsequent actions guided by them accordingly appear distorted, too (cf. neurotic symptoms). Nevertheless, the secondary aims remain means of substitutive satisfactions: ". . . psychoneuroses are substitutive satisfactions of some instinct the presence of which one is obliged to deny to oneself and others. Their capacity to exist depends on this distortion and lack of recognition" (Freud, 1910d, p. 148).

An example is seen in the Rat Man case study (Freud, 1909d). After the hostility towards his father was repressed, the object-hungry desire remained, forming secondary aims via association, which, in the Rat Man's case, led to substitutive hostility directed towards his brother. The stability of this situation is precarious, however, since these substitutes are never fully satisfying:

> Psycho-analysis has shown us that when the original object of a wishful impulse has been lost as a result of repression, it is frequently represented by an endless series of substitutive objects none of which, however, brings full satisfaction. [Freud, 1912d, p. 189; cf. Freud, 1915a, p. 165]

> The repressed instinct never ceases to strive for complete satisfaction, which would consist in the repetition of a primary experience of satisfaction. No substitutive or reactive formations and no sublimations will suffice to remove the repressed instinct's persisting tension . . . [Freud, 1920g, p. 42]

Hence repression, as a solution to conflict and perceived threat, always results in perpetual frustration, providing motivation for the return of the repressed. Since beliefs themselves are policy-neutral (i.e., simply about states of affairs) they require a motivational component to explain why they repeatedly become activated and the source of symptoms. Although Freud's account here raises difficulties in accounting for maintaining repression, it provides an explanation for the return of the repressed and a coherent basis for understanding human motivation generally.

Note

1. While Virsida (1998) notes the lack of motivational constructs in Frank's account (p. 166), he fails to emphasize that this alone makes Frank's account unsatisfactory.

CHAPTER EIGHT

The role of affects in repression

The significance of affects

W hile Freud notes the importance of drives as motivating structures he also writes that "psycho-analysis unhesitatingly ascribes the primacy in mental life to affective processes" (Freud, 1913j, p. 175) and affects are generally seen as central to both psychoanalytic therapy and theory throughout Freud's time to the present day (Breuer & Freud, 1895d; Freud, 1907a, 1924f; Brierley, 1937; Rapaport, 1953; Brenner, 1974; Green, 1977; Rangell, 1978; Schwartz, 1987; Westen, 1997; Emde, 1999). Brierley (1937), for instance, writes that "analysis is not an intellectual process but an affective one" and both pathology and success are judged by the analysand in terms of experienced affects (p. 266). Moreover, the clinically significant transference relationship is primarily emotional (Brenner, 1974; Emde, 1999; Green, 1977; Rapaport, 1953; Ross, 1975), and one of Freud's earliest views is that insight is only therapeutic if it is *emotional* insight: "Recollection [of memories] without affect almost invariably produces no result" (e.g., Breuer & Freud, 1895d, p. 6). Affects, too, have a significant role in repression, implicated as both cause and target (Freud, 1907a, pp. 48–49). The aim of the present chapter is to provide an account of affects outlining both their role in instigating, as well as their vicissitudes after, the act.

Affects in psychoanalytic theory

Despite their significance, there has been a long-standing dissatisfaction with the psychoanalytic theory of affects (Applegarth, 1977; Cavell, 1993; Green, 1977; Jacobson, 1953; McIlwain, 2007; Moore & Fine, 1990; Rangell, 1995; Rapaport, 1953; Rosenblatt, 1985; Ross, 1975; Schur, 1969; Sjöbäck, 1973). Sjöbäck (1973), for instance, writes, "the psychoanalytic theory of affects is fraught with obscurities and lacking in coherence" (p. 77), and Rangell (1995) writes concerning affects that "the understanding of their own central nature . . . has lagged behind and remains one of the most obscure areas, if not theoretical mysteries, of psychological, somatic, and psychosomatic theory" (p. 381). This latter comment draws attention to the intricacies involved with conceptualizing what involves a "complex psychobiological state" (Pally, 1998, p. 352), an issue not helped by the inconsistent and idiosyncratic use of terms such as affect, emotion, feelings, and so on. Some authors, for instance, distinguish between "affects", "emotions", and "feelings" (e.g., Moore & Fine, 1990; Pulver, 1971), others see the terms as generally interchangeable (e.g., Jacobson, 1953; Rangell, 1995; Schwartz, 1987), or claim that a distinction does not appear useful (e.g., Rapaport, 1953).

Freud's theory of affects

Freud's theory of affects was not static and several authors have identified distinct phases in Freud's thinking (Green, 1977; Rangell, 1995; Rapaport, 1953). However, one constant thread was Freud's conception of affects as the *discharge* of excitations toward the interior of the body. Unlike actions expressed in the external world, affects consist of alterations within the subject's own body:

> Affectivity manifests itself essentially in motor (secretory and vaso-motor) discharge resulting in an (internal) inhibition of the subject's own body without reference to the external world: motility in actions

are designed to effect changes in the external world. [Freud, 1915e, pp. 178–179n]

Freud views affects here as inextricably energic processes or "displaceable magnitudes" (Freud, 1910a, p. 18). The pleasurable and unpleasurable nature of affects follows from the release or inhibition of discharge (Freud, 1915e, p. 178; cf. Freud, 1916–1917, p. 395, 1926d, p. 132) and unpleasure and pleasure were first thought to relate to the raising or lowering of excitation, respectively (Freud, 1950[1895], p. 312), a view later qualified to account for temporal conditions of discharge (Freud, 1920g, p. 8, 1924c, pp. 159–160). However, although the relation of affects to pleasure and unpleasure is generally accepted (Brenner, 1974; Emde, 1999; Gillett, 1990; Jacobson, 1953; Krystal, 1978; Moore & Fine, 1990; Penrose, 1931; Rosenblatt, 1985; Solms, 1997b), the relationship of affects to discharge processes is much more problematic. Some view Freud's position as either too simplistic (e.g., Green, 1977; Zepf, 2001), or plainly false (Applegarth, 1977; Compton, 1972a,b; Rosenblatt, 1985) and Compton goes so far as to write that Freud's "energic overemphasis . . . impaired the development of affect theory from the start" (Compton, 1972a, p. 31). While contemporary discussions appear at times to treat "discharge" simply as synonymous with behavioural "activity" (e.g., Hutterer & Liss, 2006, p. 291), other authors still explicitly refer to "discharge" processes (e.g., Kaplan-Solms & Solms, 2000; Solms, 1997b). For example, Kaplan-Solms and Solms attempt to equate cortical *arousal* processes "as the physiological correlates of those mental processes that in psychoanalysis are conceptualized with the postulate of 'psychical energy'" (Kaplan-Solms & Solms, 2000, p. 267). However, it is difficult to defend the claim that cortical arousal operates in any fashion resembling Freud's claim (i.e., as discharge processes towards the body's interior—see Linke, 1998) and so, as discussed earlier, viewing terms such as "discharge" as metaphors (e.g., feeling relief) is much less problematic, even if explanations of such phenomena are still required.

Cognition and the relational view of affects

The contrast historically found in western thinking between "irrational" affects and "rational" impassionate cognition is typified by Bertrand Russell (1927) when he writes,

> The emotions are what makes life interesting, and what makes us feel important . . . But when, as in philosophy, we are trying to understand the world, they appear rather as a hindrance. They generate irrational opinions, since emotional associations seldom correspond with collocations in the external world . . . With the sole exception of curiosity, the emotions are on the whole a hindrance to the intellectual life . . . [p. 228]

However, there has been a shift in general psychological theory (e.g., Lazarus, 1991) and psychoanalytic theory towards viewing affects as complex processes that are inextricably cognitive and not necessarily irrational and obstructive (Brenner, 1974, 1994; Emde, 1999; Moore & Fine, 1990; Pulver, 1971; Rangell, 1978; Rosenblatt, 1985; Schur, 1969). The view that affects are *intentional*, or directed towards objects, is, to some extent, found in Freud's view that affects "cathect" or invest ideas (Freud, 1906c, p. 108, 1909b, p. 35). In terms of the model of cognitive processes presented earlier, this means that affects intend "ideas", ideas here understood as the *object* of the affect (cf. Wollheim, 1991). As Brentano writes,

> Every mental phenomenon includes something as an object within itself, although they do not do so in the same way. In presentation something is presented, in judgement something is affirmed or denied, in love loved, in hate hated, in desire desired and so on . . . No physical object exhibits anything like it. We can, therefore, define mental phenomena by saying that they are those which contain an object intentionally within themselves. [Brentano, 1874, pp. 88–89]

In this sense affects are not simply fear, anger, or happiness, but fear *of* something, anger *at* something, and so on. Pulver similarly notes that affects are clothed cognitively, part of which includes the object they are directed at:

> When, for example, we speak of the affect of anger as we see it in a patient, we are referring not only to the 'pure feeling' of anger, but to such closely linked components as the accompanying ideation ('that is the man I am angry at'), the feelings of impulse and desire ('I want to hit him'), the psychic representations of the physiological concomitants ('My heart is beating faster') and motor tendencies ('My fist is clenched'). [Pulver, 1971, p. 347]

Since cognition is required to mediate the emotional relation with the object (i.e., a subject S affectively related to some object x), affects must entail certain cognitive *relations*. As Thalberg (1977) notes, we cannot feel something towards an object without cognition: "As soon as we spell out what frightens, irks or gratifies the person, our report of his emotion will imply that he is thinking in some manner about the item" (Thalberg, 1977, p. 35). This view is also found in O'Neil's proposal that affects are relations between a feeling subject and things *felt* about:

> Just as striving (search and avoidance) implies a striver and a striven for, so feeling (pleasure and unpleasure) implies a feeler and a felt about. For just as seeking or an avoiding is inconceivable without something seeking or avoiding, so a being pleased or a being unpleasured is inconceivable without something being pleased or unpleased: and similarly just as a mind cannot strive without striving for something, so a mind cannot be pleased or unpleased without being pleased or unpleased with something. [O'Neil, 1934, pp. 281–282]

All affect is (partly) cognitive, and, taken as such, specifying affects requires identifying the subject and object terms of the relation and the particular type of affective relation involved.

"Objectless" anxiety

Anxiety is of particular interest in the theory of repression, since, with Freud's (1926d) reformulation, anxiety is specifically seen as the motive for repression, and although some authors subsequent to Freud believe that any unpleasant affect can motivate defence (e.g., Emde, 1999; Schur, 1969; Rangell, 1995), anxiety is, nevertheless, seen to hold a peculiar position (Brenner, 1974; Rangell, 1995, 2002). In light of the proposed view of affects here, understanding anxiety requires stipulating the subject and object terms involved. However, Freud later draws a distinction between "anxiety" and "fear":

> Anxiety [*Angst*] has an unmistakable relation to *expectation*: it is anxiety *about* something. It has a quality of *indefiniteness and lack of object*. In precise speech we use the word 'fear' [*Furcht*] rather than 'anxiety' [*Angst*] if it has found an object. [Freud, 1926d, pp. 164–165, his italics]

On the surface Freud appears here to be proposing the view that affects can be without objects (i.e., "objectless anxiety"), a position found similarly in Talvitie and Ihanus (2002) when they write, "[w]hen fear has no object . . . we are dealing with anxiety. When the object is found, an appropriate fear emerges" (p. 1317). However, the "objectless anxiety" that Freud refers to simply lacks a definite object, since it is still clearly expectant *about something* dreadful happening. Even if the object is indefinite, the affect is still about something, and whether the object is, in fact, conscious or not might be a vicissitude of repression (Boag, 2008a). This view is similarly proposed by Brenner, who argues that affects and ideas are "inseparable, that the former is not to be found without the latter, even though an affect may *seem* to be without ideational content when it is conscious and ideas connected with it are unconscious" (Brenner, 1974, p. 539, his italics). In fact, therapeutic practice assumes that, although the subject might not be conscious of the object of anxiety, he or she is still capable of coming to know it:

> we are not content to know that a patient is anxious. We wish to know, and we bend our analytic efforts to learn, *what* he is afraid of . . . The fact that a patient himself is unconscious of the nature and the origins of his fears does not deter us. We proceed on the assumption that anxiety is not merely an unpleasurable sensation, but that it includes ideas as well. [Brenner, 1974, p. 534, his italics]

Thus, the object of the affect might be unconsciously known (i.e., a person may fear x without knowing that he or she knows x), which is apparent in the case example reported by Kaplan-Solms and Solms (2000) of Mrs A, who was simultaneously suicidally depressed about her physical condition *and* yet also unaware of her physical symptoms.

Affects and drives

While affects are partly cognitive, cognition alone is insufficient for characterizing affects, and many authors note that emotions appear to energize and organize thought and action (e.g., Izard, 1991; Schwartz, 1987; Westen, 1999; Wilson, 1972). An angry person, for example, might wish to strike at the object of anger, and affects similarly appear to influence our evaluations and beliefs concerning the object of affects (Rosenblatt, 1985, p. 87). As Emde (1999) writes, "[affects] guide engagement with the world and learning throughout life" (Emde, 1999, p. 325), which all suggests that affects are intimately connected with motivational tendencies within the organism, and, given the ubiquitous nature of the instinctual drives in relation to behaviour and cognition, a candidate for understanding affects here would be in their relationship to instinctual drives.

However, some authors propose a distinction in Freud's thinking between his early pre-topographical "affect" theory and his post-topographic "instinctual drive" theory, claiming little relation between them (e.g., Jacobson, 1953; Ross, 1975). Freud, however, did not maintain such a dichotomy, and in places he directly equates affects and drives when he writes that psychoanalysis puts "emphasis on instinctual life (affectivity)" (Freud, 1924f, p. 197; cf. Freud, 1924e, p. 184). More specifically, Freud views affects as the end-product of instinctual forces:

> [Psychoanalysis] teaches us to recognise the affective units—the complexes dependent on instincts—whose presence is to be presumed in each individual, and it introduces us to the study of the transformations and end-products arising from these instinctual forces. [Freud, 1913j, p. 179]

Moreover, there are several good reasons for connecting affects to drive activity. Concerning the relationship between drives and environment, Zepf (2001) notes "there must be an affective relationship with what is desired" (p. 478) and, in some basic sense, objects associated with satisfaction become associated with "positive" emotions, while those associated with frustration become associated with "negative" emotions. Similarly, others note that affects typically arise in relation to frustration and gratification (Jacobson, 1953; O'Neil; 1934; Zepf, 2001), and Brierley (1937) suggests, "affect manifested is, in fact, the index to the fate of the impulse" (p. 262; cf. Rapaport, 1953, pp. 194–195). Although this may generally be correct, Zepf (2001) notes that rather than only reflecting the *fate* of the impulse, affects appear to accompany drive relations along the entire course of drive behaviour (though possibly the most salient instances of affects occur in regard to instances of frustration and gratification). In fact, affects may arise in anticipation of both pleasurable and unpleasurable events (Brenner, 1974; Freud, 1920g; Jacobson, 1953):

> human beings react powerfully, not only to intense unpleasure but even to the expectation or prospect of it. The mere prospect of the repetition of what was painful in the past is enough to cause unpleasure in the present, just as the prospect of what was pleasurable before is enough to cause pleasure now. [Brenner, 1974, p. 542]

The position adopted here, integrating cognitive and motivational factors, views affects as *drive-evaluative* phenomena reflecting the response of the drive systems to stimuli related to gratification or frustration (see also Boag, 2008a). Objects and events in the environment that are gratifying or frustrating become evaluated as positive or negative, and so affect might be thought of as the complex of drive and cognitive-evaluative processes and states involved. Similarly, Kaplan-Solms and Solms (2000) write, "This is the essence of Freudian affect theory: by a process of natural selection, pleasurable sensations gradually become attached to those objects and activities that are most likely to satisfy the libidinal drives . . ." (p. 236). Such sensations of pleasure and unpleasure are ultimately grounded in bodily states, and it is such physiological reactions which "contribute to what gives each emotion its unique quality" (Pally, 1998, p. 350). Such a drive account is also consistent with the claim that "[a]ffects reflect our internal feelings of goodness and badness" (Panksepp, 2003, p. 6), since they arise as evaluative responses to the interactions of the drives and conditions of gratification and frustration.

Can affects alone drive the organism?

In contradistinction to this position, some authors have opted for abandoning instinctual drives altogether and instead arguing for affects as the sole motivating structures (e.g., Cavell, 1993; Holt, 1976; Sandler, 1985; Sandler & Sandler, 1994; Schwartz, 1987; Westen, 1999). Affects are said to provide both "the affective 'fuel' that energises thought and action" (Westen, 1997, p. 535), and provide the policy behind human behaviour: "The attempt to regulate affect—to minimise unpleasant feelings and to maximise pleasant ones—is the driving force in human motivation" (Westen, 1997, p. 542; cf. Schwartz, 1987, p. 482). Western (1997) further writes that "[p]eople, like animals, tend to avoid what they have learned feels bad and approach what they have learned feels good" (Westen, 1997, p. 532).

However, some account is still needed for explaining why some situations are found to be pleasurable (or "good") and others not, especially considering that a single stimulus may provoke a variety of different affective responses from different subjects or from the same subject on different occasions. Westen, here, falls back upon "naturally selected affective proclivities" (1997, p. 542), but this simply raises the question concerning what these are precisely, and instinctual drives appear to be a sound candidate to fill in this gap. In so far as affects regulate behaviour, there is no conflict with a drive model of behaviour: affects may regulate drive systems, and it is these systems that explain why some objects and events are gratifying and pleasurable and others not (see also Maze, 1993; McIlwain, 2008; and Mills, 2004 for discussion concerning the relationship between drives and object-relations theory). Thus, when Bleichmar (2004) writes that "[i]t is always the pleasure/unpleasure dynamic interplay among beliefs, among fantasies, among behaviours that defines the course the psyche will take" (p. 1380), this can be understood in terms of the drives' affective responses determining and shaping the course of further drive activity.

There is, however, a further question concerning whether affects themselves can be seen as primary sources of motivation (rather than being ancillary to the drives). McIlwain (2007), for example, posits both drives and affects as independent motivating structures and writes that "a fully embodied theory of motivation must embrace both [drives and affects]" (McIlwain, 2007, p. 532). While there is no dispute that affects are causally relevant to behaviour, assessing whether affects act as primary motivational structures requires clearly delineating their characteristics and providing a workable mechanism for understanding how these operate (such that causes and effects are logically distinct from one another—see Boag, 2011a). However, it is not always easy to discern precisely what is meant by "affects". For instance, McIlwain (2007) provides no clear definition of affects, and, while we are told that affects have "dedicated neural substrates" (McIlwain, 2007, p. 547) and "underpin bodily pleasure" (p. 530), she also writes that affects form "part of our emotional experience"

(p. 534) or "emotional response" (p. 534), none of which is to say what affects are, but, rather (if anything), what they do (i.e., what relations they enter into). Additionally, the claim that affects are "intentional engines, that is, they reach for objects that might satisfy in psychic realities or objects outside our skin" (p. 531), similarly defines affects in terms of what they do ("reach for objects") and, while there may be affective systems doing this reaching, what is also not provided is an account for why certain objects are satisfying (or frustrating). While such an account might in principle be possible, the descriptions of affects above further suggest that affects act as both causes and effects (or exist both as a term in the affective relation, as well as constituting the relation itself). For instance, McIlwain (2007) invokes Tomkins' (1962, 1963) account of drives and affects, writing that "without affects, the drives would never motivate us" (p. 548) and that "[t]he affects are primary for Tomkins. If we respond to hunger with fear or shame, then the strength of the drive is likely to be diminished" (p. 548). However, it is difficult to see how affects then could be the primary motivating source, since they serve as *responses* to the drives (and, thus, appear, if anything, logically subsidiary to the drives). Furthermore, explaining why we respond to hunger or sexuality with shame could possibly be traced further back to drives fearing negative consequences to the activity of other drives (Maze, 1983).

However, none of this is to reduce the significance of affects; we are affective creatures, and, while it might be the case that affects are primary motivating structures (an empirical question), it might be simpler to say that affects are "feeling" relations, with the terms including neural processes, and felt bodily states to differentiate (in part) the affective responses that arise in relation to the world (see Boag, 2008a; cf. Damasio, 1994, 1998, 2001). Affects, then, are ancillary to the drives: drives determine policy (why, say, we respond with shame to desires) but affects are important regulators of drive activity, nevertheless. Thus, when Pally (1998) writes that "schematically emotion can be considered as a constellation of (a) stimulus appraisals as to their relevance to the organism, (b) brain and body changes that result from those feedbacks and (c) feedback to the brain itself of those brain and body changes" (Pally, 1998, p. 350), the "bodily state" responses can be seen to regulate the course of action taken but the "relevance" of the organism is rooted in the motivational bases of the organism (i.e., the drives).

Implications for repression

Anxiety requires knowing the object of threat

The account of affects proposed here, which is consistent with Freud's position (minus the energic concepts), has several implications for the theory of repression. The first implication is that since repression is motivated by anxiety, it appears to require a knowing subject evaluating content as a threat to explain how the affective response arises, and, in Freud's view, the subject is the ego, which *cognizes, recognizes* and *judges* that a danger situation threatens:

> as soon as *the ego recognises the danger of castration* it gives the signal of anxiety and inhibits through the pleasure–unpleasure agency (in a way which we cannot as yet understand) the impending cathectic process in the id. [Freud, 1926d, p. 135, my italics]

> *The ego notices* that the satisfaction of an emerging instinctual demand would conjure up one of the *well-remembered situations of danger*. [Freud, 1933a, p. 89, my italics]

> ... *the ego anticipates* the satisfaction of the questionable instinctual impulse and permits it to bring about the reproduction of the unpleasurable feelings at the beginning of the feared situation of danger. [Freud, 1933a, pp. 89–90, my italics]

Clearly, then, if anxiety motivates repression, then repression necessarily requires knowing some target as a threat for repression to occur. While this knowing might itself be unconscious, explaining secondary repression and resistance nevertheless requires the ego knowing what it is not meant to know. Furthermore, with respect to signal anxiety, Shill (2004) maintains that this must be a cognitively sophisticated state of affairs:

> Signal anxiety, as the outcome of an ego process, can serve to signal the presence of an impending threat only when the ego draws on the memory of *past* dangers, real or imagined, from which to extrapolate to situations of perceived similarity in the future. Hence, in construing the threat, ego processes such as memory, learning, exteroceptive perception and cognition (including sensations of the physiological changes due to sympathetic arousal), learning, symbolic and abstract reasoning, inhibition of primary process, use of secondary process,

affect regulation and tolerance, and perhaps others too, are all involved. [Shill, 2004, p. 125, his italics]

Shill here correctly notes that anxiety cannot be reduced to non-cognitive processes, since judging something to be dangerous (and comparing a present situation with past dangers) necessarily involves a psychological evaluation. Being "threatening" is not a property of anything (such as an object's shape or size), but involves an evaluation whereby x may be threatening for one person but not for another, in much the same way as someone might (for presumably a defence against oral desires) find breast-feeding "offensive".

With respect to anxiety, then, Wong (1999) proposes that there are three essential aspects of an anxiety state including: (i) the detection of stimuli; (ii) discriminating dangers from non-dangers, and (iii) taking steps to avoid danger: "any anxiety state—including anxiety as a signal—involves detection, discrimination, and action" (Wong, 1999, p. 829; cf. Brenner, 1974, 1994; Schur, 1953, 1969; Shill, 2004). Similarly, Shill (2004) concludes that "[t]here appears then to be an assessment or appraisal phase in the ego through which the existence of danger is detected, followed by an affective alarm phase in which signal anxiety is the predominant feature. Defensive functioning then ensues" (p. 118). While the action (or defence) appears to be more of a response to anxiety, nevertheless, anxiety (signal or otherwise) would appear to necessitate an evaluation of objects and events. Thus, as Schur (1969) notes, "the cognitive factor—in the case of anxiety the recognition of danger—is intrinsic to the total response" (p. 651). Anxiety is the affective attitude that frustration can be expected based upon prior experience, which requires an evaluating subject knowing the target of potential threat.

Can we make sense of unconscious anxiety?

While anxiety involves a subject evaluating a target as threatening, as many recognize, this is not to say that anxiety is itself necessarily conscious (Baumbacher, 1989; Emde, 1999; Pulver, 1971; Rangell, 1978; Schur, 1969; Wong, 1999). Freud's position here, however, is problematic, since he believes that affects, by definition, are conscious processes:

It is surely of the essence of an emotion that we should be aware of it, i.e. that it should be known to consciousness. Thus the possibility of the attribute of unconsciousness would be completely excluded as far as emotions, feelings and affects are concerned. [Freud, 1915d, p. 177; cf. Freud, 1923b, pp. 22–23]

While this position has been widely criticized (e.g., Brenner, 1974; Emde, 1999; Pulver, 1971, 1974; Rangell, 1995; Rosenblatt & Thickstun, 1977; Schur, 1969), a minority still follow Freud in this respect (e.g., Gillett, 1990; Rosenblatt, 1985). However, in the relational view of cognitive processes, the psychical component of affects must be unconscious in the first instance, and the claim that they are necessarily conscious is erroneous. Since any mental act is unconscious in the first instance and does not become conscious until taken as the object of a second mental act, anxiety itself will not be conscious until reflected upon. That is, one can feasibly be anxious about x without knowing that one is anxious about x. If "signal" anxiety is then understood as an "exciting cause" of repression (Gillett, 1990), then the ego could evaluate x as a threat (so the target of repression is known) but the threat-evaluation and anxiety (where S anxiously evaluates x) could occur unconsciously and trigger repression. In other words, repression could be motivated by intense anxiety without the anxiety itself, in fact, being known.

Thus, we can make sense of Shill's (2004) claim that

in concluding that a danger exists, a full range of ego operations are used in appraising the internal and external situations for the presence of danger, prior to the initiation of the affective stage of the process we call signal anxiety, which is the reaction to the unconscious realization that danger is indeed present. [p. 118]

It is possible for the ego to evaluate a target x as threatening, but for this evaluation to involve an "unconscious realization" whereby the act of evaluation itself is not reflected upon. Of course, we need then to consider why any intense response—which might ordinarily have attention drawn to it—does not become known itself. We would also have to conclude that, although the anxiety might occur unconsciously, the target of repression must nevertheless be known sufficiently to be judged as a threat: to evaluate a desire and its perceived consequences as a threat requires necessarily that it be known. What this means is that anxiety concerning mental content presumes awareness of them, and accounts of repression (resistance, etc.) motivated by anxiety appear to necessitate knowing these targets as threats. Thus, although anxiety itself might be unconscious, the knowing the target of repression (what is not meant to be known) cannot be avoided.

Inhibition of affective association

The second implication for repression is that this view of affects suggests a possible mechanism for understanding the repressive *effect*. Freud presents the view that repression dissociates affects from ideas, writing that "in repression a severance takes place between the affect and the idea to which it belongs, and that each then undergoes its separate vicissitude" (Freud, 1915e, p. 179). Freud's early account proposes that this severance makes ideas "weak" and incapable of conscious awareness, and problems with this view were outlined earlier. However, on the position adopted here, given that the "idea" component is the *object* of the affect, what Freud possibly means is that the affective relation between the subject and the object might be severed or otherwise disrupted. Thus understood, when Freud writes that

> the release of affect and the ideational content do not constitute the indissoluble organic unity as which we are in a habit of treating them, but that these two separate entities may be merely *soldered* together and can thus be detached from each other by analysis. [1900a, pp. 461–462, his italics]

he does not mean that the affective component is non-cognitive (or "blind") as Cavell (1993) believes.[1] Rather, Freud recognizes that the objects of affects are displaceable: hostility towards one object could be displaced on to substitutes due to factors such as repression. Thus, we can make sense of Freud's statement in terms of displacement:

> it may happen that an affective or emotional impulse is perceived but misconstrued. Owing to the repression of its proper representative it has been forced to become connected with another idea, and is now regarded by consciousness as the manifestation of that idea. [Freud, 1915e, pp. 177–178]

That is, repression disrupts the affective relationship, preventing certain objects being intended emotionally and consequently associating the affective response with other objects that appear inappropriate to the response (i.e., "irrational"). For instance, in the case of Mrs A discussed earlier (Kaplan-Solms & Solms, 2000), the actual object of her suicidal depression (the post-trauma deficit) was unconscious, and instead presented itself as suicidal depression about "losing little things". Hence, therapy of "irrational affects", such as so-called irrational phobic anxiety, consists in "recognising the affect as being . . . justified and by seeking out an idea which belongs to it but has been repressed and replaced by a substitute" (Freud, 1900a, p. 461). Furthermore, in most non-psychotic cases, it is impossible to utterly inhibit knowledge of all of the terms and relations involved in the repressed aim. For example, if the "desire to kill father" is evaluated as threatening and repressed, it would generally not be possible to remain ignorant of either the "father" term of the relation, or the "desire to kill". Both "father" and "desire to kill" would remain capable of being known independently, as is quite clearly seen in Freud's Rat Man case (Freud, 1909d). Here, the Rat Man's hostility towards his father was repressed, yet repression did not inhibit the actual terms and type of relation involved. The Rat Man was fully capable of hostility towards others, as his substitutive hostility towards his brother bears testimony, and also capable of admiring his father. Furthermore, he was aware of both these attitudes during his analysis. What was inhibited was the particular affective relationship: he remained ignorant of his hostile attitude *towards* his father. Here, the selective inhibition affected only the specific connection between hostility and the father, and not others of the same logical kind.

"Reversal" of affects

Another vicissitude that affects undergo after repression concerns the reversal or transformation of affects. In this view, Freud believes that affects can be transformed into their opposites (e.g., pleasure into disgust or anxiety; love into hatred) and *"it is precisely this transformation of affect which constitutes the essence of what we term 'repression'"* (Freud, 1900a, p. 604, his italics; cf. Freud, 1916–1917, p. 409). Freud views this as a theoretical problem, describing it as "one of the most important and yet at the same time one of the most difficult problems in the psychology of the neuroses" (Freud, 1905e, p. 28):

> The problem of repression lies in the question of how it is and owing
> to what motive forces that this transformation occurs . . . it is enough
> for us to be clear that a transformation of this kind does occur in the
> course of development—we have only to recall the way in which
> disgust emerges in childhood after having been absent to begin with—
> and that it is related to the activity of the second system. [Freud, 1900a,
> p. 604]

Specifically, since "satisfaction of an instinct is always pleasurable"
(Freud, 1915d, p .146), the problem is accounting for how this love
becomes transformed into an unpleasurable affect like hatred, a point
upon which critics of Freud have seized (e.g., Macmillan, 1991).
However, the problem stems from Freud's problematic energic postulation, which requires any magnitude or intensity being accounted for
economically (in a comparable fashion to accounting for "force" in
physics). Instead, Freud himself provides a solution to the supposed
"transformation" of affects with respect to distinct motivational–affective responses. Given that one and the same desire possessed by an
individual might lead to the anticipation of *both* gratification and frustration, we can understand competing affective responses as underlying the apparent affective transformation:

> We . . . learn that the satisfaction of an instinct which is under repres-
> sion would be quite possible, and further, that in every instance such
> a satisfaction would be pleasurable in itself; but it would be irrecon-
> cilable with other claims and intentions. It would therefore cause plea-
> sure in one place and unpleasure in another. It has consequently
> become a condition for repression that the motive force of unpleasure
> shall have acquired more strength than the pleasure obtained from
> satisfaction. [Freud, 1915d, p. 147]

Thus, since affects involve relations between drives and the environment, a parsimonious explanation for "affective transformation"
would consist of the imagined pleasure for one drive system constituting a threat to another drive system. For example, the love expressed
by one drive toward a particular object might also be believed to
occasion danger by another drive, overriding the initial affective
response with the opposite evaluative response. This account requires
not a literal transformation of affect—like water into wine—but,
rather, one affective response which incurs pleasurable anticipation

being overridden by another drive-evaluation involving anxiety, and, thus, the apparent "transformation" of affect is a result of conflicting aims.

Note

1. There is, however, some support for Cavell's point of view, since Freud, of course, also treats affects as the intensity component of feelings and beliefs (see, for example, Breuer & Freud, 1895d, p. 59; Freud, 1907a, pp. 48–49).

PART III
EXPLAINING REPRESSION

Introduction to Part III

The preceding chapters present a working account of conscious and unconscious mental processes and locate Freud's account of repression within the folk-psychological desire–belief model, with affects having a regulating role. Such a foundation is necessary for providing the context for an explanation of Freud's theory of repression, whereby: (i) the ego believes that gratifying certain desires and wishes will lead to punishing consequences; (ii) anxiety follows, so that the offending desires are repressed and no longer known; (iii) the repressed desire persists, impelling thought and behaviour such that it would become known unless prevented; (iv) repression must be a continuous activity to prevent the repressed from becoming conscious. We have seen that (iii) cannot be rejected *a priori*; given the physiological bases of desires, and their "object-hungry" nature (Gardner, 1993, p. 135), the source of a desire would remain active despite repression of its cognitive representative. The first explanatory strategy examines the possibility of a censor initiating repression before then examining whether repression can be reduced to neural processes. Finally, an account of repression is presented which avoids problems of the former two strategies, but which accounts for both the psychological and neural processes involved in explaining repression.

CHAPTER NINE

Repression and the censorship

Censoring and censorship

Possibly the most famous and yet most controversial explanation of repression is that of the repressing "censor" invoked to account for the repression of desires and wishes independently of the ego's knowing. Freud first mentions censorship in a letter to Fliess dated 22 December 1897, in which he compares the dynamics of the mind to the political oppression in late nineteenth-century Russia:

> Have you ever seen a foreign newspaper which has passed Russian censorship at the frontier? Words, whole clauses and sentences are blacked out so that the rest becomes unintelligible. A *Russian censorship* of this kind comes about in psychoses and produces the apparently meaningless *deliria*. [Masson, 1985, p. 289, Freud's italics]

A similar analogy is then drawn in the *Interpretation of Dreams* (1900a), where Freud writes again in relation to deliria of a "ruthless censorship" that acts exactly like the censorship of newspapers at the Russian frontier:

Deliria are the work of a censorship which no longer takes the trouble to conceal its operations; instead of collaborating in producing a new version that shall be unobjectionable, it ruthlessly deletes whatever it disapproves of, so that what remains becomes quite disconnected. This censorship acts exactly like the censorship of newspapers at the Russian frontier, which allows foreign journals to fall into the hands of the readers whom it is its business to protect only after a quantity of passages have been blacked out. [Freud, 1900a, p. 529]

The censorship metaphor is later developed and explicitly connected with the spatial metaphor of the topographic theory, whereby the censor was personified as a "watchman" preventing wishes in the *Ucs.* from accessing the *Pcs.*, within which consciousness resides:

The unconscious wishful impulses clearly try to make themselves effective in daytime as well, and the fact of transference, as well as the psychoses, show us that they endeavour to force their way by way of the preconscious system into consciousness and to obtain control of the power of movement. Thus the censorship between the *Ucs.* and the *Pcs.*, the assumption of whose existence is positively forced upon us by dreams, deserves to be recognised and respected as the watchman of our mental health. [Freud, 1900a, p. 567]

. . . on the threshold between these two rooms a watchman performs his function: he examines the different mental impulses, acts as a censor, and will not admit them into the drawing room if they displease him. [Freud, 1916–1917, p. 295]

This censoring agency is also invoked to explain resistance: "It is the same watchman whom we get to know as resistance when we try to lift the repression by means of the analytic treatment" (Freud, 1916–1917, p. 296). Thus, this issue of censorship and the censoring agency is an important aspect in Freud's account of repression and is not merely a "coyley disguised relative" of repression, as Macmillan (1991, p. 272) believes. Furthermore, while the "watchman" is clearly metaphorical, the same examining agency is found in Freud's more technical writings, whereby the same functional relation obtains. For instance, in his metapsychological paper on the unconscious, Freud writes that "the rigorous censorship exercises its office at the point of transition from the *Ucs.* to the *Pcs.* (or *Cs.*)" (Freud, 1915e, p. 173; cf. Freud, 1900a, pp. 177, 553, 617, 1915d, p. 153, 1915e, pp. 191–194,

1917d, p. 225) and Freud even suggests that there may even be a second censorship between the *Pcs.* and *Cs.* (Freud, 1900a, pp. 615, 617–618). Furthermore, Freud writes "that these crude hypotheses of the two rooms, the watchman at the threshold between them and consciousness as a spectator at the end of the second room, must nevertheless be very far-reaching approximations to the real facts" (1916–1917, p. 296).

Some authors argue that positing a censor (or censors) is logically justified, since it is necessary for avoiding the apparent paradox of repression, whereby the ego knows what it is not meant to know (e.g., Anspaugh, 1995; Johnson, 1998). However, the supposed explanatory value comes at a cost, since critics have seized upon this metaphor of a watchman to dismiss Freud's theory of repression as both fanciful and without empirical support (Bonanno & Keuler, 1998; Greenwald, 1992; Rofé, 2008; Sartre, 1956). Bonanno and Keuler (1998), for instance, write, "One of the primary difficulties with the repression model is that it hinges on the troublesome concept of an unconscious and autonomous regulator or 'censor'—the gatekeeper of the boundary to conscious awareness" (p. 439).

This censorship is also particularly prominent and conspicuously problematic in the context of explaining the bizarreness of dreams ("disguise-censorship"). For both proponents and critics of dream theory, this "dream-censorship" is posited to be "the heart of Freudian dream theory" (Hobson, 1999, p. 170; cf. Hobson, 1988; Hobson & Pace-Schott, 1999; McCarley & Hobson, 1977, p. 1218) and Colace (2010) recently writes that "in Freud's dream theory, [the] dream censorship mechanism remains the most important hypothesis in the explanation of dream bizarreness" (p. 130; cf. Colace, 2006, p. 25). Despite this supposed centrality, there has been very little critical discussion concerning precisely what is being attacked or defended in accounts of censorship in dreaming. Braun (1999), for instance, writes concerning the Solms–Hobson dream-debate that

> Solms never really addresses what Hobson refers to as "censorship and disguise," and indeed seems to minimise these features in his discussion of Freud's model. This represents a major failure in his argument (and his defence of Freud). [p. 199]

Indeed, Solms himself appears ambivalent on the issue of the issue of censorship: whereas he tentatively associates the censorship with the inhibitory functions of the mediobasal frontal region of the brain (Solms, 1997a, p. 174), elsewhere, when discussing the evidence for Freud's theory of dreams, no reference is made to censorship at all (e.g., Solms, 2005; Turnbull & Solms, 2007). On the other hand, Solms and Turnbull (2002) concede that the evidence for censorship is far from conclusive, and that dream-bizarreness "may [possibly] be due to the inherently 'regressive' nature of the dream process ... with no need to introduce the additional function of censorship" (p. 215).

The censor metaphor and Freud's states of mind

Two strands in Freud's thinking concerning the censor metaphor are reflected in his choice of terminology. Freud's editor, Strachey (in Freud, 1900a), notes that Freud most commonly used the German *Zensur* ("censorship"), referring either to the act of censoring or the censoring force (cf. Strachey, in Freud, 1914c, p. 97*n*). On the other hand, the German term for "censor" (*Zensor*) was not typically employed by Freud and some indication of the distinction between the terms is apparent in instances when both *Zensor* and *Zensur* occur: "We know the self-observing agency as the ego-censor [*Zensor*], the conscience; it is this that exercises the dream-censorship [*Zensur*] during the night, from which the repressions of inadmissible wishful impulses proceed" (Freud, 1916–1917, p. 429).

Here, the censor (*Zensor*) is the agency responsible for the *act* of censorship (*Zensur*) and given Freud's preference for *Zensur* over *Zensor*, it could be concluded perhaps that the "censor" agency was peripheral to Freud's thinking and to his account of repression. Furthermore, it is not until the 1914 additions to *The Interpretation of Dreams* (1900a) that this personal form (*Zensor*) is found to appear for the first time, a period corresponding with Freud's researches into narcissism and the emergence in Freud's work of the ego-ideal, the embryonic form of the superego and its function as a "self-observing agency":

> It has been shown that a part of the attention which operates during the day continues to be directed towards dreams during the state of sleep, that it keeps a check on them and criticizes them and reserves the power to interrupt them. It has seemed plausible to recognize in the mental agency which thus remains awake the censor [*Zensor*] to

whom we have had to attribute such a powerful restricting influence upon the form taken by dreams. [Freud, 1900a, p. 505, added in 1914]

In Freud's paper "On narcissism" (1914c), another instance is found where Freud uses the personal *Zensor*, but in the context of discussing the general "censorship" (*Zensur*). Freud begins by equating the censorship with one side of the repressive trends that govern the ego, and *not* as some sort of special power, a point of view that seems to reflect his earliest conceptions of it:

> We may here recall that we have found that the formation of dreams takes place under the dominance of a censorship [*Zensur*] which compels distortion of the dream-thoughts. We did not, however, picture this censorship as a special power, but chose the term to designate one side of the repressive trends that govern the ego, namely the side which is turned towards the dream-thoughts. [Freud, 1914c, pp. 97–98]

However, he continues,

> If we enter further into the structure of the ego, we may recognize in the ego ideal and in the dynamic utterances of conscience the *dream-censor* [*Zensor*] as well. If this censor is to some extent on the alert even during sleep, we can understand how it is that its suggested activity of self-observation and self-criticism ... makes a contribution to the content of the dream. [Freud, 1914c, pp. 97–98]

Although the censor is an aspect of the ego, the suggestion here is that it is a type of cognizing agency, "self-observing" (presumably, observing the ego and not itself), ever vigilant, and on alert to protect the sleeping (remaining) ego. Hence, the censor is independent enough to criticize the ego and observe it (i.e., take the ego as its object). Additionally, this censor stands above the rest of the ego; while the ego succumbs to sleep, the censor remains vigilant, albeit in an attenuated state. What this must imply, as Thalberg (1982) observes, is that the psychical apparatus is divided into two centres of consciousness (i.e., two knowers; one of the ego proper, and one that observes the ego).

This implication of independent knowers within the person carries over into Freud's later discussions of the superego in terms of an observing, judging agency:

I might simply say that the special agency which I am beginning to distinguish in the ego is conscience. But it is more prudent to keep the agency as something independent and to suppose that conscience is one of its functions and that self-observation, which is an essential preliminary to the judging activity of conscience, is another of them. And since when we recognise that something has a separate existence we give it a name of its own, from this time forward I will describe this agency in the ego as the '*super-ego*'. [Freud, 1933a, p. 60, his italics; cf. Freud, 1914c, p. 95, 1916–1917, pp. 428–429]

Freud further explicitly relates the superego to the censor of dreams when he writes, "We know the self-observing agency as the ego-censor, the conscience; it is this that exercises the dream-censorship during the night, from which the repressions of inadmissible wishful impulses proceed" (Freud, 1916–1917, p. 429).

Accordingly, Freud appears to postulate independent knowers, one of which instigates repression independently of the general ego. Nevertheless, Freud also explicitly states that the censorship should not be taken to mean a homunculus:

I hope you do not take the term [censorship] too anthropomorphically, and do not picture the 'censor of dreams' as a severe little manikin or a spirit living in a closet in the brain and there discharging his office; but I hope too that you do not take the term in too 'localizing' a sense, and do not think of a 'brain-centre', from which a censoring influence of this kind issues, an influence which would be brought to an end if the 'centre' were damaged or removed. For the time being it is nothing more than a serviceable term for describing a dynamic relation. [Freud, 1916–1917, p. 140]

In this view, the censor is merely one side of the repressing forces (or a description of a dynamic relation), the force of repression being left undefined. Notably, this is written after 1914, after his writings that first introduce the personal form of censor, and would seem to clearly dispel the notion that Freud conceived of the censor as an independent, anthropomorphic agent. However, Freud's choice of analogy does not help bear out the view that the censor is not to be regarded as an anthropomorphized agent. Consider, for instance, Freud's description of censorship in terms of a "watchman": ". . . there are occasions when that excellent fellow the night-watchman, whose business it is to guard the little township's sleep, has no alternative but to sound the alarm and waken the sleeping townspeople" (Freud, 1940a[1938], p. 171).

The use of terms such as "watchman" distinctly suggests conceptualizing the censor as an anthropomorphic, active, cognizing agent (a homunculus of sorts). It is also noteworthy that Freud's consistent reference to "agency" in relation to censorship (e.g., Freud, 1933a, p. 15) is not translated from the German equivalent, *Agentur*, but, rather, from *Instanz*, a judicial term pertaining to a court of justice such as used in the phrase "a Court of First Instance"[1] (Baumann, 1910), and Freud's usage is more or less explicit with respect to an authority that judges what may or may not pass (Strachey, in Freud, 1900a, p. 537; Laplanche & Pontalis, 1973, p. 16):

> We find that there is a 'censorship', a testing agency, at work in us, which decides whether an idea cropping up in the mind shall be allowed to reach consciousness, and which, so far as lies with its power, ruthlessly excludes anything that might produce or revive unpleasure. [Freud, 1913j, pp. 170–171; cf. Freud, 1932c, p. 221]

What all of this reveals is a tension in Freud's thinking which is reflected in comparing statements such as the "censorship exercised by the repression" (Freud, 1896b, p. 182) with Freud's comment that "what is rejected by the censorship is in a state of repression" (Freud, 1900a, p. 676); the former inferring that censorship is the effect of repression whereas the latter proposes that repression proceeds from the censorship. This confusion appears subsequently to have been inherited by other authors. For instance, Ernest Jones appears also to provide a similar "non-anthropomorphic" defence of the censorship concept:

> considerable objection has been raised . . . to Freud's use of the word Censor, but so far as I can see it is rather to the word than to the conception. It is not to be imagined that Freud understands by this term anything in the nature of a specific entity; to him it is nothing more nor less than a convenient expression to denote the *sum total of repressing inhibitions*. [Jones, in Wohlgemuth, 1923, p. 84, his italics]

That is, censorship should be seen as a description of repression rather than as an explanation (i.e., censorship simply means inhibition/repression). Nevertheless, Jones elsewhere writes, with respect to the "compartments" of the topographical systems, "There would appear to be a selective agency at work on which depends the admission of a given thought from one of the mental compartments to another" (Jones, 1949, p. 28). How else is one to understand this if not as a homuncular agency which selects what may or may not become conscious? If this is *not* to be conceptualized as a homuncular entity, then the problem remains exactly how this "selective agency" should be understood.

The censor in psychoanalysis today

Gillett (1987) claims that the censor that prevents mental contents from entering awareness is standard psychoanalytic theory: "I believe that there is general agreement today that all mental contents must pass some kind of censorship before becoming conscious. Questions remain over the number and location of the censorships" (Gillett, 1987, p. 540).

In the latter respect, Sandler and Sandler (1983) propose a "two censorship" model, which develops Freud's suggestions of a second censorship between the *Pcs.* and the *Cs.* Both censors are said to act independently of the ego, and neither constitute "conscious" reluctance, which would constitute a *third* censorship: "there exists a further censorship, a third one, between what the patient is consciously aware of and what he tells the analyst" (Sandler & Sandler, 1983, p. 417*n*).

Furthermore, such censors are, at times, explicitly discussed in terms of homuncular agencies. Colace (2010), for instance, equates the "superegoic functions" with the censorship (pp. 32, 55), writing that the superego is "a sort of special agency existing within the ego, vested with certain important functions such as moral conscience, self-observation, self-evaluation, and formation of ideals" (p. 129). Colace refers to this superego as an "intrapsychic selective mechanism . . . [that] reviews and excludes (repression) the contents unacceptable under the ethical, aesthetical, or social profile that cannot be admitted to the *Pcs.* (or *Cs.*) system because they would cause the development of unpleasant affects" (p. 30).

Additionally, while not all authors necessarily use the term "censor" explicitly, such selective agents might be invoked, nevertheless. Sandler and Joffe (1969), for instance, describe a "scanning function", which evaluates material prior to conscious awareness:

> we can make use of the concept of a *scanning function* which operates to guide the apparatus to some sort of action. . . . This scanning function is the internal sense organ of the apparatus. It is part of the non-experiential realm, but a major part of its function is to scan the material of the experiential realm *before it reaches consciousness*. [Sandler & Joffe, 1969, p. 83, their italics]

Similarly, Shill (2004) proposes an "appraisal function", and, while not explicitly invoking a censor (Shill says it is the "ego's appraisal"), a censor is implicated, nevertheless, since it acts independently of the ego and appraises "unconscious wishes" before conscious awareness (p. 129). Another example of cognizing agencies is found in Gillett's (1990) "double-prediction" model, which posits two "predictor" agencies, the first predicting "the consequences of allowing any given mental content pressing toward consciousness to become conscious" and, if "the prediction of danger alone is sufficiently great, a 'decision' is made by the censorship to initiate defence of that content" (p. 552). Alternatively, predictor two regulates "the intensity of the anxiety response in situations of intrapsychic conflict" and "attempts to predict the probable failure or success of defence against the dangerous content" (p. 553) and, thus, both predictors have a cognizing and censoring role.

On the other hand, other authors fall back on what Freud (1923b) calls the "unconscious ego" to explain repression. For instance, Langnickel and Markowitsch write that "only the *unconscious* part of the ego is supposed to be doing the repressing . . . and . . . there is no conscious process of repression by the ego" (Langnickel & Markowitsch, 2006, p. 525, their italics). While, to an extent, this claim is unproblematic (as will be discussed later), the question here is whether this "unconscious part of the ego" acts independently of the general ego so that it becomes an independent cognizing agency. It is clear that, in some cases, the unconscious ego is treated as an independent censor. For example, Gillett explicitly treats the unconscious ego as an independent agency to the ego:

> The *conscious ego* concept I endorse is similar to that of a central executive, a familiar concept in cognitive psychology. The *unconscious* ego

is also a central executive with functions limited to those required for the regulation of defence. I regard the conscious ego as distinct from the unconscious ego because it has no knowledge of the operations of the unconscious ego. Although both perform as "central executives," I see no theoretical justification for assuming they are different aspects of a single system. [Gillett, 1997, p. 482, his italics; cf. Gillett, 2001, pp. 272–273]

The question that requires addressing, then, is whether these or any other accounts of censors are capable of accounting for repression and whether multiple knowers within the individual can be coherently sustained. To assess this, the supposed functioning of the censor is assessed.

Censorship and the concept of "disguise"

A common element in the accounts of censors, above, is the view that, independent of the ego, exists at least one cognizing agency screening mental content before allowing it to become known by the ego. That is, taking Freud's metaphor literally, it appears that an *examining* function (a "watchman") cognizes and evaluates other mental processes (impulses and desires) before either allowing or forbidding them entry to consciousness. The immediate problem recognized by some of the authors above involves invoking a homunculus and all the associated problems therewith (Wegner, 2005). That is, explaining the censor's activity is still required, which would presumably fall back upon an account in terms of desires and beliefs attributed to the censor. However, the problem of the homunculus is compounded by Freud's discussion of the censor *disguising* mental content. While the censor is said to prevent wishes and desires from entering conscious awareness, it is also said to "disguise" this content, and, to this end, the censoring agency deliberately changes appearances of the target into an acceptable form for the ego: "the second agency (censorship) allows nothing to pass without exercising its rights and making such modification as it thinks fit in the thought which is seeking admission to consciousness" (Freud, 1900a, p. 144). In this respect, the censoring agency is also said to employ symbolism in order to disguise the forbidden content: "It is plausible to suppose, however, that the dream-censorship finds it convenient to make use of symbolism, since it leads towards the same end—the strangeness and incomprehensibility of dreams" (Freud, 1916–1917, p. 168).

Furthermore, Freud writes that displacement is either entirely or partly the result of the censorship and, thus, not resulting from so-called primary process mentation: "we know that it [displacement] is entirely the work of the dream-censorship" (Freud, 1916–1917, p. 174). Similarly,

> Omission, modification, fresh grouping of the material—these, then, are the activities of the dream-censorship and the instruments of dream-distortion. The dream-censorship itself is the originator, or one of the originators, of the dream-distortion . . . We are in the habit of combining the concepts of modification and re-arrangement under the term 'displacement'. [Freud, 1916–1917, p. 140]

Since a "disguise" generally involves altering appearance *in order* not to be recognized, many authors note that censoring agency operates here as a sophisticated, *rational* agent, "having beliefs and desires and exercising rational capacities" (Gardner, 1993, p. 49; cf. De Sousa, 1976; Gouws, 2000). The censor must know which wishes and desires are forbidden and acceptable, and know appropriate strategies for censoring and distorting repressed material in such a way as to make the offensive material appear innocuous to the conscious system. Critics have seized on this account of the censor by noting the implications:

> If our conscious mind cannot bear to process certain memories, then the decision to keep these memories repressed elsewhere, in "the" unconscious, could only originate in the unconscious. Consequently, "the" unconscious must have an autonomous quality—an inner "homunculus" which must somehow possess the omnipotence or wisdom to "know" what is best for the conscious self. [Bonanno & Keuler, 1998, p. 439; cf. Rofé, 2008, p. 66]

Similarly, Thalberg (1992) writes,

> Given Freud's general view of human motivation, can we suppose that any 'watchman' is 'conscientious' enough to care what happens to his fellow citizens? Why does he call them from their beds to help him quell 'disturbances'? Does he otherwise risk harm? *Any* reply we make to such questions will sound capricious—or deranged. Yet if we

were discussing ordinary sentries and villagers, we could find answers. [Thalberg, 1982, p. 254, his italics]

Thalberg's objection here is against specifying the motives of the censor in terms of intentional behaviour, which he believes is applicable only at the level of "person". However, explanations in terms of "persons" are also not immune to problems of teleology, and the problem here is not with multiple knowers *per se*, but with providing a non-teleological account within a plausible biological framework. Instead, if one is to avoid both teleology and the vacuity of homuncular accounts, then some postulation of the censor's motivation (the censor's "desire" component), as well as beliefs concerning how to avoid recognition, must be postulated. Here, Freud suggests that the censoring agency either acts altruistically (Freud, 1900a, p. 529, 1937c, p. 236), or is motivated by its own displeasure towards the repressed material (Freud, 1916–1917, p. 139):

Take up any political newspaper and you will find that here and there the text is absent and in its place nothing except the white paper is to be seen. This, as you know, is the work of the press censorship. In these empty places there was *something that displeased the higher censorship* authorities and for that reason it was removed ... [Freud, 1916–1917, p. 139; my italics]

Before evaluating this, however, another twist in Freud's thinking requires discussion: Freud postulates that the repressed itself acts as an agency deliberately disguising itself to evade the censorship.

Censorship from the repressed

If the teleology of the homuncular censor was not a big enough problem, not only does the censor act in order *to* disguise the repressed, but the repressed disguises itself *in order to* avoid repression (e.g., Freud, 1900a, p. 142, 1901a, p. 677; 1916–1917, p. 139). Here, Freud writes that "social life ... has provided us with our familiar analogy with the dream-censorship" (Freud, 1900a, p. 471), and an example given by Freud is the writer who wishes to express views deemed unacceptable by the government and so subsequently disguises their work in simile and metaphor:

A . . . difficulty confronts the political writer who has disagreeable truths to tell to those in authority. If he presents them undisguised, the authorities will suppress his words after they have been spoken, if his pronouncement was an oral one, but beforehand, if he had intended to make it in print. A writer must beware of the censorship, and on its account he must soften and distort the expression of his opinion. According to the strength and the sensitiveness of the censorship he finds himself compelled either merely to refrain from certain forms of attack, or to speak in allusions in place of direct references, or he must conceal his objectionable pronouncement beneath some apparently innocent disguise: for instance, he may describe a dispute between two Mandarins in the Middle Kingdom, when the people he really has in mind are officials in his own country. The stricter the censorship, the more far-reaching will be the disguise and the more ingenious too may be the means employed for putting the reader on the scent of the true meaning. [Freud, 1900a, p. 142]

The author has seen in advance which passages might give rise to objections from the censorship and has on that account toned them down in advance, modified them slightly, or has contented himself with approximations and allusions to what would genuinely have come from his pen. In that case there are no blank places in the paper, but circumlocutions and obscurities of expression appearing at certain points will enable you to guess where regard has been paid to the censorship in advance. [Freud, 1916–1917, p. 139]

This corresponds with what Freud refers to as "dissimulation", whereby one person deceives another through disguise.

Where can we find a similar distortion of a psychical act in social life? Only where two persons are concerned, one of whom possesses a certain degree of power which the second is obliged to take into account. In such a case the second person will distort the psychical acts or, as we might put it, will dissimulate. [Freud, 1900a, pp. 141–142; cf. p. 471]

The repressed, thus, creates the substitutes and distortions with the intention of evading the censorship, replacing objectionable material with content "that appears innocent to the censorship", and using substitutes such as symbolism or analogy (Freud, 1905c, p. 171). From this point of view, displacement, condensation, allusion, and substitution, are not the tools then simply of the censor—or the primary process operations—but, rather, the chief means for forbidden wishes to evade the censorship (Freud, 1900a, p. 322, 1905c, pp. 171–172, 1933a, p. 18). Clearly, however, for the repressed to be effective in pre-emptive censorship, it must know in advance what is forbidden and what might (possibly) act as a successful disguise. That is, the repressed must know prior to forming the substitute what is *both* objectionable *and* unobjectionable in order to disguise itself to avoid being detected and censored. Thus, there are now at least three cogniz-ing agencies; the conscious system (or ego), the censor, and the "repressed".

While it is uncommon to see references to the repressed disguising itself in contemporary psychoanalytic accounts, the teleology of disguise can be found, nevertheless, within modern psychoanalytic theorizing. Colace (2010), for instance, writes that the "inadmissible latent dream contents . . . are unconsciously disguised and distorted to become unrecognizable and innocuous to the conscious system" (p. 129). This raises the question as to whether such teleology can be recast coherently in deterministic terms and, as discussed earlier, we could propose that both the censor and "repressed" have beliefs and desires (standing as causal antecedents) to explain censorship: the censor desires to protect the ego and believes that distorting wishes will achieve this, while the repressed similarly desires expression and believes that self-censorship might allow this expression. Never-theless, Freud's account of repression, in terms of disguise and censor-ing and repressed agencies, is necessarily problematic, since it requires an impossible account of mind.

The transcendental censor

A major problem with Freud's account is that it invokes a transcen-dental agent (or agents) standing over and above the ego, an issue and brought out in Sartre's (1956) famous critique of Freud's censor in dis-cussion of self-deception or "Bad Faith" (*mauvaise foi*). Sartre attacks Freud's strategy of explaining repression by partitioning the mind into distinct agents; the repressed desire, the conscious ego, and the "censor". In line with the earlier discussion, Sartre notes that this censor must be an independent consciousness, discerning what shall and shall not become conscious; a "Second Mind", in Gardner's (1993,

p. 42) terms, since it is required to monitor and guard between the division:

> the censor in order to apply its activity with discernment must know what it is repressing. In fact if we abandon all the metaphors representing the repression as the impact of blind forces, we are compelled to admit that the censor must choose and in order to choose must be aware of so doing. How could it happen otherwise that the censor allows lawful sexual impulses to pass through, that it permits needs (hunger, thirst, sleep) to be expressed in clear consciousness? And how are we to explain that it can relax its surveillance, that it can even be deceived by the disguises of the instinct. [Sartre, 1956, p. 52]

Similarly, Sartre notes that Freud's account of the repressed disguising itself invokes another rational centre of agency:

> How can the repressed drive "disguise itself" if it does not include (1) the consciousness of being repressed, (2) the consciousness of having been pushed back because it is what it is, (3) a project of disguise? No mechanistic theory of condensation or of transference can explain these modifications by which the drive itself is affected, for the description of the process of disguise implies a veiled appeal to finality. [Sartre, 1956, p. 53]

What Sartre is drawing attention to here is that Freud is holding two seemingly contrary pictures of mind, one explicable in terms of mechanistic operations (such as primary process thinking), the other in terms of intentional behaviour and rational activity. However, while Sartre's analysis is problematic in many respects (e.g., it is based on a Cartesian view of consciousness, which cannot be coherently sustained), a valid point that he does make is that the censoring agency in Freud's view must be a cognizing entity *superior* to the conscious system (cf. Mirvish, 1990, p. 225). To fulfil its duties, the censor must be capable of transcending the various conscious and unconscious systems, since it must be capable of assessing so-called unconscious thoughts prior to the ego (Gardner, 1993; Mirvish, 1990). The censor's superordinate status thus entails knowing wishes while they are unconscious, which specifically requires knowing them when they are systematically *Ucs.* (before they become preconscious), knowing what is forbidden and what is to be allowed, being able to manipulate the workings of the mental apparatus to prevent and inhibit impulses deemed unlawful. The censor's transcendental nature is further demonstrated by the fact that the censoring agency transcends the need to sleep, remaining vigilant ("awake") while the ego sleeps:

> It has been shown that a part of the attention which operates during the day continues to be directed towards dreams during the state of sleep, that it keeps a check on them and criticizes them and reserves the power to interrupt them. It has seemed plausible to recognize in the mental agency which thus remains awake the censor [*Zensor*] to whom we have had to attribute such a powerful restricting influence upon the form taken by dreams. [Freud, 1900a, p. 505, added in 1914; cf. Freud, 1914c, pp. 97–98]

Accordingly, the relation between the censor and the ego is asymmetrical, since the censor clearly has power over the ego (with privileged access to the workings of the mind) and the ego, for the most part, is ignorant of the censor. Gardner (1993) thus concludes that the censor "must have a greater capacity than any other part of the mind for (i) representing the contents of other mental parts, and (ii) controlling mental events" (p. 48). Accordingly, the censoring agency is superior to the ego and equivalent to a transcendental, omnipotent figure inhabiting the mind. Similarly, all of these problems extend similarly to the "repressed agency", since it must, to disguise itself, have all of the capacities referred to above.

Providing a coherent origin of such an agency also appears inexplicable (Boag, 2006b). How could such a censor, superior to the ego in all respects, plausibly develop in a normal account of human development? In response, Colace (2006) believes that the origins of the censor can be explained simply in terms of the development of the superego: "The 'censor of dreams' conceptualized as superego, legitimates the hypothesis of a separate agency by virtue of which there is censorship activity" (Colace, 2006, p. 24). However, it does not follow that a *transcendental* homunculus can simply be accounted for in terms of biological and social pressures giving rise to the superego. The superego itself, if anything, arises from identification (e.g., the child identifies with the father), such that the child acts towards itself as it might imagine his or her father to do:

> The basis of the process is what is called 'identification'—that is to say, the assimilation of one ego to another one, as a result of which the first

ego behaves like the second in certain respects, imitates it and in a sense takes it up into itself. [Freud, 1933a, p. 63]

While Freud's account here of the superego involves comprehensible normal processes, the postulation of a transcendental independent agency does not follow. Furthermore, without a plausible biological (i.e., motivational) framework, there is no adequate account of the censor's motivation, and the censor is, at times, treated as an agency distinct from the drives. For instance, Solms (1997a) contrasts the "instinctual (appetitive) strivings on the one hand, which threaten to disturb sleep, and the censorship on the other hand, which only allows the appetitive strivings to be fulfilled in disguised (and hallucinatory) form" (p. 174). The immediate problem with this approach is then explaining the censor's motives: why, for instance, should the censorship desire to frustrate some and not other impulses, and if it is not based on drives, then what provides the motivational impetus for the censorship itself? In contrast, the discussion in the previous chapter shows that Freud provides a drive-based account of repression in terms of conflicting motives, whereby the belief that satisfying one drive's aims will lead to frustration of another (Freud, 1915d, p. 147). In this view, there is not a drive-independent censor frustrating drives via repression, but simply drives frustrating one another. This latter account provides both a more simple and theoretically justified account of the motivation of repression, because the act of repression becomes as "appetitive" as any other "striving".

Further problems with the censor

A further problem with postulating a censor to explain repression is that the censor is inferred from the effects to be explained (censorship): the censor, used to explain censoring, is itself solely inferred from the act of censoring. Macmillan (1991) similarly notes a general problem with using "repression" as an explanatory construct if repression simply renames the phenomenon to be explained (see also Boag, 2007a), and observing the apparent effect of censoring and invoking a "censor" then to explain it is akin to a crude faculty psychology, whereby an *ad hoc* "censoring faculty" of the mind is used to explain censoring. Explaining any phenomenon with respect to a faculty based purely upon the phenomenon to be explained is open to the charge of circular explanation (see Boag, 2011a; Gardner, 1993; Passmore, 1935). As Anspach (1998) notes, "to say that the unconscious drive is repressed by an agent of repression called the "censor" amounts to no more than putting a name on the phenomenon to be explained" (Anspach, 1998, p. 67; cf. Sartre, 1956, p. 53). Instead, if repression is to be explained via a censor, then some account of it, independent of its effects, is required. However, this is the problem: the only evidence that can be discerned for the censor is the act of censoring itself, since it is "not directly observable by any means" (Solms, 2006, p. 99). Consequently, Anspach (1998) rightly argues that Freud's account of the censor appears to reify censoring activity into an "autonomous consciousness", solely inferred from the act of censoring.

In addition to the issue of circularity and reification above, and given the account of mentality discussed earlier, whatever is considered a knower must possess its own intrinsic qualities existing independently of the act of cognition. As Neu (1988) notes, some objective manner is required for justifying one account of multiple agents over another (p. 88) and there is a problem with respect to pseudo-explanations of mental events whereby the mind becomes populated with agencies invoked from observation of effects. For instance, Gillett's (1990) double-predictor model assumes two predictors "predicting" various outcomes, yet the only evidence for these is the hypothesized predicting that they perform (i.e., no independent evidence for them exists). Without independent evidence, the mind, potentially, becomes populated with as many agencies as there are mental activities. Erdelyi (1974), however, believes that there is not a problem here, since computers can perform tasks such as repression. Responding to concerns of positing "little people" (homunculi), he writes,

> In this computer age, with man's head infested with (among other things) veritable societies of demons—e.g., feature demons, cognitive demons, decision demons, etc.—it is probably fair to say that the problem of the teleological homunculi has been over taken by time. It is clear ... that a system with control processes for internal regulation, including regulation of input, violates no sacrosanct edict of science, nor does it imply the literal existence of little men or demons in the head. [Erdelyi, 1974, p. 4]

However, shifting the responsibility of repression or censorship to either a "society of demons" or any other set of homunculi is simply *ad hoc* speculation, since sub-systems can be invented to explain any psychological phenomenon. Furthermore, sub-systems can be postulated *ad infinitum*, since any number of sub-systems can be postulated to explain any psychological activity: "Mental activity being viewed in this way, the number of possible agencies within agencies approaches infinity" (Schafer, 1973, p. 271). However, this is not to say that multiple knowers within a person do not exist, or that we must even reject talk of even a single knower, as Talvitie (2009) suggests. Yu (2006) correctly notes that any account of repression requires an "appraising organization" (p. 54), and so any account of repression requires at least one cognizing subject and there might be legitimate arguments for the existence of multiple knowers.

Mental conflict and the possibility of multiple knowers

Despite the implications of the censor discussed above, Freud explicitly rejected the concept of multiple knowers, and instead proposed that the "same consciousness turns to one or the other of these groups alternately" (Freud, 1915e, p. 171). Thus, what Freud is suggesting is that, despite conflicting motivational aims, such aims still belong to the one "person" (i.e., a single agent) (e.g., Gardner, 1993, p. 75; Schafer, 1973, p. 262). As Gardner (1993) writes, "Persons do have parts, in the sense that their personalities comprehend contrasting sources of motivation: but not in the sense that their minds have parts which function like agents" (p. 78). In this view, conflict emerges not between multiple agents, but between a single subject deciding on different courses of action. However, if the "person" acts as an executive, arbitrating between different desires, then this person must also be motivated (i.e., have his or her own desires) to explain how he or she arbitrates between one course of action and another (see Boag, 2005; Maze, 1983, 1987; Michell, 1988). If so, then there are at least two poles of agency, consisting of "person desires" and "non-person desires", and so not a single agent, as first presumed.

An alternative viewpoint, traceable to Plato, is that psychological conflict implicates a plurality of knowers (desirers), since it is difficult to account for conflicting intentions and desires within a truly unified agent (see Boag, 2005; Neu, 1988). One such account is provided by Maze (1983), who proposes that the drives themselves are the knowers and that there must be multiple drives/knowers to account for conflict and repression:

> It is only from a pluralistic view . . . that one can begin to make sense of the facts of internal conflict and of repression, of the situation in which one part of the psychological apparatus knows something that another part does not know. [Maze, 1983, p. 162]

Petocz (1999) similarly writes that "in order to accommodate the fact of mental conflict, of a conflict of interests within a single mind, there must be a plurality of drives—at least two" (p. 221). A strength of this position is that the drives can be distinguished from their effects and their activity explained deterministically rather than teleologically. Rather than "whole persons", these drives are sub-sets of neural structures (biomechanical systems utilizing cognition), which are the smallest units comprising the "knowers". Each drive is a bearer of full propositional attitude (desires, beliefs, fears) relevant to their somatic source component and subsequent policy, and so each individual is made up of a small community of these drives, "each of which is a knower and a doer" (Maze, 1987, p. 197). However, such drives are not homunculi, since,

> unlike the whole person each has, in effect, only one motive, never restrains itself from seeking satisfaction, knows only a portion of the aggregate body of information, and suffers no internal conflict. An instinctual drive can no more restrain itself from working than any motor can, once the switches are thrown. If its operation is to be arrested, then that must be through some influence external to itself—in the case of repression, from other instinctual drives. [Maze, 1987, p. 197]

Once activated, these drives are thoroughly "self'-serving" in relation to their biologically wired interests and learnt sources of gratification and frustration. In this respect, their activity is explicable via psycho-mechanical principles, fully determined by the relevant causal conditions. The behaviour of the "whole person" results from both facilitating and inhibiting influences emerging from the interaction of these drives and, since such drives are present at birth, there is no difficulty in accounting for their origins. Accordingly, an account of multiple knowers is defensible, but does not provide justification for positing a transcendental censoring agency.

If we reject the censor, need we reject "censoring"?

Given that no evidence is provided of the censoring agency independently of censoring itself, such accounts of the censor appear to be *ad hoc* devices that simply reify censoring activity into an agent responsible for censoring. Furthermore, the teleological and transcendental aspects of the censor further make the censor logically indefensible. Accordingly, any account of repression that promotes censoring agencies that stand prior to the ego and determine what can and cannot become conscious should be rejected. Subsequently, with respect to debates about empirical evidence for or against the censor, Mackay (2006) rightly notes that this "is an example of where attention to the conceptual problems in a theory would cut short a large amount of testing and debate over the empirical evidence for the theory" (p. 41). That is, there is no use attempting to empirically evaluate Freud's censor, since it is logically incoherent and so could not possibly ever be the case.

However, if censoring is simply a description of the effects of repression (i.e., certain targets are prevented from being known in their primary form), then there is no reason to reject the possibility of censoring activity. The problem is specifically with invoking a censor to explain this activity, and so a relevant question is whether this repressing activity can be coherently explained deterministically and within a comprehensible account of mind. The answer here comes from Freud himself, who, when in more sober moments, attributes repression not to a censor, but instead censoring is simply an outcome of motivational conflict whereby one drive cancels out another. The apparent censorship effect occurs due to the inhibition of associations between mental content and the subsequent forming of substitutes along associative paths. The effect of censorship still requires a dynamic explanation, since one part of the mental apparatus prevents another part from expression, leading to the formation of substitute aims (Boag, 2006b). So, for instance, a desire for *p* might be inhibited, but along associative paths the persisting desire is displaced on to substitute q (presumably under the belief that p and q are equivalent). While how, precisely, this occurs requires fleshing out, explaining this distortion of p to q does not require the teleological notion of disguise by either the censor or the repressed agency. Instead, under the pressure of inhibition, substitutes form via association. Thus, it is possible to agree with Colace (2010) that "the essence of the disguise-censorship model remains the assumption that a substantial portion of dream-bizarreness has a motivational–conflictive origin" (p. 198), but, in contradistinction to Colace's censor account, "censorship" can occur *without* postulating a censoring agency which suffers from the defects discussed above. Nevertheless, repression still appears to require at least one subject knowing the target of repression.

Note

1. The State court is the court of first instance and the Federal court the court of last instance.

CHAPTER TEN

Repression and neural processes

The role of neurological processes in repression

The increasing technical sophistication of brain imaging techniques promises much in terms of advances in understanding the biological bases of psychological processes generally. However, making the most of such advances requires a matching conceptual sophistication, and while there has been a growing willingness to understand psychoanalytic processes in terms of neuroscientific ones, it is not always clear that the logical implications of various claims have been carefully thought through. In particular, acknowledging what neuroscience *cannot* tell us is required if we are to avoid theoretically overstepping from the available findings. To illustrate this, this chapter examines some of the neural candidates for repression and discusses what can and cannot be inferred from the relevant findings.

Theoretical issues in neuroscience

Bennett and Hacker (2003) have recently drawn attention to the ongoing philosophical issues in neuroscience and note the importance of conceptual clarification for both theorizing and interpreting findings relevant to neuroscience. One issue is the "mereological fallacy", involving confusion between part/whole relations. Bennett and Hacker claim that statements such as "the brain experiences x" or "the brain believes y" should instead be phrased as "the person experiences x" or the "person believes y": "psychological predicates apply paradigmatically to the *human being (or animal) as a whole*, and *not* to the body or its parts" (Bennett & Hacker, 2003, p. 73, their italics).

While there are various strengths to this argument (to be discussed below), one initial concern is that arguing "paradigmatically" appears to rely on assertion rather than on actual argument. What is required instead is demonstration that psychological predicates cannot possibly be attributed to some part rather than the whole person. As discussed earlier, any psychological act requires a cognizing subject, and while we can in a general sense ascribe psychological predicates to the "person" (or some preconceived "whole"), we need to be careful to avoid reifying the "person" into something standing over and above the body's parts. In fact, explaining behaviour at the level of the "person" is potentially problematic, since the person then appears to decide and act rationally (freely even), when instead so-called human complexity and rationality could result from conflicting primitive drives (and the forced compromise and competition between them). Furthermore, since parts of the body can be removed from the "whole" (leaving other parts to do the psychological work), there appears to be no *a priori* problem with the claim that, in the final analysis, when the body is stripped of its cognitively superfluous machinery, it will be the brain, or parts thereof, that does the knowing via the nervous system. In fact, the claim that the brain evaluates and "decides" (say, what course of action to take) is no more problematic than attributing evaluation and decision to the "person": in both cases some mechanistic account must be provided to make such a claim intelligible (i.e., something greater than "choosing" must be posited to avoid explanatory vacuity).

Bennett and Hacker (2003) do draw attention to a legitimate problem in terms of part/whole relations, but, rather than arguing paradigmatically, the issue is better addressed with respect to whether any postulated knower has sufficient conditions to engage in cognition. For instance, while there does not seem to me any *a priori* problem with stating that the "brain knows the hand", there does appear something absurd about the claim that "the hand knows the brain". Why? The distinction appears to hinge upon whether the brain has sufficient machinery or hardware to psychologically know states of affairs (via the nervous system). Bennett and Hacker, however, write,

> The brain neither sees, *nor is it blind*—just as sticks and stones are not awake, *but they are not asleep either*. The brain makes no decisions, but neither is it indecisive. Only what *can* decide can be indecisive. So, too, the brain cannot be conscious; only the living creature whose brain it is can be conscious—or unconscious. *The brain is not a logically appropriate subject for psychological predicates*. [Bennett & Hacker, 2003, p. 72, their italics]

However, the analogy used here is plainly problematic, since the brain differs from inanimate objects such as sticks by having a blood supply (etc.) as well as access to the world via the nervous/perceptual systems. Therefore, the relevant question should be whether some structure X *has sufficient conditions for psychological activity* when considering claims about brain parts. For this reason, one would not state that a single neuron is a knower, but that a set of structures in the brain with sufficient complexity might be, and, as postulated earlier, one possibility here is that the smallest units comprising the "knowers" in the cognitive relation are the psychobiological drive structures, which, via the nervous system, know states of affairs relevant to gratification and frustration (Boag, 2005; Maze, 1983). Such an empirical question is not an easy one to answer (since it involves witnessing structure x (for instance) engage in some psychological act y), but this is not, in principle, impossible to address.

What Bennett and Hacker (2003) do draw attention to via the mereological fallacy is the problem of the teleological homunculus discussed earlier, whereby a part of the brain acts as a transcendental knower standing outside of what can be considered ordinary psychological activity. So, in addition to having sufficient components for knowing, any explanation of the part's role in the person's activities must necessarily not transcend the limits of ordinary knowing capabilities. However, we find accounts whereby "systems" and "brains" act independently of the person, regulating activity prior to the ordinary cognizing individual. For instance, in discussing brain processes related to inhibition, Chee, Sriram, Soon, and Lee (2000) refer to a "supervisory system" (p. 135), which supervises and inhibits habitual responses and which would appear functionally equivalent to a censor. Similarly, Ramachandran (1994) writes that defence mechanisms "arise because the brain tried to arrive at the most probable and globally consistent interpretation of the evidence derived from multiple sources" (p. 325), comparing the brain here to an army general planning an attack and having to "collect evidence from a large number of scouts, weigh the evidence, and arrive at a firm decision" (p. 325). In both cases the "supervisory system" or "brain as general" occur independently of the "person" (i.e., stand outside of ordinary cognitive processes) and so both functionally stand as transcendental censors.

How such systems reasonably function is unclear, but accounts suggest that these systems appear to engage in "decision making" prior to the ordinary knowing individual. For instance, under the heading "How the prefrontal cortex chooses how to respond", Pally (1998) writes that the prefrontal cortex "can shift from the automatic responses of the amygdala to decision and choices about what response is indicated based on prior experience" (p. 354). Similarly, "The prefrontal cortex, in relation to its working memory function . . . anticipates the outcome of various response options and considers what might go wrong if one's plan fails" (p. 354). This suggests that the prefrontal cortex is a separate agent to the person, and both somehow knows what available responses there are and can anticipate their outcome, prior to the individual's knowledge.

None of this is to say that certain brain structures are not necessary for particular aspects of functioning. However, what requires clarification is whether certain brain structures are simply necessary for the organism (or, perhaps more specifically, the drives) to engage in certain activities or whether such brain structures constitute an agent with desires and beliefs independent of the person. For instance, while the association between the prefrontal cortex and inhibitory functioning appears generally accepted (e.g., Kaplan-Solms & Solms, 2000; Ridderinkhof, Wildenberg, Segalowitz, & Carter, 2004; van Gaal, Ridderinkhof, Fahrenfort, Scholte, & Lamme, 2008), there is a distinction between the claim that specific brain structures are necessary for such activities (i.e., the prefrontal cortex is a necessary structure for inhibition) and another to attribute psychological activities to these structures (e.g., the prefrontal cortex "decides" what is inhibited).

The amygdala and unconscious threat detection

One relevant avenue to discussions of neural structures and repression relates to investigation of the amygdala and fear conditioning to aversive stimuli. The role of the amygdala in fear conditioning appears broadly accepted (LeDoux, 1990; 1995; LeDoux & Schiller, 2009; Liotti & Panksepp, 2004; Maren & Quirk, 2004; Öhman, 2009) and the role of the amygdala in inhibitory processes has also long been recognized (see Diamond, Balvin, & Diamond, 1963).[1] Subsequently, the amygdala has been invoked with approval by psychoanalytic writers with respect to understanding defensive functioning (e.g., Pally, 1998; Pugh, 2002) and what is of particular significance is the discussion of unconscious fear responses whereby the amygdala is "involved in the implicit, unconscious processing of emotion" (Pugh, 2002, p. 1380). Within the context of implicit memory, this unconscious processing of emotion could be taken to suggest that such processing occurs non-psychologically (e.g., Fonagy & Target, 2000, p. 414), and some non-psychoanalytic researchers do claim that the evidence suggests that fear appraisal can occur in the absence of "conscious" recognition of the eliciting stimulus via subcortical processing (Öhman, Carlsson, Lundqvist, & Ingvar, 2007, p. 181) and Öhman (2009) even writes that "awareness is not a necessary condition for fear conditioning" (p. 144). In any case, leaving aside the question as to what is precisely meant here by "unconscious", such findings have important implications for repression but have been, in certain respects, problematically embraced by some psychoanalytic authors. To illustrate this, a brief discussion of a non-problematic interpretation is proposed before turning to a problematic interpretation. To begin with, Pally (1998) discusses two functionally independent routes, one sub-cortical and the other involving cortical processes, involved in fear responses:

> In route (1) sensory information goes from the thalamus directly to the amygdala and rapidly triggers fear in response to simple stimulus cues. In route (2) sensory information is routed from the thalamus to the cortex and hippocampus and is then projected to the amygdala, taking longer to trigger fear in response to more complex stimulus objects. [Pally, 1998, p. 353]

Leaving aside some of the more complex issues (e.g., simple versus complex stimuli), Pally (1998) writes that "[s]ince conditioning can occur unconsciously through amygdala circuits, the person may not be aware of what the current stimulus trigger is" (p. 355). If the claim here is simply that a person can evaluate x to be a threat (which necessarily involves the functioning amygdala) and that this threat detection can occur unconsciously (such that S evaluates x to be a threat but is unaware of this evaluation), then this is a perfectly legitimate claim to make. As discussed in earlier chapters, for threat evaluation to occur then some target must be cognized and evaluated as a threat but such an evaluation does not necessitate that this evaluation is itself necessarily known (which would require a second mental act). Accordingly, findings relating to the amygdala and threat detection might provide evidence of the biological foundations for unconsciously occurring threat detection. Thus, the amygdala appears a prime candidate for a neurological basis of major aspects of repression (unconscious threat detection) and even critics of Freudian theory accept the evidence of unconscious threat detection (for instance, Rofé (2008) writes that "there seems to be strong evidence for unconscious sensitivity to threatening stimuli", p. 70).

However, while the above claim is non-problematic, Pally's further claim invokes the amygdala and other structures as homuncular agencies functionally equivalent to Freud's censor. For example, Pally (1998) refers to "appraisal centres" in the brain (e.g., amygdala, orbitofrontal cortex, anterior insulat cortex) and writes that these "[a]ppraisal centres evaluate stimuli as to their overall significance for the organism" (p. 350). Pally elaborates,

> It is considered that the amygdala makes more simple appraisals (is a stimulus good or bad? familiar or unfamiliar? safe or dangerous?) in response to simple stimulus cues such as large size, loud noise or wiggling motion. The orbitofrontal cortex reacts to the complex stimulus information of objects, people and events and makes appraisals that are built up from personal experience over the course of one's life. [Pally, 1998, p. 350]

In other words, these "appraisal centres" are now performing psychological activities and making decisions as if each is more or less a person in their own right. In many respects, too, these appraisal centres serve a functionally identical role to the dream censor. For instance, Pally (1998) writes that "[t]he amygdala and orbitofrontal cortex are . . . in an ideal position to *sample, extract and add emotional attributes to ongoing experience*" (p. 351, my italics), which appears to simply repackage Freud's dream censor as brain regions which create "limitations and omissions in the dream-content" and "interpolations and additions to it" (Freud, 1900a, p. 489), prior to the cognizing ego's knowing. Similarly, Joseph (1996) writes that "the amygdala can make fine discrimination between stimuli that are closely versus not so closely associated with fear . . . The amygdala can also anticipate fearful stimuli based on only fragmentary cues or sensory stimuli . . ." (Joseph, 1996, p. 228). The amygdala subsequently is functionally equivalent to a censor that screens information prior to the ego's knowing: "Because it [the amygdala] can anticipate [threat] based merely on fragmentary cues, individuals may come to feel upset, frightened, and yet not know why or what might have triggered these emotions" (Joseph, 1996, p. 228). That is, the amygdala now screens material prior to conscious awareness and protects the individual from potential threatening information.

While there is no logical difficulty with the claim that different parts of the brain might be knowers, whether the amygdala is in a position to evaluate targets and discern whether these are either threatening or non-threatening (independently of the ego), remains to be seen. One immediate problem, at least in Pally's (1998) account, follows from the claim that such decisions occur non-consciously. For instance, Pally writes: "Neuroscience asserts that emotion is processed independently of conscious awareness; not in the dynamic unconscious of Freud but in a biological unconscious governed by the rules and constraints of neural circuitry and neurophysiology" (p. 349). That is, the role of the amygdala is "biological" and non-psychological, or "non-experiential" (cf. Sandler & Joffe, 1969). Now, if the amygdala is relevant to emotional processing, as is generally accepted, and functions non-psychologically, then it is in no position to make "decisions" (at best, "decision" must be meant metaphorically). The amygdala might be a necessary part of brain machinery for repression, but the psychological threat evaluation that is necessary for repression cannot be reduced to the structure's non-psychological functioning.

Nevertheless, there are a variety of strategies attempting to explain repression non-psychologically and, as closer examination reveals, none satisfactorily can explain repression.

Non-conscious defensive processing (neural defence)

Hemispheric specialization and repression

One approach to understanding repression involves hemispheric specialization and failures in transfer across the brain's hemispheres. An early hemispheric model is Kissin's (1986), once described by Jones as the "most detailed of the neurobiological models of repression" (Jones, 1993, p. 71). While hemispheric specialization is also implicated in other accounts of repression or dissociative responses (e.g., Joseph, 1996; Ramachandran, 1994, 1996; Schore, 2001) Kissin's remains the most clearly articulated account. Kissin (1986) postulates two brain mechanisms contributing to repression. The first mechanism involves subcortical processing preventing information reaching higher cortical structures necessary for conscious awareness. These subcortical structures are located in the thalamic–basal ganglia complex close to the hypothalamus and limbic system. A postulate here is that "engrams" (unique patterns of neurophysiological events), corresponding to perceived stimuli, might either have positive or negative emotional charges, and when perceiving stimuli at the subcortical level, the "emotional component of stimuli are recognized before the cognitive component" (Kissin, 1986, p. 236). Kissin further claims that subcortical inhibitory processes could reduce the arousal potential of engrams associated with unpleasure, resulting in the cognitive component not reaching the cortex for conscious processing. Consequently, these are prevented from reaching the higher brain areas associated with conscious thinking and remain unconscious.

The more advanced second mechanism involves hemispheric specialization. Kissin postulates that each hemisphere has a peculiar relation to conscious thinking: the left hemisphere is associated with language, making mental content associated with it more readily conscious, whereas "the right hemisphere has a highly unusual kind of consciousness, if indeed it can be called consciousness at all", more similar to that of an altered state of mind (Kissin, 1986, p. 221; cf. Joseph, 1992, 1996). Different features of stimuli activate either the "cognitive/verbal" left hemisphere or the "motivational–emotional" right hemisphere, and differential channelling results in differential hemispheric processing:

> stimuli are differentially screened during upstream [subcortical] processing in the thalamus and basal ganglia with largely cognitive

(particularly verbal) stimuli producing increased activation of the left hemisphere and largely motivational–emotional impulses initiating increased activation of the right hemisphere. Under these circumstances, cognitive percepts (particularly verbal) would be more effectively processed but also more effectively *consolidated and stored* in the left hemisphere: motivational–emotional percepts would similarly be favoured in the right hemisphere. [Kissin, 1986, p. 218, his italics]

In addition to this, emotional stimuli with *negative* charges tend to activate greater reactivity in the right, "less conscious" hemisphere, whereas those with *positive* emotional charge tend to differentially stimulate the "conscious" left hemisphere. Thus, the differential processing and storage causes some material to remain unknown:

Having reached the right hemisphere for processing, such strongly threatening stimuli would tend to remain unconscious because the cognitive valence on the engram had been significantly reduced (with a consequent reduction in associated arousal). Right hemispheric material would also tend to remain unconscious when the left hemisphere was most active, i.e., in alert consciousness. [Kissin, 1986, p. 243]

Furthermore, the earlier model also combines with this hemispheric effect:

more threatening percepts would be cognitively decathected in the hierarchical system during upstream processing and would become, because of their lower energy level, less likely to reach consciousness threshold. As a consequence, they would tend to remain unconscious and . . . would probably be shunted to the right hemisphere for processing. [Kissin, 1986, p. 243]

The important issue here, however, concerns understanding what is meant by "stimuli", and how they are *screened* at the subcortical level. Given the earlier analysis, affects arise as drive-evaluative responses to situations, and so for "stimuli" to be negatively "charged" means first appraising them, which cannot occur prior to cognition (although these appraisals can occur unconsciously). If so, "screening" negative (or positive) engrams for their "emotional charge" could not occur prior to this *psychological* evaluation occurring and so the targets of repression must first be known. Furthermore, Kissin's account does not address why only some and not all right hemispheric material is prevented from consciousness, or why only some and not all unpleasurable memories are repressed. If the first mechanism were efficient, then we would never know painful perceptions, but, as Maze and Henry note,

> The question is, why are certain experiences debarred from consciousness and others not? How would the ones being repressed be 'directed to' the non-verbal right hemisphere while the others were allowed to go to the left? . . . [The] ability to reconcile discrimination of unwelcome impulses with unconsciousness of them remains unexplained. [Maze & Henry, 1996, p. 1091]

Hence, Kissin's account fails because: (i) it proposes screening of emotional stimuli prior to the cognizing subject having the affective relation, and (ii) there is no account of the selectivity of repression.

The neurological censor

Gillett's account proposes a *neurological censor*, "reacting to and transforming the patterning of brain events" (Gillett, 1988, p. 578). Gillett rejects a mental unconscious and, whereas conscious mental events are psychological, "unconscious mental events actually refer to neural events" (1988, p. 570; cf. Searle, 1992; Talvitie, 2009), and, given the complexity and possible combinations of brain cells, a "pattern of neuronal events" could represent specific situations, comparable to a "code":

> [Neural patterns] can be metaphorically regarded as a "code"—just as a foreign language dictionary is a set of correlations between the words of one language and another. If we knew the code in detail, it should be possible *in principle* (precluded practically by its complexity) to "translate" from any one of the intermediate brain events in the causal chain to the perceptual experience in which it culminates. [Gillett, 1988, p. 577]

Gillett proposes here a neurological censor capable of using these patterns to determine what will be censored before reaching conscious awareness:

> The censorship that monitors nonconscious contents for safety before admitting them to consciousness or activating defence against them

does not need to perform such a translation, but rather learns about the potential dangers of some mental contents in the "language" of the brain events at some stage preceding conscious experience. [Gillett, 1988, p. 577]

Although Gillett's censor here appears to be a cognizing subject (a decoder that monitors non-conscious content) he maintains that this censor operates non-experientially (cf. Sandler & Joffe, 1969, p. 82): "Another important point to keep in mind is that talk of the censor 'scanning' memory and forming 'judgements' must be construed as metaphorical, implying no kind of unconscious experiencing" (Gillett, 2001, p. 273; cf. Gillett, 1987, pp. 537–538). That is, the censor's "decision" to repress should be thought of metaphorically as simply a causal relation operating non-intentionally:

The word 'decision' in this context is used metaphorically, derived by analogy from the conscious-process of decision making. Such a metaphorical use of the term 'decide' is widespread in science. In the brain an individual neuron integrates excitatory and inhibitory potentials and 'decides' whether or not to fire. In a heating system the thermostat decides to turn the furnace on or off. Any process of causal interaction in nature can be described metaphorically as a 'decision' ... [Gillett, 1987, p. 537]

Gillett's account can be interpreted here as proposing that when brain state X occurs the brain automatically "switches off" (or represses) the mental act associated with X, rather than a neurological censor "knowing" brain state X, knowing that X is forbidden or threatening, and "deciding" to initiate repression. Presumably, then, after a person experiences event P and distressing affect Q, then, whenever P becomes active, the censoring mechanism here switches off P automatically. Nevertheless, this would appear to still require P's occurrence for the mechanism to operate, and so would not be sufficient for maintaining repression or for accounting for secondary repression and resistance. Furthermore, if Gillett's (1990) account of signal anxiety as an "exciting cause" is also accepted, then the subject must still anxiously know the target of repression for repression to occur, and Gillett, in his later writings, is also inconsistent with regard to his claim that the neurological censor does not enter into psychological relations. Inspection of Gillett's account reveals that he is suggesting that the censor does, in fact, make psychological judgements:

> the censor's safety judgement on a current content pressing toward consciousness is based on its judged connection (associative or symbolic) to the experiences that initially caused the conflict. The censor learns that activation of defence is negatively correlated with the expected trauma. [Gillett, 2001, p. 280]

It is difficult to understand how this "metaphor" can be translated into non-intentional neurological terms. The censor here makes anticipatory judgements concerning safety (if x occurs, then y follows), and learns that defence prevents such occurrences (if not x then not y). Furthermore, the censor appears to know what the brain states refer to (the relation between the brain state and the experience), and Gillett concedes that although "this decision [to repress], itself, is non-experiential, it is strongly influenced by unconscious beliefs about the dangers of object loss, castration, etc. which are unconscious in the dynamic sense" (Gillett, 1987, p. 538). If it is the case that the decision of the censor is influenced by unconscious beliefs about object loss, danger, and so on, then the censor must not only know a particular brain state, X, but also that brain state X refers to something other than itself (i.e., it is dangerous and needs to be censored, etc.). On the other hand, if the censor was said to know: (i) brain state X; (ii) the ego's anxiety response to that (brain state Y), and that (iii) Y implies X be repressed, then the censor is capable of inferring relations (and, hence, knowing when and what to repress) and is no less a cognizing agency. Gillett's model, thus, fails to explain repression non-psychologically and instead postulates a variety of censoring agency, with all the associated problems discussed in the previous chapter.

Non conscious neural defence

A recent neural account of repression that bears some similarity to Gillett's is found in Talvitie's (2009) account of unconscious detections and unconscious neural algorithms. Talvitie and colleagues explicitly rejects the anthropomorphic censor found in Freud's account (e.g., Talvitie & Ihanus, 2003b) and, as noted earlier, unconscious processes in Talvitie's account are best considered in terms of non-psychological neurophysiological activity (Talvitie, 2009, p. 107). In terms of defensive activity, Talvitie discusses *unconscious detections, unconscious neural algorithms,* and *selective non-attending.* While selective non-attending involves turning away from threatening stimuli (i.e., a psychological act), Talvitie's primary explanation of repression is in terms of "unconscious detections" and "unconscious neural algorithms" which are non-psychological (neural) activities. Talvitie (2009) proposes here a two-step account of repression, whereby neural repression occurs prior to selective inattention, in much the same manner as the amygdala is supposed to operate prior to awareness:

> for the first, through unconscious detections and neural loops our acts and conscious states become affected by matters by which we are not conscious. For the second, the mechanism of defensive non-attending restricts the impact of perceptions, ideas, and feelings to our acts and narrative self-consciousness. [Talvitie, 2009, p. 109]

A "conscious detection" "means that one has a sensation of hearing or seeing something" (Talvitie, 2009, p. 76), whereas an "unconscious detection" "does not give rise to a sensation, and as such it does not affect one's behaviour" (p. 77). Nevertheless, such unconscious detection might "trigger" neural algorithms (information processing modes), which might then influence how we interpret events. Accordingly, says Talvitie (2009), "defence mechanisms should . . . be seen as unconsciously [i.e., neurally] triggered information processing modes" (p. 77). Thus, it appears clear that Talvitie is proposing a neural (non-cognitive) defence as distinct from psychological avoidance. However, Talvitie is aware of the potential problem here:

> The above considerations lack one extremely crucial issue: how does the brain "know" which ideas and feelings should be (defensively) non-attended and left non-verbalized? Considering the principles of the four-level model, the answer is obvious. We are able to unconsciously detect and recognize the dangerousness of matters, too. When we have experienced a traumatic situation, we are later able to unconsciously detect stimuli that are related to that situation, and the detection triggers (the unconscious neural algorithms of) defences. [pp. 105–106]

However, Talvitie's solution here is not to explain how this is possible, but, rather, to assert that it is ("the answer is obvious. We are able to unconsciously detect and recognize the dangerousness of matters, too"), and while we might try to invoke neuroscientific explanations at a subpersonal (i.e., non-psychological) level, it is difficult to follow this through. Consider the claim that

> without conscious recognition [i.e., without psychological appraisal] the brain detects a pattern that has previously appeared in a fearful situation. This detection affects the processing of the brain and leads to reactions that refer to fear (bodily reactions, affects, certain kinds of associations and fantasies, for example). [Talvitie & Ihanus, 2005, p. 670]

For this mechanism to work requires the subject knowing the threat (and generating the mentioned responses) prior to the "detection" occurring. Accordingly, appeal to "unconscious detections, representations and neural routines" (Talvitie & Ihanus, 2005, p. 671) conceals an explanatory gap and simply evades addressing the crux of the issue: "threat" evaluation is necessarily a psychological evaluation, and, for making sense of phenomena such as "objectless anxiety", requires some psychological evaluation of a target constituting a threat, independent of the ego's knowing. In fact, Talvitie (2009) writes that "[i]f the landscape appears as threatening, unconscious defences might be triggered, or more or less conscious avoidance may take place" (Talvitie, 2009, p. 106), but, while we can talk of "triggering" or "activating" neural events in purely physical terms, it is difficult to determine how to understand "detection" without some reference to psychological detection. Threat evaluation is necessarily a psychological act (discriminating that X is a threat or non-threat) and so any non-psychological neural account of repression is bound to be problematic.

Nevertheless, despite the aforementioned problems of these accounts of repression, this is not to deny the role of brain state changes underlying the repressive process that might contribute to a more complete account of repression. In particular, the role of neural inhibition potentially provides an important contribution to a modern account of Freudian repression.

Neural inhibition

The accounts above, while problematic in certain respects, do draw attention to the possibility of certain inhibitory brain processes that might *underlie* repression as a psychological activity, and, in this respect, the concept of neural inhibition could be pertinent. The concept of inhibitory processes has had a complicated history in modern thinking, particularly with regard to early postulations of a purely excitatory nervous system (see Diamond, Balvin, & Diamond, 1963). Early accounts of inhibition tended to explain the inhibition of a response in terms of a "countervailing excitatory tendency" (Macmillan, 1992, p. 77) and, thus, account for "the inhibition of one excitatory process by its being overpowered by another" (p. 76). There is more than a passing resemblance here to Freud's discussion of a "volition . . . opposed by a counter-volition" (Freud, 1900a, p. 337) or "two opposing impulses" (Freud, 1909d, p. 192), which has been criticized by Macmillan (1992), who writes,

> unlike the many physiologists (most notably Sherrington) who began to see the need for some kind of central inhibitory process toward the end of the 19th century, Freud never recognized the necessity of such a conception. Why did Freud not draw on an independent central inhibitory process? I believe he could not. He interpreted his clinical observations in terms of an active excitatory process being repressed and maintained in the unconscious by equally active conscious excitatory processes. Whether an idea was repressed or not depended entirely on the magnitude of its quota of energy relative to the quota of energy available to the repressive agency. In this Gall-like conceptualization, an active inhibitory process would have involved too great a self-contradiction. [Macmillan, 1992, pp. 99–100]

However, Macmillan's criticism here is somewhat misleading, since there is no theoretical problem with the postulation of competing motivational sources inhibiting one another (such as postulated in Freudian conflict and repression), since the problem is one of mechanism, not of motive. In fact, the conflict of repression is not dissimilar to approach–avoidance conflict, a concept with a very long history (see Elliot, 2008), and in contemporary neuroscientific research one finds discussion of "conflicting response tendencies" (Ridderinkhof, Wildenberg, Segalowitz, & Carter, 2004, p. 129) or "competition between incompatible inputs" (Redgrave, Prescott, & Gurney, 1999, p. 1016) (i.e., conflicting motives) that can cancel each other out in terms of independent inhibitory processes. Consequently, what is required is simply a correction of a nervous system mechanism to account for how one neural event prevents or obstructs another neural event, rather than a rethinking of the Freudian account of motivational conflict.

Many varieties of neural processes exist, not all of which are motivationally orientated (e.g., spinal reflexes), and while Macmillan (1996) claims that this is problematic ("Central to the problems [of inhibitory processes] . . . is the varied nature of the phenomena and the explanatory mechanisms. It is they which create enormous problems for any single theory", p. 17; cf. 1992, p. 100), this is only a problem *if* one seeks a single theory. While a single theory would indeed be convenient, it is not really up to us to say that nature must conform to our wishes, and there is no problem with postulating varieties of inhibitory processes any more than there is with the claim that varieties of fruit exist. However, Freud's (1950[1895]) unpublished account of neural inhibition, which he termed a "side-cathexis", is problematic. Here, Freud proposes that a set of neurons constituting the ego diverts energy away from neurons previously associated with unpleasure to other neurons, a mechanism that appears both logically and empirically flawed, since not only does it require a teleological censor (i.e., the ego diverting energy—Maze, 1983), but the brain simply does not appear to work in such a manner (McCarley, 1998). Be that as it may, there is no reason to condemn Freud's theory of repression based on an ambitious account he determined not to publish during his lifetime. Instead, the relevant question to ask is whether a variety of neural inhibition, as required for repression to operate, could possibly exist. In this respect, given that there are inhibitory output cells in the central amygdala which prevent emotional reactions from occurring, and cells that further inhibit those inhibitory ones (LeDoux & Schiller, 2009), as well as brain mechanisms that inhibit motor "output" systems (Liotti & Panksepp, 2004), there appears to be no reason why there could not be inhibitory processes relevant to understanding repression.

While the determination of any such processes relevant to repression is an empirical matter, it is worth noting the importance of inhibitory processes generally for understanding human functioning. Deterministically inhibitory processes are logically necessitated to avoid the position that an organism can self-change its own behaviour (Maze, 1983). Consequently, explaining so-called normal behaviour requires an account of neural inhibition, and here Diamond, Balvin, and Diamond (1963) very early on recognize that for efficient action to occur, two responses should not merely be antagonistic, and instead co-ordinated movement requires restraint and inhibition of interfering responses:

> A nervous apparatus is not simply a means for the communication of excitations between differentiated receptor and effector cells. One very important function of a nervous apparatus is to provide an arrangement whereby, when the same organism has multiple response potentialities, one of these can be activated without simultaneously activating the others. If the several response systems are to be coordinated, and not independent, inhibition is required. [Diamond, Balvin, & Diamond, 1963, p. 69]

This has been recently discussed in terms of the "selection problem" with respect to competing responses and response selection determined by an inhibitory account provided by a "winner-takes-all" mechanism (Redgrave, Prescott, & Gurney, 1999; see also Boag, 2007a). While such accounts would appear to highlight the significance of conflicting motivational input, some discussions of inhibitory processes occur without any explicit regard to motivational inputs (e.g., Kok, 1999). Here, the Freudian drive account potentially "fills out" the study of inhibitory processes by recognizing the importance of motivational processes. Furthermore, Freud's drive account also promises to fill the vacuity associated with some discussions of "self-control" and "self-restraint", sometimes associated with "executive functions" (e.g., Barkley, 1997a,b; Salthouse, Atkinson, & Berish, 2003). For instance, Salthouse, Atkinson, and Berish (2003) postulate "capacities and abilities" to account for self-control. Alternatively, Kalenscher, Ohmann, and Güntürkün (2006) attribute "dispositions" and "willpower" to account for decisions and self-control, writing that "[t]he two dispositions that govern decisions about future consequences are called 'impulsivity' and 'self-control'" (p. 203) and that "humans and possibly other animals, too, are (at least occasionally) able to control their actions by sheer will-power" (p. 207). Accounting for self-control or inhibition by proposing a "capacity" or "disposition" is simply providing a descriptive label for that which is to be explained (see also Passmore, 1935, and Boag, 2011a for discussion of the conceptual problems associated with "abilities", "capacities" and "dispositions" as (pseudo)explanations), and, in contradistinction to these conceptually flawed proposals, Freud provides an ultimately much more satisfying proposal that takes into account both endogenous motivational factors and external factors within a developmental context that, in combination, give rise to motivated inhibition.

Another conceptual advantage of postulating a neural mechanism underlying repression is that it circumvents Macmillan's (1991) objection that repression has no potential for referring to a real process, since repression is simply a description of an effect (i.e., ignorance). Macmillan (1991, 1996) argues that, for repression to have any meaning, then it must involve a process which can be described independently of the effects, and, in this sense, neural inhibition is an obvious candidate (Boag, 2007a). Thus, while a neural mechanism could never provide the full picture of repression (since it is a psychological activity and, thus, cannot be reduced to non-psychological physical properties), and the discussion here is empirically speculative, the logical point remains, nevertheless, that there is a suitable candidate for a repressive mechanism (i.e., some species of neural inhibition).

Summary

As with any *psychological* phenomenon, the neurological mechanisms and processes amount to only part of the whole picture, and although neurological processes undoubtedly underlie repression, the general problem with non-psychological accounts of repression is that they attempt to deny the necessary psychological aspects. Specifically, *anxiety* as threat evaluation is inextricably cognitive, so that for anxiety to occur, a subject S must evaluate some event x as threatening. Accordingly, if repression is motivated by anxiety, then accounts that attempt to deny that repression involves psychological processes are necessarily limited. However, what can be taken from the available evidence is that there are neural mechanisms that allow a person to both know and evaluate a threat *without* knowing that the threat is known, which provides a plausible neural mechanism underlying the psychology of repression.

Note

1. The amygdala does, however, appear to be implicated in a variety of motivational, affective, and cognitive activities (see LeDoux & Schiller, 2009, pp. 52–53).

CHAPTER ELEVEN

A psychobiological account of Freudian repression

The developmental context of repression

As Freud repeatedly notes, both biological processes and social constraints underlie instinctual renunciation and repression. The human infant's state of helplessness and dependence upon care-givers for satisfaction and survival means that any threat to their providence (such as the loss of the parents' love) constitutes a *situation of danger* to the developing organism. The care-givers become learnt sources of gratification and their loss is felt to be tantamount to helplessness and frustration. Consequently, the "need for love" develops reflecting this concern:

> The biological factor is the long period of time during which the young of the human species is in a condition of helplessness and dependence. Its intra-uterine existence seems to be short in comparison with that of most animals, and it is sent into the world in a less finished state. As a result, the influence of the real external world upon it is intensified and an early differentiation between the ego and the id is promoted. Moreover, the dangers of the external world have a greater importance for it, so that the value of the object which can alone protect it against them and take the place of its former

intra-uterine life is enormously enhanced. The biological factor, then, establishes the earliest situations of danger and creates the need to be loved which will accompany the child through the rest of life. [Freud, 1926d, pp. 154–155]

Any situation then threatening the loss of object generates an expectation of helplessness and anxiety:

> When the infant has found out by experience that an external, percep-tible object can put an end to the dangerous situation [non-satisfac-tion] which is reminiscent of birth, the content of the danger it fears is displaced from the economic situation on to the condition which determined that situation, viz., the loss of object. It is the absence of the mother that is now the danger; and as soon as that danger arises the infant gives the signal of anxiety, before the dreaded economic situation has set in. [Freud, 1926d, pp. 137–138]

The wealth of evidence from attachment research, and the varieties of attachment pathologies, shows that Freud's position is not implau-sible, especially given evidence of extreme dissociative responses and failures of ego development in response to extremely inadequate object-relations (Schore, 2002, 2009).[1] With respect to Freudian repres-sion, socialization (whereby certain activities meet with social prohi-bition and threaten the withdrawal of parental affection) and mental conflict go hand in hand (Maze, 1983), and the apparent unity of the infant belies the existence of multiple motivational drives. One postu-lation is that it is these drives that learn that their individual gratifi-cation depends upon the care-givers and which come to associate the loss of their affection with the learnt experience of helplessness:

> In general, if a small child comes to feel (what is true by and large) that it cannot maintain its existence unaided in the face of a hostile envi-ronment, one may think that all its instinctual drives become joined in the belief that the gratification of each one is dependent on the parent's affection. [Maze, 1983, p. 170]

Since parental affection is urgently sought and generally contin-gent upon suppression of behaviours disapproved of by the care-givers, behaviours displeasing the parents (such as aggressive and sexual behaviours) become viewed as a threat to the interests of the remaining drives. As Maze notes more generally, the socialization of children involves bringing the drives into conflict with one another:

> The socialisation of children can readily be interpreted as the setting of instinctual drives against one another. Its aim is to bring about the suppression of specific instinctual impulses, particularly, in our society, of the expression of sexuality in its pregenital forms which are all represented as being 'dirty' . . . and of aggression, especially of aggression directed against 'proper authorities' (the parents themselves, in the first instance) . . . This is done by offering rewards and punishments. A reward can only be the gratification of an instinctual drive, and a punishment can only be the frustration of one. [Maze, 1983, p. 171]

The developmental conflict of the Oedipal period that occupied much of Freud's thinking can be understood in terms of the conflict between ego and libidinal instincts (Freud, 1910i), whereby infantile sexual desires towards the care-giver were associated with (imagined) retaliatory mutilation and loss of parental love. Presuming that fear of bodily damage has dominance over sexual gratification, Oedipal sexuality becomes the target of repression (cf. Rosenblatt, 1985, p. 90), and while the concept of both competition and "dominance" between drives requires fleshing out, nevertheless it is clear that that such conflict and dominance occurs. In rats, for instance, sex is always a dominant response over feeding (Halliday, 1995, p. 211).

Drives and the development of personality

While there is some merit to Rangell's (2002) claim that Freud's structural theory of id, ego, and superego is "the apex of psychoanalytic theory" (p. 1131), nevertheless, there are problems that require addressing, viz. the problem of anthropomorphic homunculi. This problem is not fatal for the Freudian account, however, and Maze (1983, 1987, 1993) provides a deterministic, non-homuncular account of the id, ego, and superego which serves here as a basis for understanding repression. In the Freudian context, the drives' dependence on parental affection mean that the parents' ideas of "good" and "bad" take on added significance as conditions of worth. Socially proscribed behaviours leading to punishment and parental reproval, threatening the loss of the parents' love (and, hence, threatening helplessness), become associated with what is "bad" and to be avoided while "good" behaviours become associated with gratification:

> What is bad is often not at all injurious or dangerous to the ego: on the contrary, it may be something which is desirable or enjoyable to the ego. Here, therefore, there is an extraneous influence at work, and it is this that decides what is to be called good or bad. Since a person's own feelings would not have led him along this path, he must have a motive for submitting to this extraneous influence. Such a motive is easily discovered in his helplessness and his dependence on other people, and it can best be designated as a fear of loss of love. If he loses the love of another person upon whom he is dependent, he also ceases to be protected from a variety of danger. Above all, he is exposed to the danger that this stronger person will show his superiority in the form of punishment. At the beginning, therefore, what is bad is whatever causes one to be threatened with loss of love. [Freud, 1930b, p. 124]

Subsequently, the drive expressions become modelled on parental injunctions under the belief that doing so is necessary for affection and survival. As Freud notes, the result is the formation of identifications and *internal* inhibitions ultimately based on the threat of the external environment:

> First comes renunciation of instinct owing to fear of aggression by the *external* authority. (This is, of course, what fear of loss of love amounts to, for love is a protection against this punitive aggression.) After that comes the erection of an *internal* authority, and renunciation of instinct owing to fear of it—owing to fear of conscience. In this second situation bad intentions are equated with bad actions, and hence come a sense of guilt and need for punishment. The aggressiveness of conscience keeps up the aggressiveness of the authority. [Freud, 1930b, p. 128, his italics; cf. Freud, 1926d, p. 128]

These internal inhibitions, motivated by an unconscious fear of punishment and loss of affection, form the *superego*: "[the] super-ego is the representative for us of every moral restriction" (Freud, 1933a, pp. 66–67). However, not only are morals maintained because of fear; they also become a secondary source of gratification, since abiding by them acts as a gratifying rationalization for renunciation:

Whereas instinctual renunciation, when it is for external reasons, is *only* unpleasurable, when it is for internal reasons, in obedience to the super-ego, it has a different economic effect. In addition to the inevitable unpleasurable consequences it also brings the ego a yield of pleasure—a substitutive satisfaction, as it were. The ego feels elevated: it is proud of the instinctual renunciation, as though it were a valuable achievement. [Freud, 1939a, pp. 116–117, his italics]

While Freud, in places, does treat the superego as a separate agency (e.g., Freud, 1923b, p. 51, 1933a, p. 60), this leads to the anthropomorphic problems associated with the censor, and it would be more parsimonious to view the superego as comprising the introjected moral *beliefs* learnt during infancy that guide (and limit) behaviour, as some appear to suggest (e.g., Brenner, 1982, 1994; Gillett, 1997; Maze, 1983, 1987). In this view: "The superego is not an entity. It is made up of innumerable demands some of which are precisely related to specific situations" (Arlow & Brenner, 1964, p. 81), and if these super-ego demands are conceptualized as *beliefs* about gratification and frustration, guiding the drives and motivating repressions (Maze, 1987, p. 197), then it is the drives themselves that inhibit and repress one another, guided by moral beliefs. Consequently, repression can be explained without reference to an additional "repressing" agency standing over and above the drives themselves, and situates Freudian repression within a biological framework of motivated conflict (e.g., Redgrave, Prescott & Gurney, 1999; Thayer & Friedman, 2002).

Understanding the "ego" in repression

Postulating the drives as the instigators of repression requires further clarifying Freud's position that it is the "ego" which instigates repression (e.g., Breuer & Freud, 1895d, p. 269; Freud, 1896b, p. 170, 1917d, p. 233, 1923b, p. 17, 1933a, p. 57). At times, Freud contrasts the "irrational" id with the ego as rational executive agent, analogous to a horse and rider:

The ego's relation to the id might be compared with that of a rider to his horse. The horse supplies the locomotive energy, while the rider has the privilege of deciding on the goal and of guiding the powerful animal's movements. [Freud, 1933a, p. 77; cf. Freud, 1923b, p. 25]

In this view, the ego is the controlling entity responsible for mediating between the "irrational" id, superego demands, and constraints of the external world (cf. Freud, 1923b, p. 55, 1940a[1938], p. 199). This separation between ego and id leads to the view that the ego is independent of the drives, acting as a set of "control functions", a position finding prominence in psychoanalytic theorizing (e.g., Arlow & Brenner, 1964; Beres, 1962, 1971, 1995; Gill, 1963; Grauer, 1958; Hartmann, 1950, 1958; Hartmann, Kris, & Loewenstein, 1949; Horowitz, 1977; Madison, 1961; Ritvo & Solnit, 1995; Stolar & Fromm, 1974; White, 1963). For instance, Mills (2004) suggests that the ego has a "degree of freedom" in controlling the drives (p. 675) and Tauber (2010) extends this view to then propose that the ego has "free will". The dissociation between drives and ego has even led to reinstating the Cartesian view that humans differ from other animals in so far as they possess a rationality faculty ("ego functions"): "Human psychic activity differs from that of animals, including, so far as we know, even the higher primates, by the mediation of ego functions between the instinctual drive stimulus, the need, and its gratification or inhibition" (Beres, 1962, p. 317).

The immediate problem, however, with postulating an "ego" independent of the drives, is that no adequate account of motivation is provided (Maze, 1987). If the ego truly mediates between the id, superego, and external world (i.e., performs certain activities and not others), then some account of how it arbitrates between these demands must be given. Claiming that the ego merely controls or neutralizes drive energy to use for its own purpose (e.g., Hartmann, 1950, p. 85) gives no basis for explaining why any given behaviour will be chosen over another and the claim that "adaptation" is the final behavioural criterion falls victim to an implicit moralism: adaptation is relative to both subject and situation, and a behaviour considered adaptive to one person might be considered maladaptive by another (see Maze, 1987).

Instead, since the ego is clearly motivated, a motivational account ultimately based on some biological deterministic mechanism is required to explain both the direction and activity of any behaviours. Freud, in fact, provides (in contrast to the "rational ego" above) a way forward here when he writes that "[t]he ego is not sharply separated from the id; its lower portion merges into it" (1923b, p. 24). Similarly, this ego developed out of the id, it forms with it a single biological unit, it is only a specially modified peripheral portion of it, and it is subject to the influences and obeys the suggestions that arise from the id. For any vital purpose, a separation of the ego from the id would be a hopeless undertaking. [Freud, 1925i, p. 133]

Here, Freud's (1910i) ego-instinct account can fill the motivational void because the ego then is motivated by the instinctual drives, in the same manner as the id (see Maze, 1983, 1993). The distinction between ego and (repressed) id emerges in relation to the social context related to gratification and frustration discussed earlier: the development of the ego occurs within a social context that is hostile to the expression of certain aims. Freud often notes that the ego assumes a dominating position within the personality (Breuer & Freud, 1895d, p. 116; Freud, 1900a, pp. 594–595, 1905e, p. 85, 1907a, p. 58), and the view here is that a dominating set of drive expressions emerges in competition with, and inhibiting, those drive expressions that threaten the withdrawal of the parents' affection:

In general, all those instinctual drives whose gratification is dependent on the parent's good will and which is employed as reward by them are mobilised in opposition to the forbidden instinctual impulses. Thus, one subset of the instinctual drives becomes organised in competition with the remainder, and treats the blocking off of the remainder as an essential part of securing its own gratification. [Maze, 1983, p. 171]

Rather than a single homuncular agent, the ego emerges as a subset of the drives and their expression, constituted by the dominant drive trends. The apparent unity of the ego follows from a drive neither knowing itself directly (nor the other drives) and instead only knowing the *whole* organism and its activities (Boag, 2005). On the other hand, those drive expressions that are split off and repressed from this main "ego" form the id. Viewed in this way, there are no *a priori* "id" drives and what becomes repressed is determined by prevailing social factors and inter-drive competition:

The actual principle of division, between the instinctual drives that are to constitute the ego and those which are to be repressed and constitute the id, would be that the former were those whose expression was not subject to *moral disapproval*, that is, those which were socially regarded as legitimate constituents of a respectable person, whereas the latter were morally condemned as impulses that no worthwhile person would have. [Maze, 1983, p. 172, his italics]

Accordingly, inclusion in either id or ego is fluid; a particular drive manifestation might at different times be either prohibited or encouraged, depending upon the prevailing social environment:

Although, according to the classical canon sexuality and aggression are id instincts . . . nevertheless certain alignments of the sexual instinct are admitted to the ego as socially acceptable: in our society, sexual interest in a human being of the opposite sex and of a suitable age, provided there are no barriers of marriage or blood, is defined as legitimate. Again, aggression is not only permitted but demanded in certain situations against certain objects. Thus, the repressing instincts do not forbid all recognition or expression of the repressed: under special circumstances some sexual and aggressive impulses are allowed temporary membership of the ego. [Maze, 1987, p. 196]

An advantage of Maze's development of the structural theory is that it extends a thread in Freud's own thinking which divests the theory of the anthropomorphic homunculi. The "ego" is not a substantive, indivisible unity, but, rather, a fluid collective of dominant drive trends that have not submitted to repression. There is no single ego acting as the agency of repression and instead, the protagonists behind repression are the instinctual drives, guided by beliefs of frustration and gratification (the superego), and preventing certain drive trends from expression (the id).

Understanding Freudian repression

While Freud typically discussed the repression of Oedipal sexuality, there is no theoretical reason to restrict repression to the Oedipal situation[2] and a potentially fertile source of repression involves the commonplace situation of sibling rivalry, where, when faced with the arrival of a new sibling, a young child might experience a mix of feelings, including hating the sibling as a rival for parental affection. A necessary condition for the occurrence of repression is that the child is

old enough to reflect on its hateful wishes and evaluate these as potential threats. For instance, the wish to harm the younger sibling might
be believed to entail the withdrawal of the care-giver's love, which
has the same effect as the imagined catastrophic consequence resulting from the Oedipus complex (i.e., some form of "helplessness")
(Freud, 1940a[1938]). There is generally enormous pressure on the
young child to deny being a "bad" person (and so pressure to not see
oneself clearly) and, thus, motivation to repress the wish could follow
from intense anxiety initiating a flight reflex response away from the
wish. As Freud (1908c) notes, "[t]he set of views which are bound up
with being 'good', but also with a cessation of reflection, become the
dominant and conscious views" (p. 214). In other words, becoming a
socialized being (which is associated with parental acceptance)
involves not only refraining from certain behaviours, but also denying
that the inclination to commit them even exists (Maze, 1987). Repression, here, involves denying self-knowledge, knowledge of what one
desires, whereby the child denies knowledge to itself of the existence
of the wish (i.e., the child attempts to flee the threatening event by
denying knowledge to itself of the desire). Consequently, this infantile
threat evaluation might remain unmodified, since, "[t]he processes of
accommodating old beliefs to new information, and assimilating new
beliefs to the old, could not occur with the repressed material" (Maze
& Henry, 1996, p. 1098; cf. Hopkins, 1995a, p. 415). That is, since knowledge of the repressed is denied, the person cannot re-evaluate his or
her attitude towards it. However, what makes Freud's account both
interesting and problematic is that simply turning away from the
desire does not put an end to the repressed any more than ignoring a
"desire to eat" puts an end to the need for nutrition. The repressed
persists, unacknowledged (the child hates without acknowledging the
hating) and undisturbed by the otherwise dominant ego trends.

Selective inattention and the psychology of repression

The discussion of repression thus far entails Freud's references to
repression in terms of "turning away" from distressing stimuli (e.g.,
Freud, 1900a, p. 600; Freud, 1911b, p. 219). Such "turning away" is
seen as a variety of selective *in*attention and discussing repression in
terms of attentional processes makes repression comprehensible

within the framework of everyday psychological functioning (Boag, 2007a; Erdelyi, 1990, 1993, 2006). Talvitie (2009), for instance, writes,

> Restriction of access to consciousness is an everyday phenomenon. When concentrating on writing, for example, bodily signs of hunger are not necessarily accessible for one, and when trying to score a goal in a football game, one might not notice a painful wound in a leg. [p. 96; cf. Talvitie & Tiitinen, 2006]

Nevertheless, the question that needs addressing is whether selective inattention is sufficient for accounting for the maintenance of repression: how does a person repeatedly ignore x when x is repeatedly presented? Since repression involves a conflict of desires, the question concerns how a person desires both that p be true while also desiring that not-p be the case, represses one of the desires, and prevents the persisting desire from being known without being aware of it.

Sullivan's (1956) model of *selective inattention* (SI) is an influential account of repression, and many variations of it exist in terms of equating repression with non-attending to distressing stimuli (e.g., Billig, 1997, 1999; Bonanno, 1990; Bower, 1990; Eagle, 2000a,b; Erdelyi, 1990, 1993; 2006; Hart, 1982; Jones, 1993; Talvitie, 2009). Although Sullivan (1956) claims that SI is not synonymous with repression (p. 63), it shares a core of common assumptions. SI is a dynamic process that involves "avoiding or minimising the anxiety that is inherent in the *unceasing struggle* to protect the self-system from the diffuse referential processes that *cannot be admitted into awareness*" (p. 4, my italics). The protected self-system is also the agent of SI filtering out threats through "controlling awareness of the events that impinge upon us" (Sullivan, 1956, p. 38). This selective awareness is achieved through concentrating on a particular situation to the exclusion of all other impinging stimuli. For example, a rifleman, when aiming wilfully, concentrates intensely on the target, to the exclusion of all else: "literally, on the rifle range, things are suspended from any disturbance of one's consciousness until it is time to notice them" (Sullivan, 1956, p. 40). The required intensive concentration is "selective" and the efficacy of SI depends upon "*how smoothly the control of awareness excludes the irrelevant and includes the relevant*" (p. 43, his italics). In particular, SI requires a selective, cognitive act: "it is quite important that what is relevant shall be almost immediately seized upon, and everything else be subjected to this selective inattention . . ." (p. 43). In a similar fashion to Freud's theory, "relevance" is related to *anxiety* serving as a *signal* to direct attention elsewhere:

> Anxiety is the symptom, you might say, of all threats to security, particularly threats from unwelcome dissociated impulses which are part of the entire personality: and the hint of anxiety is the signal ordinarily for the self-system to control the spread of awareness. [Sullivan, 1956, p. 56]

However, taking the example of the person with the rifle, if the shooter is focusing on the target *exclusively*, it is difficult to understand how he or she can *also* filter incoming stimuli *and* discern whether they are relevant or irrelevant to the goal at hand if the subject is a single mind, as Sullivan proposes. A single mind cannot be *both* exclusively aware of the target and also filtering incoming stimuli. Instead, a plurality of knowers would be required to explain how one mind part filters stimuli (a censor) while another part exclusively attends to the target. Furthermore, the perceived "relevance" (or "irrelevance") of stimuli is a *judgement*, which cannot preclude both awareness and evaluation of target material (though this need not be conscious itself). Consequently, selective inattention here requires that *all* incoming material be screened to determine whether it is or is not relevant. As Maze (1983) notes, "We may anticipate certain information as relevant, but we still have to perceive the remainder in order to see that it is irrelevant" (p. 75). Hence, a single subject would have to know all the targets in order to selectively inattend to them, and so would have to know what it is not meant to know. In other words, Sullivan's model itself fails because it requires multiple knowers to explain how one part of the mind filters out "irrelevant" material while maintaining "exclusive" awareness of a distracting stimulus.

Further, Sullivan's rifleman with minimal distractions analogy does not appear to reflect the psychoanalytic situation, whereby Freud compares the repressed to an angry intruder (Freud, 1910a, pp. 26–27). In the Freudian account, maintaining SI would be analogous to a rifleman attempting to ignore someone when that same someone is attempting to push or shake the rifle. Thus, to explain Freudian repression, the case must be more than a case where "[o]ne has *fleeting* sexual and aggressive feelings towards parents, but they break away from consciousness without closer examination—the person in question does not attend to them, and thus they are not accessible (remembered) for him or her later" (Talvitie, 2009, p. 98, my italics). If "fleeting" here means weak and inconsequential, then this is different from the case of Freudian repression, where the theory is attempting to explain how *strong* and *persistent* desires (as opposed to "fleeting" feelings) can be prevented from consciousness.

Nevertheless, that we attend to some aspects of situations and not others is indisputable, and this comparison with repression is consistent with the Freudian picture of repression as "turning away" (Freud, 1900a, p. 600, 1911b, p. 219). However, explaining how the repressed remains unconscious still requires addressing, an issue magnified by the Freudian assertion that the repressed desire persists as an activity of a person's own psyche and repeatedly re-presents itself to the subject. The desire to harm the sibling in the example above would still be present, and although the child might turn attention from this, the desire could still become known as one's own desire (i.e., it is still capable of becoming the object of a second mental act) and, hence, would still require further acts of repression.

The role of neural inhibition

Given that selective inattention alone would be insufficient for explaining how repression is maintained, then some blocking mechanism is required to explain how the repressed persists unconsciously. Maze and Henry (1996) propose here that some form of neural inhibition could occur which prevents the offending wish from becoming known ("affective blocking"). Following Kissin (1986), these authors propose that, since any specific mental act is mediated by a distinctive neural process peculiar to it (i.e., an "engram"), recollecting that mental act includes some form of reactivation of that neural process. The threat evaluation and intense anxiety during primal repression instigates a "neural condition" preventing the engram from activation and so preventing the repressed from becoming known or reflected upon (i.e., preventing the repressed from becoming the object of a second mental act):

> It would meet the formal requirements of primal repression if the
> flood of anxiety immediately consequent on any activation of an

engram mediating an instinctual presentation should set up a neural condition such that no neural impulses could pass directly from that engram to any further neural processes capable of registering that the engram existed—registering it in whatever way underlies becoming conscious that the dangerous material had occurred. The precondition of this anxious reaction would be the memory of a previous threat, real or imagined. This neural block is conceived as being automatically set up by the contiguous anxiety rather than as the result of a purposive, informed reaction; in that way the problem of having to know in order not to know would be avoided. [Maze & Henry, 1996, p. 1095]

So, in terms of the earlier example, the young child could repeatedly wish to harm the sibling (a full psychological act), but at the same time, be prevented from knowing the wish.

Invoking neural inhibition as a mechanism helps to bring Freudian repression up to date with current thinking by "[c]hanging the metaphor—from a repressive 'barrier' to repressive inhibition of neural circuits" (Westen & Gabbard, 2002, p. 89),[3] whereby the "blocking" metaphors for repression consequently become fleshed out in terms of neural processes and their effects. There are, however, two major limitations to Maze and Henry's proposal here, one with respect to behavioural inhibition and the second with respect to explaining resistance and phenomenon such as objectless anxiety. First, Maze and Henry's account would prevent knowledge of the wish, but would not stop the wish from being acted upon. Given that it is possible to act on desires without necessarily reflecting upon them (as is presumably always the case for young children), then the child could still act on the hateful desire. Freud, however, notes that an effect of repression is behavioural inhibition (e.g., Freud, 1923b, p. 17, 1932c, p. 221), and so some type of motor inhibition could be postulated, a point which Freud, in places, touches upon (e.g., Freud, 1915d, p. 157). So, in our example, the child desires to harm the sibling, but is both unaware of the desire and prevented from acting upon it. In this way the repressive process conforms to the long-standing view that repression is comparable to a form of "impulse control" or behaviour inhibition (cf. Cunningham, 1924; Dollard & Miller, 1950; Harris, 1950). Secondly, however, it is unclear whether Maze and Henry's proposal can account for secondary repression, resistance, objectless anxiety, and even the lifting of repression, since neural inhibition in their account would mean that the repressed remains unknowable.

Objectless anxiety and knowing the repressed

In Maze and Henry's (1996) account, after repression the target persists but the individual is prevented from reflecting upon it. So, in terms of the earlier example, the young child could repeatedly wish to harm the sibling (a full psychological act), but, at the same time, be prevented from knowing the wish. If that were the case, then this would explain the ongoing nature of repression and account for how the repressed persists unknowingly. However, a limitation is accounting for phenomena such as objectless anxiety and resistance, which entail the apparent paradoxical components of repression: knowing and not knowing the object of anxiety. For example, "objectless anxiety" appears to involve a subject anxious of x while not knowing that x is known. The earlier discussion of Mrs A, reported by Kaplan-Solms and Solms (2000), who, after suffering head trauma, was simultaneously suicidally depressed about her physical deficits *and* yet unaware of her physical symptoms, provides an example of this complex situation of "unconscious knowledge" (pp. 176–177): while Mrs A knew her deficits (causing suicidal depression), she was incapable of acknowledging that these existed (i.e., knowing that the deficits were known was prevented).

To account for such "blindness of the seeing eye", the proposal here is that repression does not involve simply preventing knowing the repressed, but, rather, *preventing knowing (or acknowledging) that the repressed is known*. That is, a person can know the repressed, feel anxious, but knowledge of knowing this is unavailable. The explanatory benefits of this position are seen in terms of making sense of secondary repression targeting derivatives of the repressed. However, to appreciate this, it is first worthwhile examining Maze and Henry's (1996) explanation of secondary repression in terms of neural inhibition spreading to associated content. Their account does not require the "ego" knowing the associated material, generating anxiety, and prompting secondary repression. Instead, they refer to inhibition through association:

> What becomes apparent about the relationship between primal repression and after-expulsion . . . is that the condition of being repressed spreads out, as it were, from the primally repressed to the after-expelled material, rather than being imposed on the latter by the

conscious ego. The associated perceptions are not so much expelled from consciousness as captured under the umbrella of the affective blocking mechanism as soon as the associative links are activated. [Maze & Henry, 1996, p. 1098]

Hence, the selectivity of secondary repression is explained in terms of "associative distance" to the primary repressed material:

there must be points in these manifold chains of association at which the connection with the primally repressed material becomes so attenuated that the associated items beyond those points escape after-expulsion; otherwise, simply everything would be subject to repression. [Maze & Henry, 1996, p. 1097]

This account, however, lacks explanatory power, since the only explanation for why one content and not another succumbs to secondary repression is that one is more or less "distant" from the primary repressed wish. Maze and Henry's account here is similar to Freud's account of resistance in terms of "mental distance", a position rejected earlier since it contradicts the affective and selective basis of the repressive activity (see Chapter One).

Alternatively, the current proposal maintains that repression does involve knowing the repressed (at least on some occasions), generating anxiety, but the person is prevented from knowing that the repressed is known. Developing the earlier example involving sibling rivalry, initially the young child experiences intense anxiety as it comes to reflect upon its hateful wish. This intense anxiety activates inhibitory processes that prevent the child from both acknowledging the wish's existence and acting upon it. Nevertheless, the wish persists, and since it does not lead to gratification, it leaves the child in a state of agitation and frustration which, according to Freud, provides a basis for the development of secondary aims (substitutive satisfactions), since the primary aims cannot be satisfied. The child, consequently, while prevented from acknowledging or acting upon the repressed wish, becomes prompted to desire a substitute object of hate. How this substitution occurs is not entirely clear, but plausibly involves the mistaken unconscious belief that the object of the repressed wish is equivalent with some other similar object (see Petocz, 1999) and repression would further prevent the mistake from being recognized and corrected. For instance, the child's frustrated wish to harm a sibling could be transferred on to similar targets, such as other children in similar positions to the sibling (e.g., other younger or weaker children). In the account here, after repression a person can know the repressed, but be prevented from knowing that the repressed is known. Subsequently, the similarity between the primary repressed aim and the secondary aims could also be known (to instigate secondary repression) but without the process itself being known. However, depending on, presumably, the social context and relative fear of punishment, the substitute wish might possibly also be subject to further repression, following on from perceived actual threat from the external environment (primary repression) or super-ego injunctions (secondary repression). For example, harming a family member is likely never to be considered acceptable, whereas harming an extra-familial target (say, during sport) might attract less punitive attention and moral disapproval. In all such cases, however, it is possible to know either the primary or secondary targets of repression, but neural inhibition prevents knowing that these are known.

Knowing the repressed target, but being prevented from knowing that this is known, also appears necessary for explaining the clinical phenomenon of resistance. Resistance occurs in response to approaching the repressed and yet, simultaneously, the "analysand" ostensibly has no insight into resisting or what it is in response to: although the behaviours constituting the resistance might be known (e.g., the analysand reports, "my mind has gone blank"), the cause of their occurrence is not. Furthermore, resistance entails the features of objectless anxiety, whereby the threat of the return of the repressed instigates anxiety and yet the threat is also not known. As Gillett (2001) writes, "more often defence failure is manifested only by increased levels of anxiety, whereas the warded off content remains unconscious" (p. 277). Since it is argued that anxiety necessarily involves threat evaluation, apparent objectless anxiety appears to require a subject anxiously evaluating a target resulting in the anxiety, while knowledge of what the anxiety is a response to is not. In the account of repression here, since knowledge of the repressed wish is prevented from becoming known, objectless anxiety and anxious resistance provide no theoretical difficulty: the individual might know the target of repression which instigates anxiety from threat evaluation, but be prevented from knowing that the threat is known.

The issue of reversibility and re-knowing the repressed

The lifting of repression still needs to be accounted for, and while the aims of psychoanalytic therapy appear multifarious (e.g., Blum, 2003a; Fonagy, 1999; Gabbard & Westen, 2003), Freud's theoretical description at times suggests that the primary factor that analysis needs to address is the beliefs of danger associated with wishes, rather than memories *per se*:

> Real danger is a danger that is known, and realistic anxiety is anxiety about a known danger of this sort. Neurotic anxiety is anxiety about an unknown danger. Neurotic danger is thus a danger that has still to be discovered. Analysis has shown that it is an instinctual danger. By bringing this danger which is not known to the ego into consciousness, the analyst makes neurotic anxiety no different from realistic anxiety, so that it can be dealt with in the same way. [Freud, 1926d, p. 165]

Thus, while memory is necessarily involved, knowing the past in and of itself would not have any more therapeutic effect than knowing the so-called present. Instead, since the primary motivation for repression is anxiety, then undoing repression successfully would entail changing the factors underlying this anxiety (beliefs about desires that generate anxiety). That is, once the infantile threat evaluation is replaced by a more presently realistic appraisal, then the repressive tendency is removed, and the repression lifted.

In Freud's account, repression first occurs as a response to an infantile threat evaluation. After repression this infantile attitude might remain unmodified, since, "[t]he processes of accommodating old beliefs to new information, and assimilating new beliefs to the old, could not occur with the repressed material" (Maze & Henry, 1996, p. 1098; cf. Hopkins, 1995a, p. 415). Since the infantile threat evaluation leading to the repression is insusceptible to modification after repression, re-evaluation of the repressed requires first acknowledging that the repressed exists. For this to occur requires a reversible account of neural inhibition, whereby the repression can be undone, even if momentarily, via factors such as external sources of stimulation (e.g., psychoanalytic interpretation). That is, while neural inhibition might generally prevent knowing that the repressed is known, such inhibition must be comparable to a "reversible lesion" (cf. Epstein, 1998, p. 505) and the therapeutic situation might help draw attention to acknowledging the repressed wish.

However, simply coming to acknowledge the repressed will not automatically undo the repression since the anxiety-instigating factors have not been modified (i.e., the resistance—Freud, 1910k, p. 225, 1913c, pp. 141–142, 1919a, p. 159, 1937d, p. 257). Additionally, even if the threatening wish becomes re-known, then there is no theoretical problem with re-repression and ensuing ignorance following. For re-repression to occur, the awareness of the repressed need occur only as quickly as is needed to evaluate and generate anxiety, and after re-repression knowledge of the repression is no longer known, as before. Furthermore, since the act of repression itself is unconscious in the first instance, the person must be motivated or prompted to pay attention to the repressive act for it to become conscious, and the re-repression could occur so quickly that their attention misses the act itself (and even if this act is noticed, it would promptly be made unconscious again after re-repression).

In the case of interpretation, then, it is not simply about making the unconscious conscious, but about engaging with motivational factors and guiding beliefs. Undoing repression can, thus, be seen in terms of re-learning experiences (extinction; counter-conditioning), whereby therapy presumably acts as a re-learning experience after re-evaluation of the initial threatening situations within the context of the transference relationship. The lifting of repression, and undoing the resistances, are comparable, then, to extinction-like processes whereby the threat evaluation and consequent anxiety is tempered by modifying re-evaluations of the situation as attention is drawn to the repressed (cf. Hutterer & Liss, 2006, p. 298; Schwartz, 1987, pp. 495–497). The effect of this re-evaluation could also be framed in terms of a "corrective emotional experience" (Eagle, 2000b, p. 175; Westen, 1999, p. 1086), "adaptive reappraisals" (Rosenblatt, 1985, p. 96), or a "shift in attitude":

> The demonstration to the patient of the repeated motifs, themes, and other derivatives of the repressed schema brings about a new ability for self-observation and an understanding of the anachronistic nature of the disturbing fantasies. As a consequence, there is a shift in attitude to the repressed . . . [Slap & Saykin, 1984, p. 122]

Once the infantile threat evaluation is replaced by a more presently realistic appraisal, then the repressive tendency is removed and the repression lifted. As presented here, this could only occur if knowledge of the repressed wish can, in fact, become known. The important point, however, is that maintaining repression and resistance does involve knowing the repressed, but not so that the repression is lifted and the drives now know that they know the repressed. This account also explains how it is possible that the analysand "knew the repressed all along" (Talvitie, 2009, pp. 106–107), since the person did know the repressed all along, but was prevented from knowing that the repressed is known.

Conclusion

This account allows for both knowing and not knowing the repressed, which, while apparently paradoxical, is explicable with respect to different objects of cognition (knowing the repressed as opposed to acknowledging that the repressed is known). The interesting aspect of Freudian repression that needs accounting for is that after repression the repressed continues to push for expression, requiring further repressive acts. Repression appears motivated by a person anxiously denying that the offending wish is known, which, mediated by neural inhibition, prevents knowing that the wish is known and from acting upon its original wish. Any actual neural mechanism involved is ultimately decided empirically, and there is no theoretical reason to rule out variations of neural inhibition and degrees of prevented access to beliefs and desires. However, while the above account is speculative, the account presented here only requires that such inhibition is possible, since the aim here is only to show that the concept of repression is not logically incoherent, rather than proving any specific model correct.

The resolution of the apparent paradox of repression hinges upon the recognition that repression inhibits knowledge of knowing the repressed. Here, repression is motivated by threat evaluation and anxiety, resulting in the person (or, more specifically, the drives) no longer knowing that the repressed is known. In this account, maintaining repression and resistance does involve knowing the repressed (but not so that the drives know that they know repressed) and there is no censoring agency sparing the threatened ego from the repressed. The advantage of this account is that it explains the active, dynamic nature of Freud's account of repression and resistance, which is both essential to any account of Freudian repression and the feature that most threatens to make repression appear impossible. Since the infantile threat evaluation leading to the repression is insusceptible to modification after repression, the re-evaluation of the repressed aim allows a lifting of repression so that the repressed aim is no longer believed to constitute an actual threat. This might occur through present beliefs concerning the nature of the repressed modifying the existing infantile beliefs, so that the drive(s) responsible for repression is no longer threatened.

Notes

1. Thus, an attachment perspective of defences need not necessarily conflict with a drive account, as Holmes (2000) suggests:

    The key point about defences from an attachment perspective is that they are interpersonal strategies for dealing with suboptimal environments. Their aim is not so much to preserve the integrity of the individual when faced with conflicting inner drives, as to maintain attachments in the face of forces threatening to disrupt them. [p. 161]

    As Maze (1983, 1993) argues, providing an account of what gratifies and frustrates ultimately requires a biological underpinning (see also McIlwain, 2007), and so emotional vulnerability is necessarily tied with biological vulnerability.

2. I have, however, also discussed repression within the Oedipal context (see Boag, 2007b).

3. These authors discuss neural inhibition within the framework of "cognitive neuroscience".

Postscript

T he discussion here of repression accounts for the apparently paradoxical phenomenon of *both* knowing and not knowing the target of repression. Freud, very early on, recognized this intriguing feature of repression ("blindness of the seeing eye"—Breuer & Freud, 1895d, p. 117*n*), and his attempts to account for this allow psychoanalytic theory to provide such a powerful insight into the mind's dynamics. As Erdelyi (1990, 2006) has long recognized, understanding repression is much more complex than it simply being the case that repression is *either* conscious *or* unconscious. Nevertheless, given that there remains such difficulty with conceptualizing the "mental unconscious", a major challenge for psychoanalysis (and general psychology) concerns how, precisely, to understand mentality, both conscious or unconscious. Here, there is still need for further theoretical development. The recent appeal of "implicit processes", which at times proposes a non-psychological or non-conscious "unconscious", unnecessarily denies the possibility of unconscious cognition, and it is also clear that some authors who reject unconscious mentality nevertheless imply a mental unconscious. As noted earlier, Talvitie's (2009) reductionist approach can be recast into relational terms, whereby his proposed distinction between "consciousness" (*knowing* states of affairs) and "self-consciousness" appears to suggest a distinction between knowing unconsciously and knowing that one knows (or being conscious of one's own mental acts). As Erdelyi (2004) notes here with respect to the assumed meaning of "pretheoretic" terms and proliferation of terminology for conscious, unconscious, non-conscious, a-conscious processes, "the crux of the problem is theoretical" (p. 74), and what is needed is not a greater variety of terms, but, rather, greater conceptual clarity concerning the ones already in use.[1]

The approach undertaken here involved identifying the various strands in Freud's thinking on repression and developing an account that retains what is coherent while rejecting unworkable elements. While there are significant problems with aspects of the Freudian account, Freud's theory of repression, understood within a contemporary neural-dynamic framework, provides a coherent account that is both psychological and neurological in detail. It is hoped that this account of repression contributes to a demystification of the process by positioning it within a framework of ordinary attentional responses to painful stimuli (cf. Boag, 2007a; Erdelyi, 1993, 2006), a position that has always been more or less explicit in Freud's own treatment of the subject: "Repression may, without doubt, be correctly described as the intermediate stage between a defensive reflex and a condemning judgement" (Freud, 1905c, p. 175; cf. Freud, 1936a, pp. 245–246). Repression is, then, also comprehensible in terms of natural defensive responses to painful stimuli, which situates the process firmly within a natural evolutionary context where humans are well and truly placed within the animal kingdom (cf. Gilbert, 2001).

It is also hoped that this theoretical research contributes to further empirical investigation of Freud's sophisticated account of repression, rather than the parody of the theory that is often presented when research purports to "evaluate Freudian repression" (e.g., Holmes, 1990; Rofé, 2008). While it might be premature to expect exciting new avenues of empirical research to suddenly emerge for assessing repression, providing a logically coherent of repression is necessary before comparing the theory with the evidence. Thus, philosophical analysis is essential to science, and the account of repression discussed here is potentially empirically assessable, not because repression fits neatly into contrived experimental conditions, but because the factors implicated in repression are all real terms. Rather than a "rational ego"

or "transcendental censor", the subject terms (the drives defined physiologically) and the targets of repression (e.g., instinctual representatives, such as wishes), the operation (e.g., neural inhibition) and the
types of contexts that repression could be expected to occur within
(e.g., early socialization) are all stipulated. For instance, as a form of
inhibition, repression is comprehensible within a neuro-dynamic
framework, whereby specific brain mechanisms mediate the repressive phenomenon. There might even be other relevant developmental
factors to consider (e.g., the maturation of the frontal lobes, which are
said to have initial growth phases around the ages of two and five—
Solms & Turnbull, 2002). The obvious future research directions for
repression are in terms of understanding the role of inhibitory process,
including the neural mechanisms implicated in repression (and
behaviour inhibition in general). However, current investigators of
inhibitory processes would do well also to consider the psychodynamics of inhibition (if having not done so already), and motivational
processes and conflict are already more or less implicated in discussions of inhibition (e.g., "the competition between incompatible
inputs"—Redgrave, Prescott, & Gurney, 1999, p. 1016). In fact, in a
time when psychology's diversity and construct proliferation is becoming increasingly unsustainable, integrating the insights of psychoanalysis, neuroscience, and general psychology is needed more than
ever.

Nevertheless, Kandel (1999) notes that psychoanalysis needs to
carefully develop "a sophisticated and realistic theory of motivation"
(p. 505). Such a theory will require both conceptual sophistication and
psychobiological realism, whereby psychological processes are not
reduced to biology but which, in relation to biological structures,
allow the organism sensitivity to features of situations. While much
remains to be discovered empirically, Freud's deterministic drive
approach fits well into a natural science framework, and while drive
accounts might not appeal to many clinicians, they are, nevertheless,
indispensable explanatory constructs. Furthermore, Freud's in principle position provides a viable approach to understanding their workings. As Mills (2004) writes, "Freud's thesis on drives is the most
philosophically sophisticated theory of motivation in the psychoanalytic literature for the simple fact that he begins with our natural
immediacy as embodied beings . . ." (p. 676). As embodied beings, any
account of cognition necessarily implicates motivation and emotion,

and Freud's general framework provides insight into how these components are integrated.

It is also heartening to see a growing recognition of the importance of motivation and motivational conflict for understanding human behaviour. For instance, proponents of the computer metaphor recognize the limitations of a motivationally neutral cold system and are making tentative steps to fill the gaps (Uleman, 2005), even if they appear to have little insight into how to adequately determine motivational policy. Furthermore, early critics of Freudian dream theory who so fervently claimed that motivation was irrelevant to dream formation (McCarley & Hobson, 1977) have come to concede that motivation and motivational conflict does influence dream content (e.g., Hobson, 1988, 2005). This is not to say that everything that Freud had to say has merit (as this book demonstrates), and a good distinction is provided by Fonagy and Target (2000) with respect to Freud's general framework and his specific clinical observations (e.g., Oedipal rivalry), the former standing independent of the latter. It is Freud's general framework that is a theoretical masterpiece, and to quote again Maze (1983), "Freud's metapsychology, though unfinished, was the one great systematic attempt in modern psychology to outline a deterministic, physiologically based theory of motivation and extend it to embrace all of human behaviour, bodily and mental" (Maze, 1983, pp. 142–143). For this reason, I can only agree with Kandel's (1999) oft-cited conclusion that "psychoanalysis still represents the most coherent and intellectually satisfying view of the mind" (p. 505). In terms of a final comment, while this book focuses upon repression within psychoanalytic theory, the subsequent discussion cannot but help develop and clarify Freud's general approach and demonstrate the relative conceptual sophistication that Freud brought to bear upon understanding the human condition.

Note

1. Erdelyi has pointed out to me that I have, in fact, also contributed to this proliferation with respect to the distinction between "awareness" and "conscious awareness" (see Boag, 2010a).

REFERENCES

Ågmo, A., & Ellingsen, E. (2003). Relevance of non-human animal studies to the understanding of human sexuality. *Scandinavian Journal of Psychology*, *44*: 293–301.

American Psychiatric Association (2000). *The Diagnostic and Statistical Manual of Mental Disorders* (4th edn). Washington, DC: American Psychiatric Association.

Anderson, J. (1927). The knower and the known. In: *Studies in Empirical Philosophy*. Sydney: Angus & Robertson, 1962.

Anderson, J. (1930). Realism and some of its critics. In: *Studies in Empirical Philosophy*. Sydney: Angus & Robertson, 1962.

Anderson, J. (1936). Causality and logic. In: *Studies in Empirical Philosophy*. Sydney: Angus & Robertson, 1962.

Anspach, M. R. (1998). Madness and the divided self: Esquirol, Sartre, Bateson. In: J.-P. Dupuy (Ed.), *Self-deception and Paradoxes of Rationality* (pp. 59–86). Stanford, CA: CSLI Publications.

Anspaugh, K. (1995). Repression or suppression? Freud's interpretation of the dreams of Irma's injection. *Psychoanalytic Review*, *82*: 427–441.

Applegarth, A. (1977). Psychic energy reconsidered: discussion. *Journal of the American Psychoanalytic Association*, *25*: 599–602.

Arlow, J. A., & Brenner, C. (1964). *Psychoanalytic Concepts and the Structural Theory*. New York: International Universities Press.

Auld, F., Hyman, M., & Rudzinski, D. (2005). *Resolution of Inner Conflict: An Introduction to Psychoanalytic Therapy.* Washington, DC: American Psychological Association.

Bach, K. (1998). (Apparent) paradoxes of self-deception and decision. In: J.-P. Dupuy (Ed.), *Self-deception and Paradoxes of Rationality* (pp. 163–189). Stanford, CA: CSLI Publications.

Baker, A. J. (1986). *Australian Realism.* Cambridge: Cambridge University Press.

Barkley, R. A. (1997a). *ADHD and the Nature of Self-control.* New York: Guildford Press.

Barkley, R. A. (1997b). Attention-Deficit/Hyperactivity Disorder, self-regulation, and time: toward a more comprehensive theory. *Developmental and Behavioural Pediatrics, 18*: 271–279.

Baumann, H. (1910). *Muret–Sanders Encyclopaedic English-German and German-English Dictionary*, Part 2. Berlin: Langenscheidtesche Verlagsbuchhandlung.

Baumbacher, G. D. (1989). Signal anxiety and panic attacks. *Psychotherapy, 26*: 75–80.

Baumeister, R. F., Dale, K., & Sommer, K. L. (1998). Freudian defence mechanisms and empirical findings in modern social psychology: reaction formation, projection, displacement, undoing, isolation, sublimation, and denial. *Journal of Personality, 66*: 1081–1124.

Bennett, M. R., & Hacker, P. M. S. (2003). *Philosophical Foundations of Neuroscience.* Malden, MA: Blackwell.

Beres, D. (1962). The unconscious fantasy. *Psychoanalytic Quarterly, 31*: 309–328.

Beres, D. (1965). Structure and function in psycho-analysis. *International Journal of Psychoanalysis, 46*: 53–63.

Beres, D. (1971). Ego autonomy and ego pathology. *Psychoanalytic Study of the Child, 26*: 3–24.

Beres, D. (1995). Conflict. In: B. E. Moore & B. D. Fine (Eds.), *Psycho-analysis: The Major Concepts* (pp. 477–484). New Haven: Yale University Press.

Bettelheim, B. (1983). *Freud and Man's Soul.* New York: Alfred A. Knopf.

Bibring, E. (1969). The development and problems of the theory of the instincts. *International Journal of Psychoanalysis, 50*: 293–308.

Billig, M. (1997). The dialogic unconscious: psychoanalysis, discursive psychology and the nature of repression. *British Journal of Social Psychology, 36*: 139–159.

Billig, M. (1999). *Freudian Repression: Dialogue Creating the Unconscious.* Cambridge: Cambridge University Press.

Blass, R. B., & Carmeli, Z. (2007). The case against neuropsychoanalysis: on fallacies underlying psychoanalysis' latest scientific trend and its negative impact on psychoanalytic discourse. *International Journal of Psychoanalysis, 88*: 19–40.

Bleichmar, H. (2004). Making conscious the unconscious in order to modify unconscious processing: some mechanisms of therapeutic change. *International Journal of Psychoanalysis, 85*: 1379–1400.

Blum, H. P. (2003a). Psychoanalytic controversies: repression, transference and reconstruction. *International Journal of Psychoanalysis, 84*: 497–503.

Blum, H. P. (2003b). Response to Peter Fonagy. *International Journal of Psychoanalysis, 84*: 509–513.

Boag, S. (2005). Addressing mental plurality: justification, objections and logical requirements of strongly partitive accounts of mind. *Theory and Psychology, 15*: 747–767.

Boag, S. (2006a). Freudian repression, the common view, and pathological science. *Review of General Psychology, 10*: 74–86.

Boag, S. (2006b). Freudian dream theory, dream bizarreness, and the disguise-censor controversy. *Neuro-psychoanalysis, 8*: 5–17.

Boag, S. (2006c). Can repression become a conscious process? *Behavioral and Brain Sciences, 29*: 513–514.

Boag, S. (2007a). 'Real processes' and the explanatory status of repression and inhibition. *Philosophical Psychology, 20*: 375–392.

Boag, S. (2007b). Realism, self-deception and the logical paradox of repression. *Theory and Psychology, 17*: 421–447.

Boag, S. (2007c). Pathological science and the myth of recovered memories: reply to McNally. *Review of General Psychology, 11*: 361–362.

Boag, S. (2008a). 'Mind as feeling' or affective relations? A contribution to the School of Andersonian Realism. *Theory and Psychology, 18*: 505–525.

Boag, S. (2008b). Making sense of subliminal perception. In: A. M. Columbus (Ed.), *Advances in Psychology Research* (pp. 117–139). New York: Nova Science Publishers.

Boag, S. (2008c). Is language necessary for consciousness? An assessment of Freud's 'word/thing' presentation distinction. In: S. Boag (Ed.), *Personality Down Under: Perspectives from Australia* (pp. 81–89). New York: Nova Science.

Boag, S. (2010a). Repression, suppression, and conscious awareness. *Psychoanalytic Psychology, 27*: 164–181.

Boag, S. (2010b). Description and explanation within personality psychology research. In: R. E. Hicks (Ed.), *Personality and Individual Differences: Current Directions* (pp. 21–29). Bowen Hills: Australian Academic Press.

Boag, S. (2011a). Explanation in personality research: 'verbal magic' and the Five-Factor Model. *Philosophical Psychology*, 24(2): 223–243.

Boag, S. (2011b). The role of conceptual analysis in personality research. In: S. Boag & N. Tiliopoulos (Eds.), *Personality and Individual Differences: Theory, Assessment and Application* (pp. 321–330). New York: Nova.

Boesky, D. (1995). Structural theory. In: B. E. Moore & B. D. Fine (Eds.), *Psycho-analysis: The Major Concepts* (pp. 494–507). New Haven, CT: Yale University Press.

Bonanno, G. A. (1990). Repression, accessibility, and the translation of private experience. *Psychoanalytic Psychology*, 7: 453–473.

Bonanno, G. A., & Keuler, D. J. (1998). Psychotherapy without repressed memory: a parsimonious alternative based on contemporary memory research. In: S. J. Lynn & K. M. McConkey (Eds.), *Truth in Memory* (pp. 437–463). New York: Guilford Press.

Boudreaux, G. (1977). Freud on the nature of unconscious mental processes. *Philosophy of the Social Sciences*, 7: 1–32.

Bower, G. H. (1990). Awareness, the unconscious, and repression: an experimental psychologist's perspective. In: J. L. Singer (Ed.), *Repression and Dissociation: Implications for Personality Theory, Psychopathology, and Health* (pp. 209–231). Chicago, IL: University of Chicago Press.

Brakel, L. A. W. (2005). Drive theory and primary process: a philosophical account. In: P. Giampieri-Deutsch (Ed.), *Psychoanalysis as an Empirical, Interdisciplinary Science* (pp. 75–90). Wien: Verlag der Österriechischen Akademie der Wissenschaften.

Brakel, L. A. W. (2009). *Philosophy, Psychoanalysis, and the A-Rational Mind*. Oxford: Oxford University Press.

Brakel, L. A. W. (2010). *Unconscious Knowing and Other Essays in Psycho-Philosophical Analysis*. Oxford: Oxford University Press.

Braun, A. (1999). Commentary on "The new neuropsychology of sleep: implications for psychoanalysis". *Neuro-Psychoanalysis*, 1: 196–201.

Brennen, T., Vikan, A., & Dybdahl, R. (2007). Are tip-of-the-tongue states universal? Evidence from the speakers of an unwritten language. *Memory*, 15: 167–176.

Brenner, C. (1957). The nature and development of the concept of repression in Freud's writings. *Psychoanalytic Study of the Child*, 12: 19–46.

Brenner, C. (1974). On the nature and development of affects: a unified theory. *Psychoanalytic Quarterly*, 43: 532–556.

Brenner, C. (1975). Affects and psychic conflict. *Psychoanalytic Quarterly*, 44: 5–28.

Brenner, C. (1981). Defence and defence mechanisms. *Psychoanalytic Quarterly, 50*: 557–569.

Brenner, C. (1982). The concept of the superego: a reformulation. *Psychoanalytic Quarterly, 51*: 501–525.

Brenner, C. (1994). The mind as conflict and compromise formation. *Journal of Clinical Psychoanalysis, 3*: 473–488.

Brentano, F. (1874). *Psychology from an Empirical Standpoint*, A. C. Rancurello, D. B. Terrell, & L. L. McAlister (Trans.). London: Routledge & Kegan Paul, 1973

Breuer, J., & Freud, S. (1895d). *Studies in Hysteria (1893–1895). S.E., II.* London: Hogarth.

Brierley, M. (1937). Affects in theory and practice. *International Journal of Psychoanalysis, 18*: 256–268.

Bruce, D., Dolan, A., & Phillips-Grant, K. (2000). On the transition from childhood amnesia to the recall of personal memories. *Psychological Science, 11*: 360–364.

Bucci, W. (1997). *Psychoanalysis and Cognitive Science: A Multiple Code Theory*. New York: Guilford Press.

Cavell, M. (1991). The subject of mind. *International Journal of Psycho-analysis, 72*: 141–154.

Cavell, M. (1993). *The Psychoanalytic Mind: From Freud to Philosophy.* Cambridge, MA: Harvard University Press.

Chee, M. W. L., Sriram, N., Soon, C. S., & Lee, K. M. (2000). Dorsolateral prefrontal cortex and the implicit association of concepts and attributes. *NeuroReport, 11*: 135–140.

Cheshire, N., & Thöma, H. (1991). Metaphor, neologism and 'open texture': implications for translating Freud's scientific thought. *International Review of Psycho-analysis, 18*: 429–454.

Cohen, J. (1985). Trauma and repression. *Psychoanalytic Inquiry, 5*: 163–189.

Cohen, J., & Kinston, W. (1983). Repression theory: a new look at the cornerstone. *International Journal of Psychoanalysis, 65*: 411–422.

Colace, C. (2006). Commentary on "Freudian dream theory, dream bizarreness, and the disguise-censor controversy". *Neuropsychoanalysis, 8*: 24–26.

Colace, C. (2010). *Children's Dreams: From Freud's Observations to Modern Dream Research.* London: Karnac.

Compton, A. (1972a). A study of the psychoanalytic theory of anxiety: I. The development of Freud's theory of anxiety. *Journal of the American Psychoanalytic Association, 20*: 3–44.

Compton, A. (1972b). A study of the psychoanalytic theory of anxiety: II. Developments in the theory of anxiety since 1926. *Journal of the American Psychoanalytic Association, 20*: 341–394.

Compton, A. (1981). On the psychoanalytic theory of instinctual drives: IV. Instinctual drives and the ego–id–superego model. *Psychoanalytic Quarterly, 50*: 363–392.

Cramer, P. (1998). Defensiveness and defence mechanisms. *Journal of Personality, 66*: 879–894.

Crews, F. (1995). *The Memory Wars: Freud's Legacy in Dispute*. New York: New York Review.

Cunningham, K. S. (1924). The relation of repression to mental development. *Australian Journal of Psychology and Philosophy, 2*: 96–103.

Damasio, A. R. (1994). *Descartes' Error: Emotion, Reason, and the Human Brain*. New York: Putnam.

Damasio, A. R. (1998). Emotion in the perspective of an integrated nervous system. *Brain Research Reviews, 26*: 83–86.

Damasio, A. R. (2001). Fundamental feelings. *Nature, 413*: 781.

Davies, J. M. (1996). Dissociation, repression and reality testing in the countertransference: the controversy over memory and false memory in the psychoanalytic treatment of adult survivors of childhood sexual abuse. *Psychoanalytic Dialogues, 6*: 189–218.

Davis, J. T. (2001). Revising psychoanalytic interpretations of the past: an examination of declarative and non-declarative memory processes. *International Journal of Psychoanalysis, 82*: 449–462.

Descartes, R. (1641). Objections and replies. In: *The Philosophical Writings of Descartes, Vol. II*, J. Cottingham, R. Stoohoff, & D. Murdoch (Trans.) (pp. 66–398). Cambridge: Cambridge University Press, 1984.

Descartes, R. (1648). *The Philosophical Writings of Descartes, Vol. III: Correspondence*, J. Cottingham, R. Stoohoff, D. Murdoch, & A. Kenny (Trans.). Cambridge: Cambridge University Press, 1991.

De Sousa, R. (1976). Rational homunculi. In: A. O. Rorty (Ed.), *The Identities of Persons* (pp. 217–238). Berkeley: University of California Press.

Diamond, M. J. (1997). The unbearable agony of being: interpreting tormented states of mind in the psychoanalysis of sexually traumatised patients. *Bulletin of the Menninger Clinic, 61*: 495–519.

Diamond, S., Balvin, R. S., & Diamond, F. R. (1963). *Inhibition and Choice: A Neurobehavioral Approach to the Problems of Plasticity in Behaviour*. New York: Harper & Row.

Dollard, J., & Miller, N. E. (1950). *Personality and Psychotherapy: An Analysis in Terms of Learning, Thinking and Culture*. New York: McGraw-Hill.

Dreher, A. U. (2005). Conceptual research. In: E. S. Person, A. M. Cooper, & G. O. Gabbard (Eds.), *Textbook of Psychoanalysis* (pp. 361–372). Washington, DC: American Psychiatric Publishing.

Eagle, M. N. (1998). Freud's legacy: defenses, somatic symptoms and neurophysiology. In: G. Guttman & I. Scholz-Strasser (Eds.), *Freud and the Neurosciences: From Brain Research to the Unconscious* (pp. 87–101). Vienna: Österreichischen Akademie der Wissenschaften.

Eagle, M. N. (2000a). Repression: Part I. *Psychoanalytic Review, 87*: 1–38.

Eagle, M. N. (2000b). Repression: Part II. *Psychoanalytic Review, 87*: 161–187.

Elliot, A. J. (2008). Approach and avoidance motivation. In: A. J. Elliot (Ed.), *Handbook of Approach and Avoidance Motivation* (pp. 3–14). New York: Psychology Press.

Emde, R. N. (1999). Moving ahead: integrating influences of affective processes for development and psycho-analysis. *International Journal of Psychoanalysis, 80*: 317–339.

Epstein, A. W. (1998). Neural aspects of psychodynamic science. *Journal of the American Academy of Psychoanalysis, 26*: 503–512.

Erdelyi, M. H. (1974). A new look at the new look: perceptual defense and vigilance. *Psychological Review, 81*: 1–25.

Erdelyi, M. H. (1985). *Psychoanalysis: Freud's Cognitive Psychology*. New York: W. H. Freeman.

Erdelyi, M. H. (1990). Repression, reconstruction, and defence: history and integration of the psychoanalytic and experimental frameworks. In: J. L. Singer (Ed.), *Repression and Dissociation: Implications for Personality Theory, Psychopathology, and Health* (pp. 1–31). Chicago, IL: University of Chicago Press.

Erdelyi, M. H. (1993). Repression: the mechanism and the defense. In: D. M. Wegner & J. W. Pennebaker (Eds.), *Handbook of Mental Control* (pp. 126–148). Englewood Cliffs, NJ: Prentice Hall.

Erdelyi, M. H. (2001). Defense processes can be conscious and unconscious. *American Psychologist, 56*: 761–762.

Erdelyi, M. H. (2004). Subliminal perception and its cognates: theory, indeterminancy, and time. *Consciousness and Cognition, 13*: 73–91.

Erdelyi, M. H. (2006). The unified theory of repression. *Behavioral and Brain Sciences, 29*: 499–551.

Erwin, E. (1988). Psychoanalysis and self-deception. In: B. P. McLaughlin & A. O. Rorty (Eds.), *Perspectives on Self-deception* (pp. 228–245). Berkeley, CA: University of California Press.

Fayek, A. (2005). The centrality of the system *Ucs.* in the theory of psychoanalysis: the nonrepressed unconscious. *Psychoanalytic Psychology, 22*: 524–543.

Fine, R. (1990). *The History of Psychoanalysis*. New York: Continuum.

Fingarette, H. (1969). *Self-deception*. London: Routledge & Kegan Paul.

Finkelstein, D. H. (1999). On the distinction between conscious and unconscious states of mind. *American Philosophical Quarterly, 36*: 79–100.

Fonagy, P. (1999). Memory and therapeutic action. *International Journal of Psychoanalysis, 80*: 215–233.

Fonagy, P., & Target, M. (2000). The place of psychodynamic theory in developmental psychopathology. *Development and Psychopathology, 12*: 407–425.

Frampton, M. F. (1991). Considerations on the role of Brentano's concept of intentionality in Freud's repudiation of the seduction theory. *International Review of Psycho-analysis, 18*: 27–36.

Frank, A. (1969). The unrememberable and the unforgettable: passive primal repression. *Psycho-analytic Study of the Child, 24*: 48–77.

Frank, A., & Muslin, H. (1967). The development of Freud's concept of primal repression. *Psychoanalytic Study of the Child, 22*: 55–76.

Frank, G. (1996). Beliefs and their vicissitudes. *Psychoanalytic Psychology, 13*: 421–431.

Frank, G. (1999). Freud's concept of the superego: review and assessment. *Psychoanalytic Psychology, 16*: 448–463.

Freud, A. (1968). *The Ego and the Mechanisms of Defence*. London: The Hogarth Press.

Freud, S. (1893a). On the psychical mechanism of hysterical phenomena: a lecture. *S.E., 3*: 25–39. London: Hogarth.

Freud, S. (1894a). The neuro-psychoses of defence. *S.E., 3*: 41–61. London: Hogarth.

Freud, S. (1895b). On the grounds for detaching a particular syndrome from neurasthenia under the description 'anxiety neurosis'. *S.E., 3*: 85–115. London: Hogarth.

Freud, S. (1895c). Obsessions and phobias: their psychical mechanism and aetiology. *S.E., 3*: 69–82. London: Hogarth.

Freud, S. (1895f). A reply to criticisms of my paper on anxiety neurosis. *S.E., 3*: 119–139. London: Hogarth.

Freud, S. (1896a). Heredity and the aetiology of the neuroses. *S.E., 3*: 141–156. London: Hogarth.

Freud, S. (1896b). Further remarks on the neuro-psychoses of defence. *S.E., 3*: 157–185. London: Hogarth.

Freud, S. (1896c). The aetiology of hysteria. *S.E., 3*: 187–221. London: Hogarth.

Freud, S. (1898a). Sexuality in the aetiology of the neuroses. *S.E., 3*: 261–285. London: Hogarth.

Freud, S. (1898b). The psychical mechanism of forgetfulness. *S.E.*, 3: 287–297. London: Hogarth.

Freud, S. (1899a). Screen memories. *S.E.*, 3: 299–322. London: Hogarth.

Freud, S. (1900a). *The Interpretation of Dreams. S.E.*, 4–5. London: Hogarth.

Freud, S. (1901a). On dreams. *S.E.*, 5: 629–686. London: Hogarth.

Freud, S. (1901b). The psychopathology of everyday life. *S.E.*, 6. London: Hogarth.

Freud, S. (1905a). On psychotherapy. *S.E.*, 7: 255–268. London: Hogarth.

Freud, S. (1905c). *Jokes and their Relation to the Unconscious. S.E.*, 8. London: Hogarth.

Freud, S. (1905d). *Three Essays on the Theory of Sexuality. S.E.*, 7: 123–246. London: Hogarth.

Freud, S. (1905e). *Fragment of an Analysis of a Case of Hysteria. S.E.*, 7: 1–122. London: Hogarth.

Freud, S. (1906a). My views on the part played by sexuality in the aetiology of the neuroses. *S.E.*, 7: 269–279. London: Hogarth.

Freud, S. (1906c). Psycho-analysis and the establishment of the facts in legal proceedings. *S.E.*, 9: 97–114. London: Hogarth.

Freud, S. (1907a). Delusions and dreams in Jensen's *Gradiva. S.E.*, 9: 1–96. London: Hogarth.

Freud, S. (1907b). Obsessive actions and religious practices. *S.E.*, 9: 115–128. London: Hogarth.

Freud, S. (1908c). On the sexual theories of children. *S.E.*, 9: 205–226. London: Hogarth

Freud, S. (1908d). 'Civilized' sexual morality and modern nervous illness. *S.E.*, 9: 179–204. London: Hogarth.

Freud, S. (1908e). Creative writers and day-dreaming. *S.E.*, 9: 141–154. London: Hogarth.

Freud, S. (1909b). *Analysis of a Phobia in a Five-year-old Boy. S.E.*, 10: 1–150. London: Hogarth.

Freud, S. (1909d). *Notes upon a Case of Obsessional Neurosis. S.E.*, 10: 151–318. London: Hogarth.

Freud, S. (1910a). Five lectures on psycho-analysis. *S.E.*, 11: 1–56. London: Hogarth.

Freud, S. (1910c). *Leonardo da Vinci and a Memory of his Childhood. S.E.*, 11: 57–138. London: Hogarth.

Freud, S. (1910d). The future prospects of psycho-analytic therapy. *S.E.*, 11: 139–152. London: Hogarth.

Freud, S (1910h). A special type of choice of object made by men (contributions to the psychology of love I). *S.E.*, 11: 163–176. London: Hogarth.

Freud, S. (1910i). The psycho-analytic view of the psychogenic disturbance of vision. *S.E.*, *11*: 209–218. London: Hogarth.

Freud, S. (1910k). 'Wild' psycho-analysis. *S.E.*, *11*: 219–228. London: Hogarth.

Freud, S. (1911b). Formulations on the two principles of mental functioning. *S.E.*, *12*: 213–226. London: Hogarth.

Freud, S. (1911c). *Psycho-analytic Notes on an Autobiographical Account of a Case of Paranoia (Dementia Paranoides)*. *S.E.*, *12*: 3–82. London: Hogarth.

Freud, S. (1912b). The dynamics of transference. *S.E.*, *12*: 97–108. London: Hogarth.

Freud, S. (1912c). Types of onset of neurosis. *S.E.*, *12*: 227–238. London: Hogarth.

Freud, S. (1912d). On the universal tendency to debasement in the sphere of love (contributions to the psychology of love II). *S.E.*, *11*: 179–190. London: Hogarth.

Freud, S. (1912g). A note on the unconscious in psycho-analysis. *S.E.*, *12*: 256–266. London: Hogarth.

Freud, S. (1912–1913). *Totem and Taboo*. *S.E.*, *13*. London: Hogarth.

Freud, S. (1913c). On beginning the treatment (further recommendations on the technique of psycho-analysis I). *S.E.*, *12*: 121–144. London: Hogarth.

Freud, S. (1913i). The disposition to obsessional neurosis: a contribution to the problem of choice of neurosis. *S.E.*, *12*: 311–326. London: Hogarth.

Freud, S. (1913j). The claims of psycho-analysis to scientific interest. *S.E.*, *13*: 163–190. London: Hogarth.

Freud, S. (1913m). On psycho-analysis. *S.E.*, *12*: 205–212. London: Hogarth.

Freud, S. (1914c). On narcissism: an introduction. *S.E.*, *14*: 67–102. London: Hogarth.

Freud, S. (1914d). On the history of the psycho-analytic movement. *S.E.*, *14*: 1–66. London: Hogarth.

Freud, S. (1914g). Remembering, repeating and working-through (further recommendations on the technique of psycho-analysis II). *S.E.*, *12*: 145–156. London: Hogarth.

Freud, S. (1915a). Observations on transference-love (further recommendations on the technique of psycho-analysis III). *S.E.*, *12*: 157–171. London: Hogarth.

Freud, S. (1915c). Instincts and their vicissitudes. *S.E.*, *14*: 109–140. London: Hogarth.

Freud, S. (1915d). Repression. *S.E.*, *14*: 141–158. London: Hogarth.

Freud, S. (1915e). The unconscious. *S.E.*, *14*: 159–215. London: Hogarth.

Freud, S. (1916–1917). *Introductory Lectures on Psycho-analysis. S.E., 15–16.* London: Hogarth.

Freud, S. (1917a). A difficulty in the path of psycho-analysis. *S.E.*, *17*: 135–144. London: Hogarth.

Freud, S. (1917d). A metapsychological supplement to the theory of dreams. *S.E.*, *14*: 217–235. London: Hogarth.

Freud, S. (1918b). *From the History of an Infantile Neurosis. S.E., 17*: 1–124. London: Hogarth.

Freud, S. (1919a). Lines of advance in psycho-analytic therapy. *S.E.*, *17*: 157–168. London: Hogarth.

Freud, S. (1919d). Introduction to *Psycho-analysis and the War Neuroses. S.E., 17*: 205–216. London: Hogarth.

Freud, S. (1919e). 'A child is being beaten': a contribution to the study of the origin of sexual perversions. *S.E.*, *17*: 175–204. London: Hogarth.

Freud, S. (1919g). Preface to Reik's *Ritual: Psycho-analytic Studies. S.E., 17*: 257–264. London: Hogarth.

Freud, S. (1920g). *Beyond the Pleasure Principle. S.E., 18*: 1–64. London: Hogarth.

Freud, S. (1923a). Two encyclopaedia articles. *S.E.*, *18*: 233–260. London: Hogarth.

Freud, S. (1923b). *The Ego and the Id. S.E., 19*: 1–66. London: Hogarth.

Freud, S. (1924b). Neurosis and psychosis. *S.E.*, *19*: 147–154. London: Hogarth.

Freud, S. (1924c). The economic problem of masochism. *S.E.*, *19*: 155–170. London: Hogarth.

Freud, S. (1924d). The dissolution of the Oedipus complex. *S.E.*, *19*: 171–180. London: Hogarth.

Freud, S. (1924e). The loss of reality in neurosis and psychosis. *S.E.*, *19*: 181–188. London: Hogarth.

Freud, S. (1924f). A short account of psycho-analysis. *S.E.*, *19*: 189–210. London: Hogarth.

Freud, S. (1925d). An autobiographical study. *S.E.*, *20*: 1–74. London: Hogarth.

Freud, S. (1925e). The resistances to psycho-analysis. *S.E.*, *19*: 211–224. London: Hogarth.

Freud, S. (1925i). Some additional notes on dream-interpretation as a whole. *S.E.*, *19*: 123–138. London: Hogarth.

Freud, S. (1925j). Some psychical consequences of the anatomical distinction between the sexes. *S.E.*, *19*: 241–258. London: Hogarth.

Freud, S. (1926d). *Inhibitions, Symptoms and Anxiety. S.E., 20*: 75–176. London: Hogarth.

Freud, S. (1926e). The question of lay analysis. *S.E., 29*: 177–258. London: Hogarth.

Freud, S. (1926f). Psycho-analysis. *S.E., 20*: 259–270. London: Hogarth.

Freud, S. (1928b). Dostoevsky and parricide. *S.E., 21*: 173–194. London: Hogarth.

Freud, S. (1930b). *Civilization and Its Discontents. S.E., 21*: 57–146. London: Hogarth.

Freud, S. (1932c). My contact with Josef Popper-Lynkeus. *S.E., 22*: 217–224. London: Hogarth.

Freud, S. (1933a). *New Introductory Lectures on Psycho-analysis. S.E., 22*. London: Hogarth.

Freud, S. (1936a). A disturbance of memory on the Acropolis. *S.E., 22*: 237–248. London: Hogarth.

Freud, S. (1937c). Analysis terminable and interminable. *S.E., 23*: 209–254. London: Hogarth.

Freud, S. (1937d). Constructions in analysis. *S.E., 23*: 255–270. London: Hogarth.

Freud, S. (1939a). *Moses and Monotheism: Three Essays. S.E., 23*: 1–138. London: Hogarth.

Freud, S. (1940a[1938]). *An Outline of Psycho-analysis. S.E., 23*: 139–208. London: Hogarth.

Freud, S. (1940b[1938]). Some elementary lessons in psycho-analysis. *S.E., 23*: 279–286. London: Hogarth.

Freud, S. (1940e[1938]). Splitting of the ego in the process of defence. *S.E., 23*: 271–278. London: Hogarth.

Freud, S. (1942a[1905]). Psychopathic characters on the stage. *S.E., 7*: 303–310. London: Hogarth.

Freud, S. (1950[1895]). *Project for a Scientific Psychology. S.E., 1*: 283–397. London: Hogarth.

Fulgencio, L. (2005). Freud's metapsychological speculations. *International Journal of Psychoanalysis, 86*: 99–123.

Gabbard, G. O., & Westen, D. (2003). Rethinking therapeutic action. *International Journal of Psychoanalysis, 84*: 823–841.

Gardner, S. (1993). *Irrationality and the Philosophy of Psychoanalysis.* Cambridge: Cambridge University Press.

Gay, V. P. (1982). Semiotics as metapsychology: the status of repression. *Bulletin of the Menninger Clinic, 46*: 489–506.

Geisler, C. (1985). Repression: a psychoanalytic perspective revisited. *Psychoanalysis and Contemporary Thought, 8*: 253–298.

Gilbert, P. (2001). Evolutionary approaches to psychopathology: the role of natural defences. *Australian and New Zealand Journal of Psychiatry, 35*: 17–27.

Gill, M. M. (1963). *Topography and Systems in Psychoanalytic Theory*. New York: International Universities Press.

Gillett, E. (1987). The relationship of repression to the unconscious. *International Journal of Psychoanalysis, 68*: 535–546.

Gillett, E. (1988). The brain and the unconscious. *Psychoanalysis and Contemporary Thought, 11*: 563–578.

Gillett, E. (1990). The problem of unconscious affect: signal anxiety versus the double-prediction theory. *Psychoanalysis and Contemporary Thought, 13*: 551–600.

Gillett, E. (1997). Revising Freud's structural theory. *Psychoanalysis and Contemporary Thought, 20*: 471–499.

Gillett, E. (2001). Signal anxiety from the adaptive point of view. *Psychoanalytic Psychology, 18*: 268–286.

Gouws, A. (2000). Will the real Freud please stand up? The distribution of power between the unconscious and the preconscious according to the *Traumdeutung*. *International Journal of Psychotherapy, 5*: 227–239.

Grauer, D. (1958). How autonomous is the ego? *Journal of the American Psychoanalytic Association, 6*: 502–518.

Green, A. (1977). Conceptions of affect. *International Journal of Psychoanalysis, 58*: 129–156.

Greenwald, A. G. (1992). New Look 3: unconscious cognition reclaimed. *American Psychologist, 47*: 766–779.

Grossman, W. I., & Simon, B. (1969). Anthropomorphism: motive, meaning, and causality in psychoanalytic theory. *Psychoanalytic Study of the Child, 24*: 78–111.

Halliday, T. R. (1995). Motivational systems and interactions between activities. In: F. M. Toates & T. R. Halliday (Eds.), *Analysis of Motivational Processes* (pp. 205–220). London: Academic Press.

Harris, H. I. (1950). Repression as a factor in learning theory. *Psychoanalytic Quarterly, 19*: 410–411.

Hart, W. D. (1982). Models of repression. In: R. Wollheim & J. Hopkins (Eds.), *Philosophical Essays on Freud* (pp. 180–201). Cambridge: Cambridge University Press.

Hartmann, H. (1950). Comments on the psychoanalytic theory of the ego. *Psychoanalytic Study of the Child, 5*: 74–96.

Hartmann, H. (1958). *Ego Psychology and the Problem of Adaptation*. New York: International Universities Press.

Hartmann, H., Kris, E., & Loewenstein, R. M. (1949). Notes on the theory of aggression. *Psychoanalytic Study of the Child, 3*: 9–36.

Hayman, A. (1969). What do we mean by "id"? *Journal of the American Psychoanalytic Association, 17*: 353–380.

Henderson, J. (1999). *Memory and Forgetting*. London: Routledge.

Hibberd, F. J. (2009). Anderson's development of (situational) realism and its bearing on psychology today. *History of the Human Sciences, 22*: 1–30.

Hobson, J. A. (1988). *The Dreaming Brain*. New York: Basic Books.

Hobson, J. A. (1999). The new neuropsychology of sleep: implications for psychoanalysis. *Neuro-Psychoanalysis, 1*: 157–183.

Hobson, J. A. (2005). In: bed with Mark Solms? What a nightmare! Reply to Domhoff (2005). *Dreaming, 15*: 21–29.

Hobson, J. A., & Pace-Schott, E. F. (1999). Response to commentaries. *Neuro-Psychoanalysis, 1*: 206–224.

Holmes, D. S. (1990). The evidence for repression: an examination of sixty years of research. In: J. L. Singer (Ed.), *Repression and Dissociation: Implications for Personality Theory, Psychopathology, and Health* (pp. 85–102). Chicago, IL: University of Chicago Press.

Holmes, J. (2000). Attachment theory and psychoanalysis: A *rapprochement*. *British Journal of Psychotherapy, 17*: 157–172.

Holt, E. B., Marvin, W. T., Montague, W. P., Perry, R. B., Pitkin, W. B., & Spaulding, E. G. (1912). *The New Realism*. New York: Macmillan.

Holt, R. R. (1976). Drive or wish? A reconsideration of the psycho-analytic theory of motivation. In: M. Gill & P. Holzman (Eds.), *Psychology vs Metapsychology: Psycho-analytic Essays in Memory of George Klein. Psychological Issues*, Monograph 36, Vol. 9 (pp. 158–197). New York: International Universities Press.

Hopkins, J. (1988). Epistemology and depth psychology: critical notes on *The Foundations of Psycho-analysis*. In: P. Clark & C. Wright (Eds.), *Mind, Psychoanalysis and Science* (pp. 33–60). Oxford: Basil Blackwell.

Hopkins, J. (1995a). Introduction to *Philosophical Essays on Freud*. In: C. Macdonald & G. Macdonald (Eds.), *Philosophy of Psychology: Debates on Psychological Explanation*, Vol. I (pp. 409–432). Oxford: Blackwell.

Hopkins, J. (1995b). Reply: irrationality, interpretation and division. In: C. Macdonald & G. Macdonald (Eds.), *Philosophy of Psychology: Debates on Psychological Explanation*, Vol. I (pp. 461–484). Oxford: Blackwell.

Horowitz, M. H. (1977). The quantitative line of approach in psychoanalysis: a clinical assessment of its current status. *Journal of the American Psychoanalytic Association, 25*: 559–579.

Hospers, J. (1959). *An Introduction to Philosophical Analysis*. New Jersey: Prentice-Hall.

Hutterer, J., & Liss, M. (2006). Cognitive development, memory, trauma, treatment: an integration of psychoanalytic and behavioural concepts in light of current neuroscience research. *Journal of the American Academy of Psychoanalysis and Dynamic Psychiatry, 34*: 287–302.

Izard, C. E. (1991). *The Psychology of Emotions*. New York: Plenum.

Jacobson, E. (1953). The affects and their pleasure–unpleasure qualities in relation to psychic discharge processes. In: R. M. Loewenstein (Ed.), *Drives, Affects, Behaviour* (pp. 38–66). New York: International Universities Press.

Jaffe, D. S. (1991). Beyond the what, when, and how of transference: a consideration of the why. *Journal of the American Psychoanalytic Association, 39*: 491–512.

Johnson, A. (1998). Repression: a reexamination of the concept as applied to folktales. *Ethos, 26*: 295–313.

Jones, B. P. (1993). Repression: the evolution of a psycho-analytic concept from the 1890's to the 1990's. *Journal of the American Psychoanalytic Association, 41*: 63–95.

Jones, E. (1948). Psycho-analysis and the instincts. In: *Papers on Psycho-analysis* (pp. 153–169). Boston: Beacon Press.

Jones, E. (1949). *What is Psycho-analysis?* London: George Allen & Unwin.

Jones, E. (1953). *Sigmund Freud: Life and Work*, Vol. 1. London: Hogarth.

Jones, E. (1955). *Sigmund Freud: Life and Work*, Vol. 2. London: Hogarth.

Joseph, R. (1992). *The Right Brain and the Unconscious: Discovering the Stranger Within*. New York: Plenum.

Joseph, R. (1996). *Neuropsychiatry, Neuropsychology, and Clinical Neuroscience*. Baltimore: Williams & Wilkins.

Kalenscher, T., Ohmann, T., & Güntürkün, O. (2006). The neuroscience of impulsive and self-controlled decisions. *International Journal of Psychophysiology, 62*: 203–211.

Kandel, E. R. (1999). Biology and the future of psychoanalysis: a new intellectual framework for psychiatry revisited. *American Journal of Psychiatry, 156*: 505–524.

Kaplan-Solms, K., & Solms, M. (2000). *Clinical Studies in Neuro-psycho-analysis: Introduction to a Depth Psychology*. London: Karnac.

Kendall, T., & Speedwell, K. (1999). On the existence of the unconscious. In: C. Feltham (Ed.), *Controversies in Psychotherapy and Counselling* (pp. 15–24). London: Sage.

Kihlstrom, J. F. (1987). The cognitive unconscious. *Science, 237*: 1445–1452.

Kissin, B. (1986). *Conscious and Unconscious Programs in the Brain.* New York: Plenum.

Klein, M. (1928). Early stages of the Oedipus conflict. In: M. Klein (Ed.), *Love, Guilt and Reparation and Other Works, 1921–1945* (pp. 186–198). London: Karnac, 1992.

Klein, M. (1933). The early development of conscience in the child. In: M. Klein (Ed.), *Love, Guilt and Reparation and Other Works, 1921–1945* (pp. 248–257). London: Karnac, 1992.

Kok, A. (1999). Varieties of inhibition: manifestations in cognition, event-related potentials and aging. *Acta Psychologica, 101*: 129–158.

Krystal, H. (1978). Trauma and affects. *Psychoanalytic Study of the Child, 33*: 81–116.

Kubie, L. S. (1947). The fallacious use of quantitative concepts in dynamic psychology. *Psycho-analytic Quarterly, 16*: 507–518.

Langnickel, R., & Markowitsch, H. (2006). Repression and the unconscious. *Behavioural and Brain Sciences, 29*: 524–525.

Laplanche, J., & Pontalis, J.-B. (1973). *The Language of Psychoanalysis.* London: Karnac.

Lazarus, R. S. (1991). *Emotion and Adaptation.* New York: Oxford University Press.

LeDoux, J. E. (1990). *The Emotional Brain.* New York: Simon & Schuster.

LeDoux, J. E. (1995). Emotion: clues from the brain. *Annual Review of Psychology, 46*: 209–235.

LeDoux, J. E., & Schiller, D. (2009). The human amygdala: insights from other animals. In: P. J. Whalen & E. A. Phelps (Eds.), *The Human Amygdala* (pp. 43–60). New York: Guilford Press.

Linke, D. B. (1998). Discharge, reflex, free energy and encoding. In: G. Guttman & I. Scholz-Strasser (Eds.), *Freud and the Neurosciences: From Brain Research to the Unconscious* (pp. 103–108). Vienna: Österreichischen Akademie der Wissenschaften.

Liotti, M., & Panksepp, J. (2004). Imaging human emotions and affective feelings: implications for biological psychiatry. In: J. Panksepp (Ed.), *Textbook of Biological Psychiatry* (pp. 33–74). Hoboken, NJ: Wiley-Liss.

Locke, J. (1690). *An Essay Concerning Human Understanding.* London: J. M. Dent, 1947.

Loftus, E., & Ketcham, K. (1994). *The Myth of Repressed Memory.* New York: St. Martin's Press.

Lothane, Z. (1999). The perennial Freud: method versus myth and the mischief of Freud bashers. *International Forum of Psychoanalysis, 8:* 151–171.

Machado, A., & Silva, F. J. (2007). Toward a richer view of the scientific method: the role of conceptual analysis. *American Psychologist, 62:* 671–681.

MacIntyre, A. C. (1958). *The Unconscious: A Conceptual Analysis.* London: Routledge & Kegan Paul.

Mackay, N. (1994). Cognitive therapy, constructivist metatheory, and rational explanation. *Australian Journal of Psychology, 46:* 7–12.

Mackay, N. (1996). The place of motivation in psychoanalysis. *Modern Psychoanalysis, 21:* 3–17.

Mackay, N. (1999). Reason, cause, and rationality in psychological explanation. *Journal of Theoretical and Philosophical Psychology, 19:* 1–21.

Mackay, N. (2006). Commentary on "Freudian dream theory, dream bizarreness, and the disguise-censor controversy". *Neuropsychoanalysis, 8:* 40–42.

Macmillan, M. (1991). *Freud Evaluated: The Completed Arc.* North-Holland: Elsevier Science.

Macmillan, M. (1992). Inhibition and the control of behaviour: from Gall to Freud via Phineas Gage and the frontal lobes. *Brain and Cognition, 19:* 72–104.

Macmillan, M. (1996). The concept of inhibition in some nineteenth century theories of thinking. *Brain and Cognition, 30:* 4–19.

Madison, P. (1956). Freud's repression concept: a survey and attempted clarification. *International Journal of Psychoanalysis, 37:* 75–81.

Madison, P. (1961). *Freud's Concept of Repression and Defense: Its Theoretical and Observational Language.* Minneapolis, MN: University of Minnesota Press.

Mancia, M. (2006). Implicit memory and early unrepressed unconscious: their role in the therapeutic process (How the neurosciences can contribute to psychoanalysis). *International Journal of Psychoanalysis, 87:* 83–103.

Maren, S., & Quirk, G. J. (2004). Neuronal signalling of fear memory. *Nature Reviews Neuroscience, 5:* 844–852.

Martindale, C. (1975). The grammar of altered states of consciousness: a semiotic reinterpretation of aspects of psychoanalytic theory. *Psychoanalysis and Contemporary Science, 4:* 331–354.

Masling, J. M. (1992). What does it all mean? In: R. F. Bornstein & T. S. Pittman (Eds.), *Perception without Awareness: Cognitive, Clinical, and Social perspectives* (pp. 259–276). New York: Guilford Press.

Masson, J. M. (Ed.) (1985). *The Complete Letters of Sigmund Freud and Wilhelm Fliess, 1887–1904*. Cambridge: Belknap Press.

Matte-Blanco, I. (1975). *The Unconscious as Infinite Sets: An Essay in Bi-Logic*. London: Duckworth.

May, U. (1999). Freud's early clinical theory (1894–1896): outline and context. *International Journal of Psychoanalysis, 80*: 769–781.

Maze, J. R. (1954). Do intervening variables intervene? *Psychological Review, 61*: 226–234.

Maze, J. R. (1983). *The Meaning of Behaviour*. London: Allen & Unwin.

Maze, J. R. (1987). The composition of the ego in a deterministic psychology. In: W. J. Baker, M. E. Hyland, H. Van Rappard, & A. W. Staats (Eds.), *Current Issues in Theoretical Psychology* (pp. 189–199). North Holland: Elsevier Science.

Maze, J. R. (1993). The complementarity of object-relations and instinct theory. *International Journal of Psychoanalysis, 74*: 459–70.

Maze, J. R., & Henry, R. M. (1996). Problems in the concept of repression and proposals for their resolution. *International Journal of Psychoanalysis, 77*: 1085–1100.

McCarley, R. W. (1998). Dreams: disguise of forbidden wishes or transparent reflections of a distinct brain state? In: R. M. Bilder & F. F. LeFever (Eds.), *Neuroscience of the Mind on the Centennial of Freud's Project for a Scientific Psychology* (pp. 116–133). New York: New York Academy of Sciences.

McCarley, R. W., & Hobson, J. A. (1977). The neurobiological origins of psychoanalytic dream theory. *American Journal of Psychiatry, 134*: 1211–1221.

McDougall, W. (1923). *An Outline of Psychology*. London: Methuen.

McIlwain, D. (2001). The dynamic unconscious revisited: the role of motivation, affect, embodiment and intersubjectivity in catching ourselves unawares. In: J. R. Morss, N. Stephenson, & H. van Rappard (Eds.), *Theoretical Issues in Psychology* (pp. 379–392). Boston, MA: Kluwer.

McIlwain, D. (2007). Rezoning pleasure: drives and affects in personality theory. *Theory and Psychology, 17*: 529–561.

McIntosh, D. (1986). The ego and the self in the thought of Sigmund Freud. *International Journal of Psychoanalysis, 67*: 429–448.

McMullen, T. (1996a). Psychology and realism. In: C. R. Latimer & J. Michell (Eds.), *At Once Scientific and Philosophic: A Festschrift for John Philip Sutcliffe* (pp. 59–66). Brisbane: Boombana.

McMullen, T. (1996b). John Anderson on mind as feeling. *Theory and Psychology, 6*: 153–168.

McNally, R. J. (2007). Do certain readings of Freud constitute "pathological science"? A comment on Boag (2006). *Review of General Psychology,* 11: 359–360.

Medlow, S. (2008). *The 'Paradox' of Mental Causation: Solutions From Anomalous Monism and Direct Realism.* Saarbrücken: VDM.

Merlan, P. (1945). Brentano and Freud. *Journal of the History of Ideas,* 6: 375–377.

Metcalfe, J., & Shimamura, A. P. (1994). *Metacognition: Knowing About Knowing.* Cambridge, MA: MIT Press.

Michell, J. (1988). Maze's direct realism and the character of cognition. *Australian Journal of Psychology,* 40: 227–249.

Michell, J. (2000). Normal science, pathological science and psychometrics. *Theory and Psychology,* 10: 639–667.

Mills, J. (2004). Clarifications on *Trieb:* Freud's theory of motivation reinstated. *Psychoanalytic Psychology,* 21: 673–677.

Mirvish, A. (1990). Freud contra Sartre: repression or self-deception? *Journal of the British Society for Phenomenology,* 21: 216–233.

Moore, B. E., & Fine, B. D. (Eds.) (1990). *Psychoanalytic Terms and Concepts.* New Haven, CT: American Psychoanalytic Association.

Morley, R. E. (2000). The self-blinding of Oedipus and the theory of repression. *Psychoanalytic Studies,* 2: 159–176.

Nagel, E. (1959). Methodological issues in psychoanalytic theory. In: S. Hook (Ed.), *Psychoanalysis, Scientific Method and Philosophy* (pp. 38–56). Washington Square: New York University Press.

Nesse, R. M. (1990). The evolutionary functions of repression and the ego defenses. *Journal of the American Academy of Psychoanalysis,* 18: 260–285.

Neu, J. (1988). Divided minds: Sartre's "bad faith" critique of Freud. *Review of Metaphysics,* 42: 79–101.

Öhman, A. (2009). Human fear conditioning and the amygdala. In: P. J. Whalen & E. A. Phelps (Eds.), *The Human Amygdala* (pp. 118–154). New York: Guilford Press.

Öhman, A., Carlsson, K., Lundqvist, D., & Ingvar, M. (2007). On the unconscious subcortical origin of human fear. *Physiology & Behaviour,* 92: 180–185.

Oliner, M. M. (2000). The unsolved puzzle of trauma. *Psychoanalytic Quarterly,* 69: 41–61.

Oliphant, G. (1994). Connectionism, psychology and science. In: J. Wiles, C. Latimer, & C. Stevens (Eds.), *Collected Papers from a Symposium on Connectionist Models and Psychology,* Technical Report No. 289. Queensland: University of Queensland.

O'Neil, W. M. (1934). Mind as feeling? *Australasian Journal of Psychology and Philosophy,* 12: 280–287.

Pally, R. (1998). Emotional processing: the mind-body connection. *International Journal of Psychoanalysis, 79*: 349–362.

Panksepp, J. (1999). Emotions as viewed by psychoanalysis and neuroscience: an exercise in consilience. *Neuro-psychoanalysis, 1*: 15–38.

Panksepp, J. (2001). The long-term psychobiological consequences of infant emotions: prescriptions for the twenty-first century. *Infant Mental Health Journal, 22*: 132–173.

Panksepp, J. (2003). At the interface of the affective, behavioural, and cognitive neurosciences: decoding the emotional feelings of the brain. *Brain & Cognition, 52*: 4–14.

Panksepp, J. (2005). Affective consciousness: core emotional feelings in animals and humans. *Consciousness & Cognition, 14*: 30–80.

Panksepp, J., & Moskal, J. (2008). Dopamine and SEEKING: subcortical "reward" systems and appetitive urges. In: A. J. Elliot (Ed.), *Handbook of Approach and Avoidance Motivation* (pp. 67–87). New York: Psychology Press.

Pasnau, R. (1997). *Theories of Cognition in the Later Middle Ages*. Cambridge: Cambridge University Press.

Passmore, J. A. (1935). The nature of intelligence. *Australasian Journal of Psychology and Philosophy, 13*: 279–289.

Pataki, T. (1997). Self-deception and wish-fulfilment. *Philosophia, 25*: 297–322.

Pataki, T. (2000). Freudian wish-fulfilment and sub-intentional explanation. In: M. P. Levine (Ed.), *The Analytic Freud: Philosophy and Psychoanalysis* (pp. 49–84). London: Routledge.

Peled, A. (2008). *Neuroanalysis: Bridging the Gap Between Neuroscience, Psychoanalysis and Psychiatry*. London: Routledge.

Penrose, L. S. (1931). Freud's theory of instinct and other psycho-biological theories. *International Journal of Psychoanalysis, 12*: 87–97.

Peskin, M. M. (1997). Drive theory revisited. *Psychoanalytic Quarterly, 66*: 377–402.

Petocz, A. (1999). *Freud, Psychoanalysis, and Symbolism*. Cambridge: Cambridge University Press.

Petocz, A. (2006). Commentary on "Freudian dream theory, dream bizarreness, and the disguise-censor controversy". *Neuropsychoanalysis, 8*: 48–53.

Plato (1928). *The Republic*. New York: Charles Schribner's Sons.

Pugh, G. (2002). Freud's 'problem': cognitive neuroscience and psychoanalysis working together on memory. *International Journal of Psychoanalysis, 83*: 1375–1394.

Pulver, S. E. (1971). Can affects be unconscious? *International Journal of Psycho-analysis, 52*: 347–354.

Pulver, S. E. (1974). Unconscious versus potential affects. *Psychoanalytic Quarterly, 43*: 77–84.

Pulver, S. E. (1995). Psychoanalytic process and mechanisms of therapeutic change. In: B. E. Moore & B. D. Fine (Eds.), *Psycho-analysis: The Major Concepts* (pp. 81–94). New Haven, CT: Yale University Press.

Ramachandran, V. S. (1994). Phantom limbs, neglect syndromes, repressed memories, and Freudian psychology. *International Review of Neurobiology, 37*: 291–333.

Ramachandran, V. S. (1996). The evolutionary biology of self-deception, laughter, dreaming and depression: some clues from anosognosia. *Medical Hypotheses, 47*: 347–362.

Rangell, L. (1978). On understanding and treating anxiety and its derivatives. *International Journal of Psycho-analysis, 59*: 229–236.

Rangell, L. (1995). Affects. In: B. E. Moore & B. D. Fine (Eds.), *Psycho-analysis: The Major Concepts* (pp. 381–391). New Haven: Yale University Press.

Rangell, L. (2002). The theory of psychoanalysis: vicissitudes of its evolution. *Journal of the American Psychoanalytic Association, 50*: 1109–1137.

Rantzen, A. J. (1993). Constructivism, direct realism, and the nature of error. *Theory & Psychology, 3*: 147–171.

Rapaport, D. (1953). On the psycho-analytic theory of affects. *International Journal of Psychoanalysis, 34*: 177–198.

Redgrave, P., Prescott, T. J., & Gurney, K. (1999). The basal ganglia: a vertebrate solution to the selection problem? *Neuroscience, 89*: 1000–1023.

Richfield, J. (1954). An analysis of the concept of insight. *Psychoanalytic Quarterly, 23*: 390–408.

Ridderinkhof, V. K., Wildenberg, W. P. M., Segalowitz, S. J., & Carter, C. S. (2004). Neurocognitive mechanisms of cognitive control: the role of the prefrontal cortex in action selection, response inhibition, performance monitoring, and reward-based learning. *Brain & Cognition, 56*: 129–140.

Ritvo, S., & Solnit, A. J. (1995). Instinct theory. In: B. E. Moore & B. D. Fine (Eds.), *Psycho-analysis: The Major Concepts* (pp. 327–333). New Haven, CT: Yale University Press.

Rofé, Y. (2008). Does repression exist? Memory, pathogenic, unconscious and clinical evidence. *Review of General Psychology, 12*: 63–85.

Rosenblatt, A. D. (1985). The role of affect in cognitive psychology and psychoanalysis. *Psychoanalytic Psychology, 2*: 85–97.

Rosenblatt, A. D., & Thickstun, J. T. (1977). Energy, information, and motivation: a revision of psycho-analytic theory. *Journal of the American Psychoanalytic Association, 25*: 537–558.

Ross, N. (1975). Affect as cognition: with observations on the meanings of mystical states. *International Review of Psycho-analysis, 2*: 79–93.

Rudy, J. W., & Morledge, P. (1994). Ontogeny of contextual fear conditioning in rats: implications for consolidation, infantile amnesia, and hippocampal system function. *Behavioural Neuroscience, 108*: 227–234.

Russell, B. (1927). *An Outline of Philosophy*. London: George Allen & Unwin.

Salthouse, T. A., Atkinson, T. M., & Berish, D. E. (2003). Executive functioning as a potential mediator of age-related cognitive decline in normal adults. *Journal of Experimental Psychology: General, 132*: 566–594.

Sandler, J. (1974). Psychological conflict and the structural model: some clinical and theoretical implications. *International Journal of Psychoanalysis, 55*: 53–62.

Sandler, J. (1985). Towards a reconsideration of the psycho-analytic theory of motivation. *Bulletin of the Anna Freud Centre, 8*: 223–244.

Sandler, J., & Joffe, W. G. (1969). Towards a basic psychoanalytic model. *International Journal of Psychoanalysis, 50*: 79–90.

Sandler, J., & Sandler, A.-M. (1983). The 'second censorship', the 'three box model' and some technical implications. *International Journal of Psychoanalysis, 64*: 413–425.

Sandler, J., & Sandler, A.-M. (1994). The past unconscious and the present unconscious: a contribution to a technical frame of reference. *Psychoanalytic Study of the Child, 49*: 278–292.

Sandler, J., & Sandler, A.-M. (1997). A psychoanalytic theory of repression and the unconscious. In: J. Sandler & P. Fonagy (Eds.), *Recovered Memories of Abuse: True or False?* (pp. 163–181). Madison, NY: International Universities Press.

Sandler, J., Dreher, A. U., & Drews, S. (1991). An approach to conceptual research in psychoanalysis illustrated by a consideration of psychic trauma. *International Review of Psychoanalysis, 18*: 133–141.

Sartre, J.-P. (1956). *Being and Nothingness*, H. E. Barnes (Trans.). New York: Philosophical Library.

Schafer, R. (1968). The mechanisms of defence. *International Journal of Psychoanalysis, 49*: 49–62.

Schafer, R. (1973). The idea of resistance. *International Journal of Psychoanalysis, 54*: 259–285.

Schore, A. N. (2001). The right brain as the neurobiological substratum of Freud's dynamic unconscious. In: D. E. Scharff (Ed.), *The Psychoanalytic Century: Freud's Legacy for the Future* (pp. 61–88). New York: Other Press.

Schore, A. N. (2002). Dysregulation of the right brain: a fundamental mechanism of traumatic attachment and the psychopathogenesis of posttraumatic stress disorder. *Australian and New Zealand Journal of Psychiatry, 36*: 9–30.

Schore, A. N. (2009). Relational trauma and the developing right brain: an interface of psychoanalytic self psychology and neuroscience. *Self and Systems, 1159*: 189–203.

Schur, M. (1953). The ego in anxiety. In: R. M. Loewenstein (Ed.), *Drives, Affects, Behaviour* (pp. 67–103). New York: International Universities Press.

Schur, M. (1969). Affects and cognition. *International Journal of Psychoanalysis, 50*: 647–653.

Schwartz, A. (1987). Drives, affects, behavior—and learning: approaches to a psychobiology of emotion and to an integration of psychoanalytic and neurobiologic thought. *Journal of the American Psychoanalytic Association, 35*: 467–506.

Searle, J. R. (1992). *The Rediscovery of the Mind*. Cambridge, MA: MIT Press.

Searle, J. R. (1995). Consciousness, explanatory inversion and cognitive science. In: C. Macdonald & G. Macdonald (Eds.), *Philosophy of Psychology: Debates on Psychological Explanation*, Vol. I (pp. 331–355). Oxford: Blackwell.

Sewards, T. V., & Sewards, M. A. (2002). The medial pain system: neural representations of the motivational aspect of pain. *Brain Research Bulletin, 59*: 163–180.

Sewards, T. V., & Sewards, M. A. (2003). Representations of motivational drives in mesial cortex, medial thalamus, hypothalamus and midbrain. *Brain Research Bulletin, 61*: 25–49.

Shevrin, H. (1990). Subliminal perception and repression. In: J. L. Singer (Ed.), *Repression & Dissociation: Implications for Personality Theory, Psychopathology, & Health* (pp. 103–119). Chicago, IL: University of Chicago Press.

Shill, M. A. (2004). Signal anxiety, defense, and the pleasure principle. *Psychoanalytic Psychology, 21*: 116–133.

Sjöbäck, H. (1973). *The Psychoanalytic Theory of Defensive Processes: A Critical Survey*. Lund: CWK Gleer Up.

Slap, J. W., & Saykin, A. J. (1984). On the nature and the organisation of the repressed. *Psychoanalytic Inquiry, 4*: 107–124.

Slavin, M. O. (1985). The origins of psychic conflict and the adaptive function of repression: an evolutionary biological view. *Psychoanalysis and Contemporary Thought*, 8: 407–440.

Slavin, M. O. (1990). The dual meaning of repression and the adaptive design of the human psyche. *Journal of the American Academy of Psychoanalysis*, 18: 307–341.

Slavin, M. O., & Grief, D. (1995). The evolved function of repression and the adaptive design of the human psyche. In: H. R. Conte & R. Plutchik (Eds.), *Ego Defenses: Theory and Measurement* (pp. 139–175). New York: John Wiley & Sons.

Smith, S. M. (2006). Resolving repression. *Behavioral & Brain Sciences*, 29: 534–535.

Solms, M. (1995). Is the brain more real than the mind? *Psychoanalytic Psychotherapy*, 9: 107–120.

Solms, M. (1997a). *The Neuropsychology of Dreams: A Clinic-anatomical Study*. Mahweh, NJ: Lawrence Erlbaum Associates.

Solms, M. (1997b). What is consciousness. *Journal of the American Psychoanalytic Association*, 45: 681–703.

Solms, M. (2003). Do unconscious phantasies really exist? In: R. Steiner (Ed.), *Unconscious Phantasy* (pp. 89–105). London: Karnac.

Solms, M. (2005). Neuroscience. In: E. S. Person, A. M. Cooper, & G. O. Gabbard (Eds.), *Textbook of Psychoanalysis* (pp. 535–546). Washington, DC: American Psychiatric Publishing.

Solms, M. (2006). Commentary on "The psychic apparatus, metapsychology, and neuroscience". *Neuropsychoanalysis*, 8: 99.

Solms, M., & Turnbull, O. (2002). *The Brain and the Inner World: An Introduction to the Neuroscience of Subjective Experience*. New York: Other Press.

Sperling, S. J. (1958). On denial and the essential nature of defence. *International Journal of Psychoanalysis*, 39: 25–38.

Spitz, R. A. (1961). Some early prototypes of ego defenses. *Journal of the American Psychoanalytic Association*, 9: 626–651.

Stolar, D., & Fromm, E. (1974). Activity and passivity of the ego in relation to the superego. *International Review of Psychoanalysis*, 1: 297–311.

Sullivan, H. S. (1956). *Clinical Studies in Psychiatry*. New York: W. W. Norton.

Suppes, P., & Warren, H. (1975). On the generation and classification of defence mechanisms. *International Journal of Psychoanalysis*, 56: 405–414.

Talvitie, V. (2009). *Freudian Unconscious and Cognitive Neuroscience: From Unconscious Fantasies to Neural Algorithms*. London: Karnac.

Talvitie, V., & Ihanus, J. (2002). The repressed and implicit knowledge. *International Journal of Psychoanalysis, 83*: 1311–1323.

Talvitie, V., & Ihanus, J. (2003a). On the nature of repressed contents—a working-through of John Searle's critique. *Neuro-psychoanalysis, 5*: 133–142.

Talvitie, V., & Ihanus, J. (2003b). Response to commentaries. *Neuro-psycho-analysis, 5*: 153–158.

Talvitie, V., & Ihanus, J. (2005). Biting the bullet: the nature of unconscious fantasy. *Theory & Psychology, 15*: 659–678.

Talvitie, V., & Ihanus, J. (2006). The psychic apparatus, metapsychology, and neuroscience: toward biological (neuro)psychoanalysis. *Neuro-psychoanalysis, 8*: 85–98.

Talvitie, V., & Tiitinen, H. (2006). From the repression of contents to the rules of the (narrative) self: a present-day cognitive view of the 'Freudian phenomenon' of repressed contents. *Psychology and Psychotherapy: Theory, Research and Practice, 79*: 165–181.

Tauber, A. I. (2010). *Freud, the Reluctant Philosopher*. Princeton, NJ: Princeton University Press.

Thalberg, I. (1977). *Perception, Emotion and Action*. Oxford: Basil Blackwell.

Thalberg, I. (1982). Freud's anatomies of the self. In: R. Wollheim & J. Hopkins (Eds.), *Philosophical Essays on Freud* (pp. 241–263). Cambridge: Cambridge University Press.

Thayer, J. F., & Friedman, B. H. (2002). Stop that! Inhibition, sensitization, and their neurovisceral concomitants. *Scandinavian Journal of Psychology, 43*: 123–130.

Thornton, E. M. (1999). Does the unconscious mind really exist? In: C. Feltham (Ed.), *Controversies in Psychotherapy and Counselling* (pp. 7–14). London: Sage.

Tomkins, S. (1962). *Affect, Imagery, Consciousness: Vol. 1. The Positive Affects*. New York: Springer.

Tomkins, S. (1963). *Affect, Imagery, Consciousness: Vol. 2. The Negative Affects*. New York: Springer.

Turnbull, O. H., & Solms, M. (2004). Depth psychological consequences of brain damage. In: J. Panksepp (Ed.), *Textbook of Biological Psychiatry* (pp. 571–595). Hoboken, NJ: Wiley-Liss.

Turnbull, O. H., & Solms, M. (2007). Awareness, desire, and false beliefs: Freud in the light of modern neuropsychology. *Cortex, 43*: 1083–1090.

Uleman, J. S. (2005). Introduction: becoming aware of the new unconscious. In: R. R. Hassin, J. S. Uleman, & J. A. Bargh (Eds.), *The New Unconscious* (pp. 3–15). Oxford: Oxford University Press.

van Gaal, S., Ridderinkhof, K. R., Fahrenfort, J. F., Scholte, H. S., & Lamme, V. A. F. (2008). Frontal cortex mediates unconscious triggered inhibitory control. *Journal of Neuroscience, 28*: 8053–8062.

Virsida, A. R. (1998). Cognition and its disembodiment: some comments on Freud scholarship. *Psychoanalytic Psychology, 15*: 164–167.

Wagner, H. (1999). *The Psychobiology of Human Motivation*. London: Routledge.

Wallerstein, R. S. (1977). Psychic energy reconsidered: introduction. *Journal of the American Psycho-analytic Association, 25*: 529–535.

Wegner, D. M. (2005). Who is the controller of controlled processes? In: R. R. Hassin, J. S. Uleman, & J. A. Bargh (Eds.), *The New Unconscious* (pp. 19–36). Oxford: Oxford University Press.

Weinberger, J. (2003). Commentary on "On the nature of repressed contents". *Neuro-psychoanalysis, 5*: 152–153.

Weinberger, J., & Westen, D. (2001). Science and psychodynamics: from arguments about Freud to data. *Psychological Inquiry, 12*: 129–166.

Weintraub, R. (1987). Unconscious mental states. *Philosophical Quarterly, 37*: 423–432.

Weiskrantz, L. (1997). Memories of abuse, or abuse of memories? In: J. Sandler & P. Fonagy (Eds.), *Recovered Memories of Abuse: True or False?* (pp. 3–25). Madison, NY: International Universities Press.

Westen, D. (1986). The superego: a revised developmental model. *Journal of the American Academy of Psychoanalysis, 14*: 181–202.

Westen, D. (1997). Towards a clinically and empirically sound theory of motivation. *International Journal of Psychoanalysis, 78*: 521–548.

Westen, D. (1999). The scientific status of unconscious processes: is Freud really dead? *Journal of the American Psychoanalytic Association, 47*: 1061–1105.

Westen, D., & Gabbard, G. O. (2002). Developments in cognitive neuroscience: I. Conflict, compromise, and connectionism. *Journal of the American Psychoanalytic Association, 50*: 53–98.

White, R. W. (1963). Ego and reality in psychoanalytic theory. In: *Psychological Issues*, Vol. 3, Monograph 11. New York: International Universities Press.

Whyte, L. L. (1962). *The Unconscious Before Freud*. London: Tavistock.

Wiedeman, G. H. (1972). Comments on the structural theory of personality. *International Journal of Psycho-analysis, 53*: 307–313.

Wilson, J. R. S. (1972). *Emotion and Object*. Cambridge: Cambridge University Press.

Wohlgemuth, A. (1923). *A Critical Examination of Psycho-analysis*. London: George Allen & Unwin.

Wollheim, R. (1991). *Freud.* London: Fontana Press.

Wollheim, R. (1993). *The Mind and its Depths.* Cambridge, MA: Harvard University Press.

Wong, P. S. (1999). Anxiety, signal anxiety, and unconscious anticipation: neuroscientific evidence for an unconscious signal function in humans. *Journal of the American Psychoanalytic Association, 47*: 817–841.

Young-Bruehl, E., & Bethelard, F. (1999). The hidden history of the ego instincts. *Psychoanalytic Review, 86*: 823–851.

Yu, C. K-C. (2006). Commentary on "Freudian dream theory, dream bizarreness, and the disguise-censor controversy". *Neuropsychoanalysis, 8*: 53–58.

Zepf, S. (2001). Incentives for a reconsideration of the debate on metapsychology. *International Journal of Psychoanalysis, 82*: 463–483.

Zola, S. M. (1998). Memory, amnesia, and the issue of recovered memory: neurobiological aspects. *Clinical Psychology Review, 18*: 915–932.

INDEX

affect(s), 5, 10, 13–17, 19–21, 28, 36,
   45, 49–50, 52, 83, 96, 104, 108,
   114–115, 119, 123–139, 143, 152,
   159, 175–177, 179–180, 184,
   186–188, 191–192, 196, 199
aggression, 44, 94, 186–188, 192, 195
Ågmo, A., 119, 209
American Psychiatric Association,
   xvii, 209
amnesia
   hysterical, 36, 103
   infantile, 34–35, 94
Anderson, J., xxiii, 72–73, 209
anger, 15, 76, 98, 126, 128, 195
Anspach, M. R., 162, 209
Anspaugh, K., 147, 209
anthropomorphism, xx–xxi, 47,
   49–50, 150–151, 178, 187, 189,
   192
anxiety
   automatic, 45–46
   intense, 63, 135, 193, 196, 199
   moral, 47, 50
   neurotic, 44–47, 50, 201

objectless, 127–128, 180, 197–198,
   200
realistic, 46–47, 201
separation, 106
signal, 45–46, 49–50, 58, 133–135,
   177
use of, 48–49
Applegarth, A., 124–125, 209
Arlow, J. A., 39, 100, 102, 189–190,
   209
Atkinson, T. M., 183, 230
attachment, 15–16, 186, 204
Auld, F., 56, 58, 210

Bach, K., 62–63, 210
Baker, A. J., 73, 210
Balvin, R. S., 171, 181–183, 214
Barkley, R. A., 183, 210
Baumann, H., 151, 210
Baumbacher, G. D., 134, 210
Baumeister, R. F., 62, 210
behaviour *see also*: sexual
   bad, 53
   conscious, 81

For Product Safety Concerns and Information please contact our EU
representative GPSR@taylorandfrancis.com
Taylor & Francis Verlag GmbH, Kaufingerstraße 24, 80331 München, Germany